W9-CNU-294

# MAKING SENSE
## OF GOVERNANCE

# MAKING SENSE OF GOVERNANCE

## Empirical Evidence from Sixteen Developing Countries

Goran Hyden,
Julius Court, and
Kenneth Mease

LYNNE
RIENNER
PUBLISHERS

BOULDER
LONDON

JF
130
.H93
2004

Published in the United States of America in 2004 by
Lynne Rienner Publishers, Inc.
1800 30th Street, Boulder, Colorado 80301
www.rienner.com

and in the United Kingdom by
Lynne Rienner Publishers, Inc.
3 Henrietta Street, Covent Garden, London WC2E 8LU

© 2004 by Lynne Rienner Publishers, Inc. All rights reserved

**Library of Congress Cataloging-in-Publication Data**
Hyden, Goran, 1938–
    Making sense of governance  :  empirical evidence from sixteen
developing countries  /  Goran Hyden, Julius Court, and Kenneth Mease.
        p.  cm.
    Includes bibliographical references and index.
    ISBN 1-58826-267-7 (hardcover  :  alk. paper)
    1. Comparative government—Research.   2. Developing
countries—Politics and government.   I. Court, Julius.   II. Mease,
Kenneth, 1951–   III. Title.
    JF130.H93   2004
    320.9172'4—dc22
                                                        2004003784

**British Cataloguing in Publication Data**
A Cataloguing in Publication record for this book
is available from the British Library.


Printed and bound in the United States of America

The paper used in this publication meets the requirements
⊗ of the American National Standard for Permanence of
Paper for Printed Library Materials Z39.48-1992.


5   4   3   2   1

545366653

# Contents

# Tables and Figures

## Tables

## Figures

# Acknowledgments

This project was begun in 1999 by Julius Court when he served as program officer at the United Nations University (UNU) in Tokyo. Subsequently, Goran Hyden was invited to serve as joint coordinator, and together they developed the World Governance Survey, a project that generated the database on which this book is based. The instrument for the survey was developed and refined in several sessions both at UNU and with advice from the United Nations Development Programme (UNDP). It was first applied in late 2000 and early 2001, when country coordinators in twenty-three countries, mostly in the developing world, administered the questionnaire to a cross section of people concerned with national governance issues, referred to in the text below as well-informed persons (WIPs). Kenneth Mease joined the team in 2001 at the analysis stage, and the book has benefited enormously from his expertise.

This is the first consolidated and comprehensive report on the World Governance Survey. Our intention was to develop a way to generate comprehensive, comparative governance assessments. This raised major conceptual and methodological challenges: the survey was logistically complex, and measuring governance is politically sensitive (though less so than we expected). Nevertheless, it was an enormously rewarding exercise. We are extremely grateful to partners around the world who have helped in developing a framework, testing different approaches, and gathering systematic data on issues that are so important yet so challenging. It is appropriate, therefore, that we acknowledge the contributions of several colleagues and friends.

At UNU, we would especially like to mention the contributions of Monica Blagescu, Soisik Habert, Edward Newman, and Keiko Suzuki. The work was coordinated and largely funded by UNU, and we are grateful to Hans van Ginkel and Ramesh Thakur—respectively rector and vice rector for peace and governance. The project also benefited from substantive, financial, and logistical support from the UNDP. This was largely facilitated by Kanni Wignaraja, to whom we owe a great deal, but we are also grateful to many others in that organization. We thank several academic colleagues for help as we developed the program, notably John Harbeson of the City University of New York Graduate Center, Ashutosh Varshney of the University of Michigan, Yasutami Shimomura of Hosei University in Tokyo, and Mette Kjaer of Aarhus University in Denmark.

We must also include a special thanks to the country coordinators, the majority of them academics, who carried out the project in the field. They provided valuable insights on substantive as well as methodological issues. Some preferred not to be named, but we wish every one of them to know how much we appreciate their efforts. The other anonymous group to whom we owe a great deal is represented by the respondents, who took the time to provide ratings and comments on governance in their countries in contexts that are often far from ideal.

In analyzing the findings, we have benefited from comments at academic meetings and presentations at international organizations. At the UNDP we are grateful to Shabbir Cheema, José Cruz-Osorio, Sakiko Fukuda-Parr, Omar Noman, Richard Ponzio, Mounir Tabet, Paul Oquist, and Robertson Work. At the World Bank we benefited from comments from David Cieslikowski, Daniel Kaufmann, Steve Knack, Mark Kugler, Francesca Recanatini, and Pablo Zoido-Lobaton. We were grateful for the opportunity to present the work at two European meetings on statistics and human rights: particular thanks to Dirk Berg-Schlosser, Paul Graham, Nigel Thornton, and Thomas Wollnik. We are grateful to David Brown, Tim Forsyth, Simon Maxwell, and James Putzel for comments at a discussion seminar at the Overseas Development Institute. We want to thank David Figlio and Chris McCarty of the University of Florida, as well as Fritz Scheuren of the National Organization for Research at the University of Chicago, for sound advice on the data analysis and sampling. During the writing phase we benefited from the assistance of Vilma Fuentes and Kelli Moore, Ph.D. candidates in the Department of Political Science at the University of Florida. Finally, we extend our thanks to two anonymous reviewers of the manuscript for extensive and constructive suggestions.

The coauthors are solely responsible for the final result of this book. Joint authorship is always a challenge, but it has been a great pleasure on this important project.

# Introduction

The purpose of this book is to demonstrate the value of research on governance. Using a comprehensive framework and drawing on a new set of data on governance collected in sixteen countries, the book provides a complementary perspective on democratization and the relationship between politics and development. It also complements studies on specific aspects of governance in which the issue of corruption occupies a particularly important place. The countries included here come from those regions of the world that are labeled *developing* or *transitional*. In Africa, we have data from Tanzania and Togo; in Asia, from China, India, Indonesia, Mongolia, Pakistan, the Philippines, and Thailand; in Eastern Europe and the former Soviet Union, from Bulgaria, Kyrgyzstan, and Russia; in Latin America, from Argentina, Chile, and Peru; and in the Middle East, from Jordan.

There are good reasons for developing a more rigorous, systematic, and theory-based approach to governance. One is the growing sense of the inadequacy of studies of democratization. The dilemma facing researchers in this area is that of steering clear of conceptual stretching and the identification of an infinite number of so-called diminished subtypes.[1] Related to this problem is a tendency for studies of democratization to be so heavily loaded with normative assumptions and preferences that political issues are analyzed from a narrow perspective.

We believe that to understand the relationship between politics and development it is necessary to transcend such limitations and to move up the conceptual ladder by focusing on regime. Although it may take away some of the specificity that comes with studying a particular subtype or demonstrating how well a country's political reform efforts match a specific model, notably the Western liberal version of democracy, a step upward to the regime level allows for a more open-ended examination of countries undergoing political reform. For decades some scholars doing large N studies have devoted time to examining how far democracy and development go together. Other than agreements about broad correlations, we don't know which way the causal links go or which variable is important in what context and when. It is not only the relationship between democracy and development that is so interesting; it is also the relationship between other types of regime and development.

By focusing on regime, we are proposing a shift in the study of governance. This book defines *governance* in reference to how the rules of the political game are managed. Rules are typically formal but may well be informal. The important thing is that they are "rules-in-use"—they are operational. The rules of the regime provide the context in which policy and administration are carried out. In practice, these activities are interconnected, but for analytical reasons they are best separated. Governance refers to the *voluntarist* intervention at the level of the regime to protect, amend, or just sustain specific rules that are important for how the political system functions and the political process operates. The extent to which these overarching rules are perceived as legitimate says a lot about the way citizens relate to politics and what we can expect from politics in terms of national development. Because political processes are embedded in historical and cultural contexts, it is inevitable that the basis for assessing rules will vary from one country to another, even from one social group to another within the same country. Governance is a structurally contingent activity in the sense that *agency* is not completely free but to varying extents shaped by structural and/or institutional factors that are specific to time and space.

Another reason to focus on governance is a lack of analytical usage of the concept. Governance first became a tool for program design in many international organizations and bilateral aid agencies. It was used as a catchall phrase to allow these agencies to support and finance particular types of activities linked to economic, administrative, and political reforms. As we discuss in Chapter 1, there are different interpretations of what governance refers to, but they typically reflect the ideology and culture of each funding agency. In more recent years, these organizations have tried to reach a greater consensus on what *good* governance means—an assortment of measures that largely reflects the historical experience of Western societies. This has given the concept a sharper normative edge, but it also made it more operational than analytical.

There is also growing evidence that perceptions of the macropolitical structures and their performance are important for investors. A recent study of the business climate in Eastern Europe and the former Soviet Union indicates that the perceptions business persons have of the political system at large is important for their decision whether or not to invest.[2] Whenever they have an optimistic view of it, they tend to invest; but when they have a more pessimistic opinion, they tend to hold back. Thus studies that deal with the rules of the game are of practical value to those who are involved in economic activities.

Yet another reason to focus on governance is that the roads to good governance are not paved in a linear or identical fashion. There are historical differences among regions, bound to affect the way forward. For instance, many Asian countries, with a legacy of strong indigenous institutions, are likely to chart a different path from Africa, Latin America, and the former Soviet Union. Research on governance can help throw light on questions such as which rules matter when and how, as well as on the contextual factors that explain similarities and differences among countries. In short, it can enrich the study of political and economic reform beyond the snapshot presentations that cross-sectional studies of democratization or any other aspect of national development provide.

Because of the various problems associated with the governance concept, most academics have stayed away from using it. We understand this caution, yet a serious effort to demonstrate the usefulness of governance as an analytical tool is timely. By moving in this direction, we offer the opportunity for new insights into key relationships between politics and development. We do not merely look at issues of interest to specific groups or clients. We do not, as studies of democratization do, merely look at the issues of how elections foster democracy and how civil society contributes to civil and political liberties. We take in a comprehensive view of the full dimensions of the political process, allowing for a more open investigation of which explanatory variables count where and when.

It is important to make a distinction between governance performance indicators and governance process indicators. *Performance indicators* refer to the quality of governance in terms of a normative outcome, such as the level of corruption. *Process indicators* refer to the quality of governance in terms of how outcomes are achieved. As highlighted in Chapter 1, an emphasis on governance process stems from a rights-based approach to development. Although there has been considerable improvement in monitoring governance outcomes, the monitoring of processes is limited. The challenge, therefore, is how to measure governance cohesively and systematically in terms of critical *processes*.

For this reason, we adopt a *political-process approach*. The concept is linked to rules that guide the process at large—the regime. But in order to capture the governance dynamics, we divide the process into six separate arenas: (1) civil society, (2) political society, (3) government, (4) bureaucracy, (5), economic society, and (6) judiciary. Each arena corresponds to key points where rules make a difference to both process and outcome. Thus civil society socializes individuals to believe in certain things that form the basis for articulating ideas and interests. Political society adopts and aggregates such *inputs* from civil society. It helps put them together in policy packages. Government, which corresponds to the executive function, is where key decisions are made for society at large. It provides policy the stamp of authority. As such, it sets the stage for policy implementation, the function that is associated with bureaucracy. The way the latter operates has a bearing on how the public perceives rules of putting policies into practice. Economic society refers to how relations between state and market are structured. The function of economic society is to obtain a satisfactory equilibrium between concerns for efficiency and distribution. The judicial arena, finally, is fulfilling the need for a mechanism to resolve conflicts between actors in different arenas.

The challenge for students of governance is to identify the most suitable indicators for each of the six arenas. Note that we are not interested in finding out specific substantive outcomes within each arena. That is what students of policy and/or administration do. We focus on the rules in use, that is, how operational rules shape specific outcomes. For instance, are the rules applying to civil society legitimate in the eyes of key actors? For a comparative study like ours it is imperative to strike a meaningful balance between *universally applicable* norms associated with particular rules and the *contextually derived* norms that are important in particular countries. For instance, it has become necessary to ask questions that make sense in different cultural contexts yet are not so watered down that they lose significance. In this study, we decided to identify five indicators—questions—for each arena that would serve as the basis for any measurement of the quality of governance within each arena and, by extension, for each country as a whole. They are introduced in further detail in Chapter 1.

We should explain the fact that this survey covers only sixteen countries, far short of covering the whole world. To be sure, if we were to take the total populations of the countries included, it would amount to more than half the world's population. The reason for the relatively small $N$ stems from our decision that in order to complete such a huge undertaking as a worldwide survey, it is first necessary to test the instrument and refine it before extending it to a larger number of countries. The important thing is that we provide—for the first time—a set of systematically collected primary data on governance that can be used by other academics and analysts or practitioners interested in these issues.

Our approach to governance is based on interviews with a cross section of well-informed persons (WIPs) in the sixteen countries. What we report, therefore, are subjective perceptions of governance in different countries. The WIPs have been chosen from different categories—government servants, parliamentarians, media folk, lawyers and judges, businesspeople, religious leaders, academics, and representatives of civil society and international organizations. Each respondent has answered the same questions, and many provided qualitative commentaries to back up their ratings. Even though the total number of respondents per country is small, this cross section is important to paint an aggregate picture that is representative of a range of informants. As might be expected, we found that state actors generally had a higher appreciation of governance than did nonstate actors, but because we had a cross section of both types we believe our survey is valid. We discuss this issue at some length in Appendix 1. There, we also discuss other methodological issues, such as the fact that we had to cut out six countries that were initially part of the study because we could not obtain a sufficient number of respondents, or because those included were too numerous from either the state sector or civil society. Finally, we should add here that we also rely in our write-up on the substantive reports provided by the country coordinators of our field research.

We ruled out public opinion surveys as being too costly and in some countries impractical. After trying out focus groups with local community representatives, we decided that such a method would not add anything at the country level. Although we gained insights about important issues that applied to local governance, we did not have the resources to extend our study beyond the national level.

We are the first to accept that with a relatively small number of respondents per country, we are not in a position to go into detailed discussions of trends and events in individual countries. Our principal objective is to demonstrate the value and feasibility of studying governance and then to relate it to studies of democracy and development. Thus, in handling substantive issues we try as much as possible to stay with the specific information that our survey provides in relation to each indicator, arena, and country.

This book begins with an overview of the international development debate and why, as well as how, governance has become a major concern. Chapter 1 also presents our approach to governance and how it complements and relates to studies of democratization. Chapter 2 provides an aggregate view of governance performance in the sixteen countries included. It compares performance across countries as well as across arenas. Chapters 3–8 report the findings for each of the arenas identified above. It places the analysis in the context of major issues covered by the literature, thus providing a more detailed comparison with other sources. Chapter 9 draws the main conclusions from this study and discusses its implications for future research on governance, as well as how this project compares with other governance studies. We have included two appendices, the first a discussion of how we went about collecting and analyzing data, the second containing the survey instrument used in this study.

The study of governance has come a long way from the early days, when it surfaced in conference papers and eventually obtained a place of prominence in a few edited volumes (see Goran Hyden and Michael Bratton, eds., *Governance and Politics in Africa*, 1992). This book is evidence that governance can be used to assess how rules relate to both democratization and development. We have a dataset that serves as baseline or takeoff point for further studies on the subject. We hope that the insights here spur more research on governance and its relationship to development.

## Notes

1. David Collier and Steven Levitsky, "Democracy with 'Adjectives': Conceptual Innovation in Comparative Research," *World Politics* 49, no. 3 (April 1997): 430–451.

2. See notably the Business Environment and Enterprise Performance Survey (BEEPS), carried out jointly by the World Bank and the European Bank for Reconstruction and Development in 27 "transitional" societies in Eastern Europe and the former Soviet Union. A first report on the findings of this survey was presented by Joel Hellman and Alan Rousso at the Eleventh International Anti-Corruption Conference organized by Transparency International in Seoul, Korea, May 25–28, 2003.

# Governance, Democracy, and Development

G overnance has become a key concept in the international development debate. It marks an intriguing transformation in focus from micro-level to macro-level issues. It also poses fresh challenges to those interested in relating socioeconomic outcomes to macropolitical interventions. After more than a decade of efforts to make sense of governance in development, many of these basic challenges remain. What is the relationship between governance and development? What does *governance* really mean? How can the concept be best put into analytical usage? What analytical advantages does it have? How does it compare to democracy as an analytical lens? This introductory chapter tries to address these questions as a precursor to the analytical effort attempted in this volume.

## From Micro-Level to Macro-Level Interventions

In order to fully understand the importance that governance has acquired, it is helpful to trace the most significant shifts that have taken place in thinking about development since the end of World War II. Much has happened since the concept of development—in the context of President Harry Truman's postwar Four Point Program that led to the Marshall Plan for European recovery—was adapted for use at the international level in the late 1940s and early 1950s. The history is long and has many twists. What is often overlooked, however, is that shifts are the result of an unsatisfactory, if not negative, experience with the way that the development concept has been operationalized. Development itself, in other words, has always been a moving target, constantly generating demands for new approaches. It is possible to identify at least four distinct ways by which the international community has tried to make operational sense of development.

The initial tack goes back to the Marshall Plan, the first major transfer of public capital to enhance the pace of international development. Influenced by the success that the Marshall Plan had in the reconstruction of Western Europe, economic analysts began to turn the same Keynesian ideas on which it rested into universal recipes. With these efforts, a new field—*development economics*—was born. In the perspective of these economists, development in the emerging states of what has since become the third world would be best achieved through transfers of capital and technical expertise.[1] This philosophy prevailed in the last days of colonial rule and the early years of independence in Africa. It was also applied to Asia and Latin America with few modifications. Being lodged in a modernization paradigm—implying that development is a move from traditional to modern society—this approach was characterized by great confidence and optimism. Although it was not reconstruction but development that was attempted in these instances, the challenge looked easy. Defined largely in technocratic terms, development was operationalized with little or no attention to context. The principal task was to ensure that institutions and techniques that had proved successful in modernizing the Western world could be replicated.

The intellectual efforts were concentrated in two directions. One approach was to produce comprehensive national development plans as guides for which policies should be prioritized. These plans stated the anticipated macroeconomic conditions under which specific program and project activities should and could be developed. Projects took on special significance. They constituted the means by which macro-level goals could be realized. Good project design was the key to success. It is no exaggeration to suggest that during this first phase of development thinking, which lasted into the latter part of the 1960s, the *project level* was regarded as most important. Project design, however, was the prerogative of technical experts. It was done on behalf of potential beneficiaries without their input. Government and other public institutions were identified as responsible for ensuring effective implementation. Private and voluntary sector organizations were ignored. Development, then, was a top-down exercise by public agencies *for the people*.

The second phase began in the latter part of the 1960s, when analysts and practitioners had begun to recognize that a singular focus on projects in the context of national plans was inadequate. The critique followed at least two lines. First, projects designed with little attention to context typically had more unanticipated than anticipated outcomes. For instance, the assumption that development would trickle down from the well endowed to the poor, thus generating ripple effects, proved to be mistaken. Second, projects were inevitably enclave types of intervention with little or no positive externalities. For example, evaluations confirmed the absence of meaningful backward or forward linkages in this type of intervention. Analysts concluded that the project approach failed to realize improvements, especially in the conditions of the poorer segments of the population. Convinced that something else had to be done to reduce global poverty, the international community decided that a *sectoral approach* would be more effective. Farmers would no longer be approached merely as producers but as people with genuine needs as human beings responsible for other members in the household. In operational terms, this meant substituting *project* for *program* as the principal concern.

The important thing in this second phase, therefore, became how to design integrated programs that addressed not a single dimension of human needs but the whole range of them. For example, integrated rural development programs became fashionable instruments of action. As a sequitur, governments also engaged in administrative reforms that stressed the value of decentralizing authority to lower levels of government organization to enhance coordination and management of these new sectoral programs.[2] Another element was the growing emphasis on education and training of the masses. Human capital mattered. Whereas capacity-building in the first phase had been concentrated on the elite, in the second phase the focus was on such areas as adult education and universal primary education, the assumption being that these were integral parts of a poverty-oriented approach to development.[3] That is why during this phase the main idea can be said to have been development *of the people*.

At the end of the 1970s there was a third phase, this time of even greater consequence than the first. It was becoming increasingly clear that governments could typically not administer the heavy development burden that had been placed on their shoulders. This was most apparent in sub-Saharan Africa, where states lacked the technical capacity, but it was also acknowledged elsewhere because of bureaucratic shortcomings.[4] Government agencies simply did not work efficiently in the development field. Placing all development eggs in one basket, therefore, was increasingly questioned as the most useful strategy. So was the role of the state in comparison with the market as an allocative mechanism of public resources.[5] As analysts went back to their drawing boards, the challenge was no longer how to manage or administer development as much as it was identifying the incentives that may facilitate it. The strategic focus was shifted to the level of *policy*.

The World Bank, mandated by its governors, took the lead on this issue and, with reference to sub-Saharan Africa, the most critical region, produced a major policy document outlining the proposed necessary economic reforms.[6] This report became the principal guide for structural adjustment in Africa during the 1980s, although the strategy was also applied in other regions. These reforms, in combination with parallel financial stabilization measures imposed by the International Monetary Fund (IMF), were deemed necessary to get the prices right and to free up state-controlled resources that could be potentially better used and managed by other institutions in society—particularly the private sector. Most important, it also assumed that individuals would act rationally in the marketplace. Although most discussion of structural adjustment focused on the structural reforms and their consequences for ordinary citizens, one of the most important theoretical points was that individuals—on their own or in cooperation with others—can make a more significant contribution to development than can the state bureaucracy. This period thus witnessed an increase in voluntary organizations around the world and preliminary efforts to bring such organizations into the development process. With more responsibilities delegated to the market, private and voluntary organizations could play a more significant role in working with people to realize their aspirations, whether individual or communal.[7] Small-scale activities mattered and could make a difference. Even though the economic reforms tended to create social inequities, the basic premise was that nongovernmental organizations (NGOs) could do *with* the people what the government had failed to do *for* the people. Seen from the pedestal of international development agencies, this implied a significant change. People were no longer targets of development policies but rather partners that could be induced to make a difference for themselves and their country. Again, the perception of development had changed, this time to being an exercise done *with the people*.

The fourth phase, since the 1990s, has been the growing recognition that development is not only about projects, programs, and policies but also about *politics*. For a long time, politics and development were seen as two separate and distinct activities. Development analysts, especially economists, preferred to treat development as apolitical. Out of respect for national sovereignty, donors and governments upheld this dichotomy for a long time. This has been challenged. Although it is controversial in government circles in the third world, there is a growing recognition that getting politics right is, if not a precondition, at least a requisite of development. The implication is that conventional notions of state sovereignty are being challenged and undermined by the actions taken by the international community, notably international finance institutions and bilateral donors. United Nations agencies also find themselves caught in this process. For example, human rights violations, including those that limit freedoms of expression and association, are being invoked as reasons for not only criticizing governments of other countries but also withholding aid if no commitment to cease such violations and improvement is made. Underlying this shift toward creating a politically enabling environment is the assumption that development, after all, is the product of what people decide to do to improve their livelihoods. People, not governments (especially those run by autocrats), constitute the principal force of development. They must be given the right incentives and opportunities not only in the economic arena but also the political arena. They must have a chance to create institutions that respond to needs and priorities. Development is no longer a benevolent, top-down exercise, not even a charitable act by nongovernmental organizations, but instead is a bottom-up process. As such, development is now seen primarily in terms of something done *by the people*.

This overview of how development ideas have changed (see Table 1.1) since World War II is brief and does not explain the nuances that many involved in the development business would recognize and wish to emphasize. We believe, however, that the basic distinctions made above reflect principal shifts in how we conceive development and the measures that go with it. Two points need to be made about this process. The first is that each approach or emphasis has lasted only a decade or a little more. The urge to abandon one approach in favor of another has come as a result of evaluations indicating serious shortcomings but also of the general impatience and need for quick results that characterize international development funders. For instance, these agencies, through the United Nations, used to identify development in terms of decades, each with its own emphasis. Global blue-ribbon commissions made up of influential persons helped set the new agenda, thus pushing agencies away from what they were already engaged in. The idea of development decades has now been abandoned, indicating—perhaps—that the international community recognizes that development is a complex activity and that results come in incremental and often infinitesimal steps.

The second point is that the global development agenda is still very much the product of the views of dominant states and institutions. Although more voices are being raised today, not the least by social movements and nongovernmental organizations, theirs are still alternatives to mainstream thinking as reflected in documents issued by the World Bank, the United Nations, and bilateral donors.[8] Apart from the UN conferences during the 1990s, third world governments and other organizations typically have very little say. This is increasingly controversial in a period when development includes calls for reforms of the political setup in individual countries. It is

Table 1.1  **Shifts in Development Thinking and Emphasis from the 1950s to the Present**

| Period | Focus | Emphasis |
|---|---|---|
| 1950s–1960s | Project | For the people |
| 1960s–1970s | Program | Of the people |
| 1980s | Policy | With the people |
| 1990s–present | Politics | By the people |

no coincidence, therefore, that the international community, especially the World Bank and the IMF, has taken refuge in the concept of governance or institutions when referring to things political.

## Defining Governance

Despite the recent popularity of governance at both the practical and theoretical levels, the concept continues to mean different things to different people. Academics and practitioners often talk past one another, as do scholars in different academic disciplines and fields. A review of the literature, however, suggests that such differences tend to crystallize along two separate lines, one regarding the substantive content of governance, the other regarding its character in practice. Along the first line, there is a difference between those who view governance as concerned with the rules of conducting public affairs versus those who see it as steering or controlling public affairs. One might say that the rules approach tends to emphasize the institutional determinants of choice, whereas the steering approach concentrates on how choices get implemented.

Along the second line, the difference is between governance as related to performance or process. Some analysts treat governance as reflected in human intention and action. It is possible to see the results of governance interventions. Others, however, view governance as an activity that guides the process by which results are reached. Practitioners tend to adopt the former position; many academics end up taking the latter. As Figure 1.1 indicates, one can identify four major positions on how governance has been defined and used. Students of public administration share with analysts and practitioners in international development agencies the notion that governance is about steering and control, but they differ in that the former regard it as a process, whereas the latter see it as performance-related. For example, representatives of the donor community wish to see measurable results of governance—hence their concern with developing results-based indicators. Students of public administration, by contrast, are content with recognizing that managing public affairs—and thus controlling outcomes—is no longer confined to traditional jurisdictions but influenced by processes that transcend such boundaries. International relations scholars share with students of comparative politics the notion that governance is about the rules of the game, but they have divergent views on its character, the former treating it as process, the latter more in terms of performance. For example, students of international relations recognize that creating new rules for global governance is a process involving multiple actors at different levels—hence the difficulty of overcoming tendencies among national governments to stick with realist principles. Comparativists, by contrast, look at

**Figure 1.1  Different Uses of the Governance Concept**

governance as a voluntarist act that can make a positive difference to social and economic development.[9] For example, there is in the field of comparative politics a consistent effort to determine the relationship between democracy and development (see Figure 1.1).

In order to sort out the basic issues surrounding the uses of the concept, it may be helpful to elaborate a little on each of these four positions. Beginning with public administration, governance has emerged as a popular way of dealing with the fact that conventional jurisdictional boundaries of administration no longer have the same exclusivity. Substantive issues cut across boundaries. Formulation and implementation of policy, therefore, often require cooperation among representatives of different organizations. European scholars first noted this when they began studying the effects of European integration and the growth of new institutional formulas in the social welfare sector. In one of the first and more comprehensive treatments of governance from a public administration perspective,[10] it was argued that governance is composed of purposeful action to guide, steer, and control society. The authors recognized that this is not achieved with a single measure but is a process that takes time and involves both governmental and nongovernmental organizations. Governance, they argued, is the regularized, institutional patterns that emerge from the interactions of these organizations. This view of governance also reflects the normative change that took place in Europe during the 1980s when economic liberalization reduced the role of the welfare state as the sole agent of policy implementation and paved the way for public-private partnerships. Needs were no longer confined to society, capacity to government. Needs and capacities became both public and private. They are today embedded in both state and society in their mutual interdependencies.

Thus governance transcends the conventional boundaries of public administration. Other students of European governments,[11] for whom self-organizing, interorganizational networks constitute the essential ingredients of the governance process, make the same point. In the context of a disarticulated state (i.e., one with reduced capacity to solve public problems), it is in governance theory that public administration gets to wrestle with problems of representation, the political control of bureaucracy, and the democratic legitimacy of institutions and networks.

This view is also shared by a growing number of students of public administration in the United States. Although the impetus for turning to governance has been primarily the issue of the disconnect between the scope of public issues and the jurisdictional boundaries of public agencies, they tend to approach governance in a fashion similar to their European counterparts. Thus, for example, it has been argued that governance links values and interest of citizens, legislative choice, executive and organizational structures and roles, and judicial oversight in a manner that suggests interrelationships among them that might have significant consequences for performance.[12] Governance is a process that brings administrators into new collaborative relations in which the prospect for results is deemed to be better than within conventional organizational settings.

An international relations literature on governance emerged after the collapse of communism and the bipolar world order. It accepts that interdependence is an increasingly important feature of a new world order and argues that this calls for commonly accepted norms, rules, and patterns of behavior that facilitate international cooperation.[13] Contrary to the realist or neorealist approaches to international politics that stress the overwhelming importance of perceived national interest, governance is typically associated with a constructivist approach, in which rules as regimes are viewed as key ingredients for stabilizing international relations. Cooperation across both national and issue boundaries requires the initiation of a process involving actors ready to transcend narrow national interest concerns. Governance, therefore, is a process involving multiple actors in the international arena that produces new norms and rules for working together to solve global problems or conflicts.[14]

Interest in governance among students of comparative politics has also emerged as a result of the collapse of communism. Their study of the rules of the game is associated with an increasing concern around the world to bring about democracy. In this context, governance is studied as part of regime transition. In the first attempt to delineate the concept, *governance* was defined as the "conscious management of regime structures with a view to enhancing the legitimacy of the public realm."[15] By focusing on rules as reflected in regime structures and how they are managed, this view of governance emphasizes the institutional framework within which public decisions and policies are made. It calls for attention to constitutional and legal issues in ways that conventional political economy studies focusing on how resources are allocated do not. Governance is a product of human agency that helps define the relations and interactions between state and society. Others have adopted a similar perspective, arguing that governance "involves affecting the framework within which citizens and [state] officials act and politics occurs."[16] Rules affect outcomes—hence the importance of selecting them as an object of study in comparative politics. Their view of governance as institutional frameworks for the realization of democratic ideals also tallies with the interpretation by public administration scholars in that it recognizes the revision of rules in order to meet the demands of more complex societal systems.

It is appropriate that the discussion of the perspective of international development agencies be a little longer here. Although there tends to be agreement about governance as an activity aimed at steering societies in desired directions, these agencies have typically adopted the concept to suit their own programmatic needs. Their entry points differ. The United Nations Development Programme, for example, has adopted a definition that sees governance as "the exercise of economic, political, and administrative authority to manage a country's affairs at all levels."[17] In this perspective, governance comprises the mechanisms, processes, and institutions through which citizens and groups articulate interests, exercise legal rights, meet obligations, and mediate conflicts. Governance is said to have three legs: economic, political, and administrative. *Economic governance* includes decisionmaking processes that affect a country's economic activities and its relationship with other economies. *Political governance* involves the formulation of policy. *Administrative governance* is the system of policy implementation. As can be seen from this and similar definitions used by international development agencies, governance is an all-encompassing concept. It permeates all sectors, and it makes no distinction between governance, policymaking, and policy implementation.

The World Bank has its own interpretation of governance that is of special interest because its official mandate prevents it from dealing with political issues. To cope with this, the World Bank makes a distinction between governance as an analytic framework and governance as an operational framework, leading it to identify three aspects of governance: (1) the form of political regime; (2) the process by which authority is exercised in the management of a country's economic and social resources for development; and (3) the capacity of governments to design, formulate, and implement policies and discharge functions.[18] The World Bank has professed to confine itself only to the second and third aspects of governance, but it has found itself under increasing pressure from Western bilateral donors to address also the first. Its recent recognition of human rights as an essential aspect of governance seems to be a manifestation of this extended operational use of the concept.

The problem with the definitions used by international development agencies is twofold. By being a catchall concept it fails to make distinctions that are important for any attempt to assess governance. It resembles the notion of development management that was employed in the 1970s to identify what governments in developing countries were doing. More specifically it fails to make a distinction between governance, policy, and administration. Governance folds into the latter two without a distinct meaning to it. This means that it is difficult to know whether it is actually the quality of policymaking and implementation rather than something peculiar known as governance that really is supposed to make a difference. For example, it is possible that the same kind of governance setup in two separate countries may produce different outcomes because of variations in policy formulation or implementation capacity. And by watering down its political character, governance loses its distinction in relation to the economy. Where does governance begin and end as a variable expected to cause specific outcomes? How can one meaningfully say something about the impact of governance unless it has some specificity? These are key definitional challenges that these agencies have not adequately addressed but which we try to address here.

*    *    *

For the purpose of this volume, a definition of governance is adopted that focuses on the importance of rules rather than results. It examines process, not performance. Governance is treated as both activity and process in the sense that it is viewed as reflective of human intention and agency but is itself a process that sets the parameters for how policy is made and implemented. Analytically speaking, governance becomes a meta-activity that influences outcomes, such as reducing transaction costs and protecting human rights, depending on the nature of the rules adopted. With this in mind, the following working definition is adopted for this study: *Governance refers to the formation and stewardship of the formal and informal rules that regulate the public realm, the arena in which state as well as economic and societal actors interact to make decisions.* Governance, then, refers to behavioral dispositions rather than technical capacities.

It is a quality of the political system that in the current development debate serves as an independent variable, an explanatory factor. In this perspective, governance deals with the constitutive side of how a political system operates rather than its distributive or allocative aspects that are more directly a function of policy. In order to clarify the way governance is conceived and how it relates to other concepts that international development agencies tend to fuse it with, Table 1.2 sets out the principal differences.

It is important to emphasize that these different levels are empirically

**Table 1.2    Governance and Its Relations to Other Concepts and Activities**

| Level | Activity | Concept |
|---|---|---|
| Meta | Politics | Governance |
| Macro | Policy | Policymaking |
| Meso | Program | Public administration |
| Micro | Project | Management |

interconnected, but there are good reasons for keeping them analytically apart. Rules are, empirically speaking, set at different levels. For example, a community may decide to change the rules by which its members abide in order to improve the prospects of a better life. Such a revision of rules—the local community regime—has a bearing on how decisions are made and implemented or singular project activities managed. Governance is also present at higher levels, ultimately in terms of establishing and managing constitutional principles at national or international levels.

With this definition in mind, it is possible to sustain the distinction between a *constitutive* and a *distributive* side of politics. What is new in the contemporary international setting is that the distributive side is no longer solely important. The classical political economy question, originally attributed to Harold Lasswell—Who gets what, when, and how?—that has been underlying previous approaches to development is now being challenged by another important concern: Who sets what rules, when, and how? It is this constitutive side of politics that needs to be highlighted and emphasized in the name of governance. Without being separated from the concerns associated with resource allocation, it is impossible to know whether political behavior makes a difference to development. Governance does not influence such outcomes directly, but it does so indirectly by changing the rules for how policies are made. The best analogy is that governance is to policy and administration what a house is to its occupants: it sets the limits and opportunities for those inside. Any sense of comfort is determined by how they experience its physical boundaries for social interaction. In a political setting, the rules of the game—whether formal or informal—do the same. As they assess governance, they are commenting on the degree of legitimacy that they attribute to these rules.

If governance is about rules, the question inevitably arises as to which rules are important for shaping policy processes and, by extension, development outcomes. There is a tendency among analysts and development agencies alike to adopt those that fit most closely their own programmatic mandate. A governance survey project has to transcend such limits. It must measure governance on a global scale using indicators applicable across national boundaries. Given the connection to policy, implementation, and development, the choice here is to focus on the various dimensions of the political process that produce outcomes. The assumption is that how the political process is structured (i.e., how state, society, and economy interact) is important for development.

In deciding what dimensions of the political process are important, an examination of how policy comes about may be especially helpful. It allows us to design the survey to reduce normative biases associated with the way governance has been applied thus far. Yet by virtue of its inclusivity, this approach covers what the vast majority of analysts and agencies consider relevant and important. It also makes specific references to the various arenas in which these dimensions are performed and the purpose of the rules associated with each dimension. The scheme is summarized in Table 1.3.

In order to fully appreciate this approach and what it entails, it is necessary to elaborate on its rationale and the substantive content of each governance arena.

## Civil Society

This arena is where persons become familiar and interested in public issues and how rules tend to affect the articulation of interests from society. The way rules are constituted in order to channel participation in public affairs is generally considered an important aspect of governance. For example, much of the recent literature on democratization indicates the important role that citizens have played in reshaping the rules in order to enhance their own input into the making of public policy. Robert Putnam's study of

**Table 1.3   The Functional Dimensions of Governance and Their Institutional Arenas**

| Process Dimension | Institutional Arena | Purpose of Rules |
|---|---|---|
| Socializing | Civil society | To shape the way citizens become aware of and raise issues in public |
| Aggregating | Political society | To shape the way issues are combined into policy by political institutions |
| Executive | Government | To shape the way policies are made by government institutions |
| Managerial | Bureaucracy | To shape the way policies are administered and implemented by public servants |
| Regulatory | Economic society | To shape the way state and market interact to promote development |
| Adjudicatory | Judicial system | To shape the setting for resolution of disputes and conflicts |

making democracy work in Italy is a case in point.[19] He emphasizes, like Alexis de Tocqueville before him, the importance of local associations in building trust and confidence in institutions as well as among people.

In Latin America and Eastern Europe, political reforms have been the result of socialization in the context of social movements, intensified political communications, and an enhanced articulation of interests that previously were latent for fear of public authority. As Juan Linz and Alfred Stepan note in their account of the democratic transition and consolidation in these two regions,[20] civil society was rightly considered the "celebrity" of democratic resistance and transition in many countries. However, the opportunity for articulating citizen voices on public issues is still limited in many countries. A recent global survey found that not having a voice in policy formulation is a source of frustration even in countries where elections are held on a regular basis.[21] On a more positive note, at the micro level, World Bank research[22] shows that water projects with participation are not only better designed and constructed; participation also enhances the likelihood of sustained support required for long-term maintenance of such schemes. Much more evidence could be garnered for support of the position that it matters how civil society is organized. Suffice it to add here that for any survey of how governance relates to development, this dimension is of doubtless significance.

## Political Society

This arena deals with how ideas and interests are aggregated into specific policy proposals. Much of the difficulty in consolidating democracy in regions like Latin America is seen by students of politics to be rooted in the problem of how contending social classes and interest groups are to be connected to the governing process.[23] This arena is usually referred to as political society (i.e., the place where public demands get tackled by specific political institutions such as political parties and legislative bodies). Rules for aggregating issues into policy vary. One major distinction in democratic polities is between *pluralist* and *corporatist* systems. The former is competitive, whereas the latter is directed. Many authoritarian regimes find the transition in political society especially hard since rules of this arena dictate who gets to power. Thus the design of electoral systems tends to influence the party system, the party system the way the legislature operates. Many countries in political transition prefer a presidential system over a parliamentary one based on the assumption—often mistaken—that a strong executive can control political society and provide greater political stability. Much has been written on this subject based on the experience of a range of countries, especially in Latin America.[24] Many of the governance concerns of the international community have also centered on this dimension. Designing electoral systems, monitoring elections to assess their fairness, as well as strengthening the technical capacity of parliaments to make them more effective in formulating policy and holding public officials accountable are measures that the international community has sponsored in developing and transitional countries.[25] Think tanks and other institutions that try to assess progress toward democracy give particular attention to the rules affecting performance of political society.[26] Its relevance to the objectives of this project cannot be called into question.

## Government

Governments do not merely make policy. They are also responsible for creating a climate in which people enjoy peace and security. The rules that they set to shape the relation between state and society in the broader security area are of growing importance not only in societies in transition but also in established political systems.[27] This is an aspect of governance that has often been overlooked due to the emphasis in the democratization literature on institutional reform. One important issue in transitional societies is clearly how the political leadership structures its relations with the military. In many such societies, the military has held political power in the past and is unlikely to relinquish it without insisting on certain conditions favorable to its members. To the extent that the civil-military relations have featured in the literature, it has focused on the pacting that takes place between outgoing military rulers and incoming civilian ones.[28]

Dealing with violence and poverty in society is another set of issues that transcends the boundaries of individual policy and enters the governance realm. Development, as Amartya Sen has argued, is very much a product of the freedom that citizens are able to enjoy.[29] What rules, formal and informal, do governments put in place to meet popular expectations of freedom from fear and want? These are systemic concerns that no other institution but government has ultimate responsibility for. Taking on these big issues is not easy, and many governments are unwilling to rise to the challenge. How government organizes itself and the rules it puts in place for its own operations are also important aspects of how societies function; in other words, governance influences popular perceptions of the regime.[30]

## The Bureaucracy

This arena refers to how the policy implementation machinery is organized. Public servants working in bureaucracies and bureaucratic-type organizations are engaged in formulating as well as implementing policy and delivering services. Their public impact, however, comes foremost from the role they play in carrying out policy. It is the most visible part of that role. How bureaucracy is structured and how it relates to the political leadership have been issues of great significance to academics and practitioners alike since Max Weber. The idea that rules must be legal-rational (i.e., formal and logical) has dominated especially in modern democracies. Many assume that bureaucracies can function efficiently and effectively only in such conditions.[31] Others, however, have also pointed to the problems of combining formal rules and procedures with positive substantive outcomes. Bureaucracy in this type of study is viewed in negative terms.[32] Comparative studies of how bureaucratic rules affect economic development have emerged.[33] They indicate the importance of viewing the bureaucracy in the context not only of policy implementation but also of governance, since its rules and procedures tend to have an influence on how people perceive the political system at large. As we know, many contacts that citizens have with government are with first-level bureaucrats, responsible for processing requests for services and assistance.

Bureaucracy, therefore, is an integral part of any governance assessment. The democratization literature typically ignores this arena; yet it is important in shaping overall perceptions of how a political system functions. At the same time, by placing it side by side with the other five dimensions of governance, the public impression of its performance is not blown out of proportion, as is the case when graft or improper practices are chosen as the only major indicators of poor governance.

## Economic Society

State-market relations have become of increasing importance to governance. No less an advocate of the invisible hand of the market than Adam Smith acknowledged that the state is necessary to perform certain economic functions. Most important of these is to deal with market failures—situations when the market fails to aggregate private choices in an optimal fashion. State institutions, therefore, are often created and called upon to regulate the economy. We refer to this arena as economic society, a term that we borrow from Linz and Stepan.[34] One common assumption is that when private firms have an opportunity to influence the way rules are formulated and implemented, this regulatory dimension is more effectively managed. It helps making policy better and also enhances regime legitimacy among key economic actors. The norms and institutions that are put in place to regulate how corporations operate, how property is owned and protected, as well as how capital may be transferred and trade conducted are

all important aspects of governance. This subject has gained greater prominence by theorists like Douglass North.[35] The compatibility of market and
democracy is also a subject of study by Adam Przeworski[36] and John
Dryzek.[37]

This arena is of special interest given that many analysts see economic
liberalization and political democratization as complementary processes.
Studies to date indicate that the relationship between the two is complex
and certainly not linear (as the collapse of Argentina's economy in late
2001 has indicated). This dimension is also important because it features
significantly in the strategies of many development agencies, where economic liberalization is viewed as a precondition for political democracy.

### The Judiciary

Each political system develops its own structures for conflict and dispute
resolution. How such institutions operate has a great bearing on popular
perceptions of regime performance. For example, persons who have been
mistreated by public officials or find themselves in conflict with others
must have an authoritative instance to call upon for a fair hearing. The
importance of this arena has been recognized by political theorists like John
Locke[38] and Charles de Montesquieu,[39] as well as by anthropologists like
Max Gluckman.[40] The adjudicatory function, however, goes beyond the
boundaries of individual cases. It also includes how conflicts between
groups in society are handled, even conflicts with other countries. One
important governance question is what rules apply to resolving such conflicts. The legal culture that develops as a result of how arbitration in this
broader sense is carried out is important for how people perceive not only
the judiciary but also the political system at large. Although the notion of
rule of law is important, many societies also have informal mechanisms for
resolving conflicts between government and private actors. Such is the
case, for example, in many Asian countries. There is little doubt that the
adjudicatory dimension is important for governance, especially in developing and transitional societies where rules are in flux. How they can be stabilized and turned into institutions that enjoy the confidence of citizens is
of vital significance.

### Operationalizing Governance

Measuring governance poses challenges that are not encountered in the
economic or social development fields. It is possible to provide firm indicators of such things as economic growth, level of unemployment, primary

school enrollment, and so forth. It is much more difficult to find and agree upon indicators of a macropolitical phenomenon like governance. Attempts to do so[41] confirm this but also indicate that aggregate measures of such phenomena as the rule of law are useful. More and better data are needed to provide a firmer basis for identifying statistically significant differences in governance across countries as well as for country-specific in-depth governance diagnostics. There is a need for systematic as well as longitudinal data that cover not only specific aspects of government activities, like corruption or transaction costs, but also the whole political process—from input to output. This book is an attempt to address such needs.

The tendency in international development circles has been to treat *governance* as a synonym for *liberal democracy.* In other words, features found in the political systems of Western societies have been elevated by the dominant agencies in the international development community to the level of being universally desirable. There are understandable reasons for such a move. With the collapse of the communist systems—at least the majority of them—liberal democracies can claim that they have proved to be the most sustainable. They continue to enjoy an acceptable level of legitimacy, and even though they do not work perfectly they combine efficiency with justice in ways that other systems do not. Nonetheless, there are many countries where liberal democratic values are questioned as the basis for better governance. There are others (e.g., China) that do very well in economic development terms and give economic reform priority over political changes. It is understandable that leaders as well as citizens in these countries view calls for good governance as a cover for extending Western influence in the global arena. In short, any attempt to measure governance is fraught with controversy over which norms should prevail.

It is not easy to develop a survey that does justice to cultural variations, acknowledges the possibility that factors in development interact in many different ways, and can still lay claim to addressing universally acceptable values. There may be other approaches, but following a long consultation with academics, as well as policy analysts in the international development community, we turned to the human rights arena, because this is where (at least officially) the broadest consensus on what constitutes *universally acceptable principles of rule* may be found. More specifically, fifty-eight UN member states signed the Universal Declaration of Human Rights (UDHR)—the secular equivalent of the Ten Commandments and similar statements in world religions—in 1948. And in 1993, 171 countries reaffirmed their commitment to the UDHR at the World Conference on Human Rights in Vienna. In addition, it should be noted that every country in the world has ratified at least one of the six other principal human rights treaties. And more than half the countries of the world have ratified all six principal human rights treaties—up from just 10 percent in 1990. A special millennium survey conducted by Gallup International indicates that the protection of human rights is of great concern to ordinary people around the world. The same survey also shows that people believe that governments are not doing enough to address human rights problems.[42] Although defining what exactly constitutes universal values will continue to be a source of controversy in the global arena, there is clearly a growing consensus to move in that direction, current U.S. unilateralist thinking notwithstanding. Latching on to the fledgling global human rights regime makes sense because rights relate to rules in the same way as needs relate to policy. The difference between a rights-based and a needs-based approach to development is summarized in Table 1.4.[43]

Relating rights to governance has many advantages. First, it shifts the focus from government to citizen. Good governance is a public good that citizens should be entitled to. Second, by focusing on entitlements, it recognizes that poverty is not merely a matter of being economically deprived. It is defined and sustained by a sense on the part of the poor of helplessness, dependence, lack of opportunities, and a lack of self-confidence and self-respect. The language of rights makes clear that the poor are not the subject of charity and benevolence by governments or the rich but instead are entitled to a decent standard of living and that rights are the vehicles for participation and empowerment. As Amartya Sen[44] argues, development should include a broad range of freedoms or rights such as the basic capabilities to avoid starvation, undernourishment, and premature mortality, as well as rights to education and being able to participate in the political process. This argument is echoed in the 2000 Human Development Report,[45] which discusses the relationship between human rights and human development approaches. The third—and most important—aspect of a rights-based approach is that it draws attention to the importance of norms and rules.

**Table 1.4  Differences Between a Needs Approach and a Rights Approach to Development**

| Needs Approach | Rights Approach |
| --- | --- |
| Needs are met or satisfied | Rights are realized |
| Needs do not imply duties or obligations | Rights always imply correlative duties |
| Needs are not necessarily universal | Human rights are universal |
| Needs can be met by outcome strategy | Rights can be realized only by paying attention to both outcome and process |
| Needs can be ranked in a hierarchy of priorities | Rights are indivisible because they are interdependent |
| Needs can be met through charity and benevolence | Charity is obscene in a rights perspective |

How a society is governed and how it achieves its development is as important in this perspective as what these processes accomplish. That is why this study is justifiably focusing on rules-in-use, not just results. The quantitative indicators of development—social or economic—should be analyzed in terms of how they were achieved. It is how these specific arena rules, aggregated into a particular political regime, are perceived that gives us the clues to how good governance is.

We recognize that the choice of human rights as the place from which to choose universal values is not free of controversy. But in the light of the other options available, it seemed to us to be the most relevant and promising for selecting our indicators and thus created the basis for a systematic and relevant data analysis. More specifically, we chose three principles that bear on how the state relates to society, in addition to three others that help us measure state performance: participation, fairness, decency, efficiency, accountability, and transparency.

The first three of these governance principles refer to *state-society relations*, the last three to *how the state operates*. The first set covers the way public authorities treat citizens. The second set relates to how public authorities go about realizing public policy objectives. It is obvious to us that both sets of principles are necessary for a complete coverage of the political process.

Two other considerations have been important to the design of our survey. The first is the number of indicators to include. This has a bearing on how detailed or disaggregated any measure will be. In striking a balance between being comprehensive and analytically specific, the survey consists of thirty indicators. This amounts to five indicators for each governance arena. These are inevitably aggregate variables, but we believe that they are meaningful and often more significant in understanding governance than more specific measures. The survey, therefore, does not probe governance issues in depth within individual countries as much as it provides the basis for an aggregate assessment of governance over time within and among countries. In so doing, our study may serve as a springboard for country-specific governance surveys and debates.

The second consideration is whether each dimension is of equal importance. Should each be weighted equally? The survey has been designed on the premise that each dimension and each indicator does indeed carry the same weight (i.e., each is made up of five indicators using the same rating scale of 1-5 points). This does not rule out the possibility that one set of indicators may at a particular time prove more important than others. Our premise, however, is that over time any such differences are neutralized. The alternative of differentiating the governance dimensions in terms of weight in this survey would make the analysis more difficult and arbitrary.

## Why Governance?

The last question could also have been the first: Why should we work with the concept of governance rather than democratic transition or democratic consolidation, which are more established in the literature on political change? We have already alluded to some of the reasons above, but in order to make clearer why governance may have an advantage at this point in the study of political changes, we shall discuss all of them here.

The first is that we are interested in the quality of regimes, not how they are transformed. Studies of democratic transition and consolidation tend to focus on the origins of a regime in structural terms or focus on the success of key actors to find agreement on a set of new constitutional rules. Although such studies have their value, they also have problems: structuralist studies because of their tendency to assume path dependency, voluntarist studies because they exaggerate actor autonomy.[46]

A second problem with the studies of democratization has become increasingly obvious, as we learn more and more about its rich empirical variety. As noted in one review of this literature, the core concept of democracy is increasingly "watered down" by the endless creation of "diminished subtypes" such as "illiberal," "delegative," or "electoral" democracy.[47] The result is that it is increasingly difficult to know where democratic consolidation begins and ends. Countries labeled as being in transition or undergoing consolidation end up in a conceptual no-man's land.

Some authors[48] have suggested that we should focus our study on democratic quality rather than transition or consolidation. We think this is a step in the right direction, but we are also concerned about the lack of consensus regarding what democratic quality is. The latter tend to focus only on such issues as representation, competition, and cooperation in the political arena. Although Larry Diamond uses a broader definition that includes references to the main indices in the Freedom House Index, we find his indices too tightly associated with the Western type of liberal democracy. Moreover, it overlooks important aspects of politics, notably the role that bureaucracy plays in determining outcomes. The time has come to find a concept that focuses on the concept of regime, a higher level of abstraction that allows us to explore more effectively whether governance makes a difference if constituted along liberal lines. By moving in this direction, we include in our selection of cases those that are not seen as being in the process of democratic consolidation.

In going forward with the World Governance Survey and analyzing our data, we are interested in examining how governance and democratization relate to one another. We shall return to this issue in Chapter 9, where we draw conclusions from this study.

Governance, then, in spite of the problems it has encountered, offers a potential that academic writers may appreciate more today than in the past when the focus—understandably—was squarely on understanding the dynamics of democratic transition. It offers a chance for comparative politics to be more universal in outlook, in how we assess regimes and regime change. As we propose in this book, governance can be treated as both a dependent and an independent variable. In the former case, it is likely to be analytically embedded in sets of thick variables that help us understand in individual countries or regions what the key variables are that explain the quality of governance. In the latter case, it is seen as having an effect on specific policy outcomes. As such, it responds to the concerns of the international community, which believes that good governance makes a difference when it comes to social and economic development. The basic analytical framework used here is summarized in Figure 1.2.

The analysis builds on existing works[49] that try to link institutional features to development. Our ambition is in some respects more limited, but also more realistic. By showing how a cross-section of well-informed persons perceives governance, we try to demonstrate the extent to which rules in use enjoy legitimacy. As such, our survey provides data that is complementary to other datasets but of equal importance, because the scores we provide for each country are an independent guide for businesspeople and others with a stake in development.

Finally, in treating governance as a dependent variable, we recognize that it is context-specific; any subjective perceptions thereof must be explained by specific events or trends. Although the extent to which this book allows us to engage in in-depth country analysis is limited, we do want to be sensitive to both the historical legacy and the international environment in which governance is being practiced in developing societies.

These points have definite implications for how we present our material in the substantive data chapters. The analysis and discussion center on the survey data that we obtained. Comparisons are made to highlight

**Figure 1.2　Framework for Analyzing Governance**

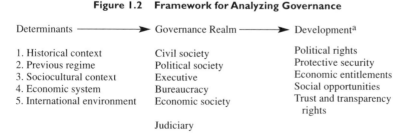

| Determinants | Governance Realm | Development[a] |
|---|---|---|
| 1. Historical context | Civil society | Political rights |
| 2. Previous regime | Political society | Protective security |
| 3. Sociocultural context | Executive | Economic entitlements |
| 4. Economic system | Bureaucracy | Social opportunities |
| 5. International environment | Economic society | Trust and transparency rights |
| | Judiciary | |

*Note:* a. Our definition of development is an adaptation from Amartya Sen (1999).

changes over time in perceptions of governance as well as between high-, medium-, and low-scoring countries. In the individual arena chapters, our discussion begins with a review of the literature that is relevant to governance indicators. The analysis proceeds from the aggregate to the individual indicator level, providing insight into events in individual countries. For most of the discussion of the indicators, we rely on complementary qualitative data drawn from comments made by the respondents and/or the country coordinators. These comments are important in letting us discuss governance as a dependent variable (i.e., explain differences with regard to specific factors at play). Finally, we should add that each of these chapters also includes a concluding summary of the main points and raising issues with implications for both research and policy practice.

## Notes

1. John Rapley, *Understanding Development: Theory and Practice in the Third World* (Boulder, CO: Lynne Rienner Publishers, 1996).
2. For an overview of the very wide range of administrative activities that took place in the 1970s, see Gerald E. Caiden, *Administrative Reform Comes of Age* (Berlin and New York: Walter de Gruyter, 1991).
3. This first phase devoted to poverty reduction was very much inspired by the works of Simon Kuznets, who argued that the central factor in equalizing income is the rising income of the poorer segments of the population. See his article "Economic Growth and Income Inequality," *American Economic Review* 45, no. 1 (March 1955): 17–26.
4. See, e.g., R. B. Jain (ed.), *Bureaucratic Politics in the Third World* (New Delhi: Gritanjali Publishing House, 1989).
5. M. Meyer et al., *Limits to Bureaucratic Growth* (New York and Berlin: Walter de Gruyter, 1985).
6. World Bank, *Accelerated Development in Sub-Saharan Africa* (Washington, DC: World Bank, 1981).
7. Path-breaking for this new move toward greater emphasis on voluntary action by people themselves were E. Schumacher, *Small is Beautiful* (New York: Harper & Row 1973), and D. Korten and R. Klauss (eds.), *People-Centered Development: Contributions Toward Theory and Planning Frameworks* (West Hartford CT: Kumarian Press, 1985).
8. An interesting illustration of this is the rapid growth of the World Social Forum (WSF), constituted by new social movements as a counterweight to the World Economic Forum, which is made up of representatives of governments and business. The WSF and other like-minded initiatives, however, continue to operate in the shadow of the dominant agenda, currently dominated by the Millennium Development goals approved by the United Nations General Assembly.
9. We are grateful to Vilma Fuentes, who helped us sort out the governance literature along the lines discussed here.
10. Jan Kooiman (ed.), *Modern Governance: New Government-Society Interactions* (London: Sage Publications, 1993).

11. See, e.g., R. A. W. Rhodes, *Understanding Governance: Policy Networks, Governance, and Accountability* (Buckingham, UK: Open University Press, 1997); and Jon Pierre and Guy Peters, *Governance, Politics, and the State* (London: Macmillan, 2000).

12. L. E. Lynn Jr., C. Heinrich, and C. J. Hill, "The Empirical Study of Governance: Theories, Models, Methods," paper presented at the Workshop for the Empirical Study of Governance, Tucson, University of Arizona, 1999.

13. K. J. Holsti. "Governance without Government: Polyarchy in the 19th Century European International Politics," in James N. Rosenau and E-O Cziempel, eds., *Governance Without Government: Order and Change in World Politics* (Cambridge, UK: Cambridge University Press, 1992).

14. E.g., Rosenau and Cziempel, *Governance Without Government*; and P. Redfern and M. Desai, *Global Governance: Ethics and Economics of the World Order* (New York: Pinter, 1997).

15. Goran Hyden, "The Study of Governance," pp 1–26 in G. Hyden and M. Bratton, eds., *Governance and Politics in Africa* (Boulder: Lynne Rienner Publishers, 1992).

16. James G. March and Johan P. Olsen, *Democratic Governance* (New York: Free Press, 1998), p. 6.

17. United Nations Development Programme, *Reconceptualizing Governance* (New York: UNDP, 1997), pp. 2–3.

18. World Bank, *Governance and Development* (Washington, DC: World Bank, 1992).

19. Robert Putnam, *Making Democracy Work: Civic Traditions in Modern Italy* (Princeton, NJ: Princeton University Press, 1993).

20. Juan Linz and Alfred Stepan, *Problems of Democratic Transition and Consolidation: Southern Europe, South America, and Post-Communist Europe* (Baltimore: Johns Hopkins University Press, 1996).

21. R. Sprogard and M. James, "Governance and Democracy: The People's View. A Global Opinion Poll," presented at the United Nations University's Millennium Conference, Tokyo, January 19–21, 2000.

22. D. Narayan, R. Patel, K. Schafft, A. Rademacher, and S. Koch-Schulte, *Voices of the Poor: Can Anyone Hear Us?* (Washington, DC: World Bank, 2000).

23. See, e.g., Scott Mainwaring and T. R. Scully (eds.), *Building Democratic Institutions: Party Systems in Latin America* (Stanford, CA: Stanford University Press, 1995); Larry Diamond, *Developing Democracy: Towards Consolidation* (Baltimore: Johns Hopkins University Press, 1999).

24. M. Shugart and J. M. Carey, *Presidents and Assemblies: Constitutional Design and Electoral Dynamics* (Cambridge, UK: Cambridge University Press, 1992); also, A. Stepan and C. Skach, "Constitutional Frameworks and Democratic Consolidation: Parliamentarism versus Presidentialism," *World Politics* 46, no. 1 (1996): 1–22.

25. Andrew Reynolds and Timothy Sisk (eds.), *Elections and Conflict Resolution in Africa* (Washington, DC: United States Institute of Peace Press, 1997).

26. International Institute for Democracy and Electoral Assistance, *The International IDEA Handbook of Electoral System Design* (Stockholm: International IDEA, 1997).

27. After the terrorist attacks in New York and Washington, DC, on September 11, 2001, this issue has become increasingly salient in the United States, where

national security concerns to administration officials are interpreted to override conventional emphasis on individual civil liberties.

28. E.g., Samuel P. Huntington, *The Third Wave: Democratization at the End of the 20th Century* (Norman: University of Oklahoma Press, 1991); Adam Przeworski, *Democracy and the Market* (New York: Cambridge University Press, 1991).

29. Amartya Sen, *Development as Freedom* (New York: Random House, 1999).

30. N. Campos and J. Nugent, "Development Performance and the Institutions of Governance: Evidence from East Asia and Latin America," *World Development* 27, no. 3 (1999): 439–452.

31. E.g., Peter Blau, *The Dynamics of Bureaucracy: A Study of Interpersonal Relations in Two Government Agencies* (Chicago: University of Chicago Press, 1963), and *Exchange and Power in Social Life* (London: J. Wiley, 1964).

32. Michel Crozier, *The Bureaucratic Phenomenon* (Chicago: University of Chicago Press, 1964).

33. E.g., Peter Evans and J. Rauch, "Bureaucratic Structure and Bureaucratic Performance in Less Developed Countries," *Journal of Public Economics* 75 (2000): 49–71.

34. Linz and Stepan, *Problems of Democratic Transition.*

35. Douglass North, *Institutions, Institutional Change, and Economic Performance* (Cambridge, UK: Cambridge University Press, 1990).

36. Przeworski, *Democracy and the Market.*

37. John Dryzek, *Democracy in Capitalist Times: Ideals, Limits, and Struggles* (Oxford: Oxford University Press, 1996).

38. John Locke, *The Second Treatise of Civil Government* (Oxford, UK: Blackwell, 1946); and *Two Treatises of Government* (Cambridge, UK: Cambridge University Press, 1960).

39. C. Montesquieu, *Spirit of the Laws* (New York: Free Press, 1970).

40. Max Gluckman, *Politics, Law, and Ritual in Tribal Society* (Oxford, UK: Blackwell, 1965).

41. D. Kaufmann, A. Kraay, and P. Zoido-Lobaton, "Aggregating Governance Indicators," *Policy Research Working Paper No. 2195* (Washington, DC: World Bank, 1999).

42. Sprogard and James, "Governance and Democracy."

43. We are grateful to Urban Jonsson and Bjorn Ljungqvist of UNICEF for ideas included in this table.

44. Sen, *Development as Freedom.*

45. United Nations Development Programme, *Human Development Report 2000* (New York: Oxford University Press, 2000).

46. Goran Hyden and Ole Elgstrom (eds.), *Development and Democracy: What Have We Learnt and How?* (London: Routledge, 2002).

47. David Collier and Stephen Levitsky, "Democracy with 'Adjectives': Conceptual Innovation in Comparative Research," *World Politics* 49, no. 3 (April 1997): 430–451.

48. Diamond, *Developing Democracy.* Herbert Kitschelt, Z. Mansfeldova, R. Markowski, and G. Toka, *Post-Communist Party Systems: Competition, Representation, and Inter-Party Competition* (New York: Cambridge University Press, 1999).

49. See, e.g., Daniel Kaufmann, Aart Kraay, and Pablo Zoido-Lobaton, "Governance Matters II—Updated Indicators for 2000/01," *World Bank Policy*

*Research Department Working Paper No. 2772* (Washington, DC: World Bank, 2002). For further materials on governance produced by Kaufmann's team, see www.worldbank.org/wbi/governance; S. Knack and O. Keefer, "Institutions and Economic Performance: Cross-Country Tests Using Alternative Institutional Measures," *Economics and Politics* 7 (1995): 207–227; R. LaPorta, F. Lopez-de-Silanes, A. Shleifer, and R. Vishny, "The Quality of Government," *NBER Working Paper Series No. 6727* (Cambridge, MA: National Bureau of Economic Research, 1999).

# 2

# Governance Performance: The Aggregate Picture

This chapter reports the aggregate findings of the World Governance Survey. It is important to note that the study of governance is not the same as the study of democracy, although there is overlap. Students of the process of democratization have been caught in a debate about whether to adopt a minimalist definition of democracy, implying a focus on measurable variables. The latter are typically related to the two dimensions of Robert Dahl's notion of *polyarchy*—contestation and participation.[1] Although we recognize the value of such a more specific focus, we also acknowledge (with the many critics of the minimalist approach[2]) that it omits many dimensions that are important in determining political reform in transitional and developing societies. The study of governance at the empirical level differs from mainstream studies of democratization in two important respects: (1) it provides a thick definition that allows for an assessment of a broader set of variables than those typically included in studies of democratization; and (2) by focusing on the regime level, it is not a priori loaded in the direction of favoring the liberal-democratic model of democracy. We do not expect, therefore, that our findings will automatically correlate well with studies that draw on the liberal-democratic model for its primary indicators. At the same time, we are interested in determining how much overlap there is in the explanatory variables used here and in other attempts at measuring governance (or specific aspects thereof).

This chapter is divided into two major sections. The first presents an aggregate profile of governance performance in each of the sixteen countries included in this study. To facilitate the analysis, it groups the countries in terms of high, medium, and low governance scores based on the 2000 survey. It also discusses changes that have taken place over the five-year period respondents were asked to consider. Attention is paid to explaining the major changes that have taken place, whether positive or negative, in

33

individual countries. The second section discusses governance ratings by arena with a view to identifying which seems to be particularly volatile.

## Understanding Changes in Governance

This section reports on how our respondents—the WIPs—assessed governance in their respective countries in 2000. It is organized to provide an aggregate profile for each country, as well as a composite picture of each arena. In addition to discussing the perceived quality of each arena, any outlying or interesting cases are included. We focus on comments made by the experts and country coordinators that clearly support the differences in numerical ratings (see Figure 2.1).

In order to differentiate among our sixteen cases, we decided to group them in terms of high, medium, and low scorers, based on their aggregate ratings from the 2000 survey.[3] Our goal is to examine the characteristics of each group to better understand the similarities and differences among the groups.[4] Beginning with the high scorers, below we present aggregate scores for each group.[5]

### High-Scoring Countries

This group consists of six countries: Chile, India, Jordan, Mongolia, Tanzania, and Thailand (see Figure 2.2). They all have an aggregate score of 85 points or above for all six arenas. This is approximately in the middle of the numerical scale but clearly above average regarding perceptions by respondents. It indicates that respondents have been aware that if the various dimensions of governance—or all the arenas—are adequately considered,

**Figure 2.1   WGS Scores for All Sixteen Countries, 1995 and 2000**

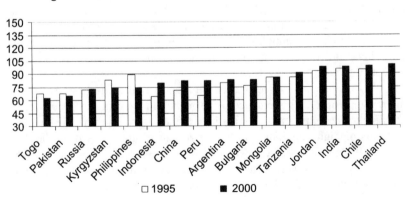

**Figure 2.2     Countries with High Governance Scores, 1995 and 2000**

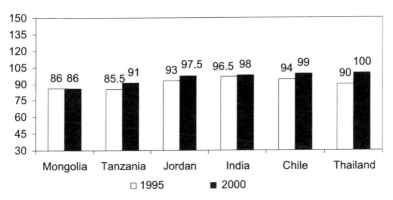

there are shortcomings even in the countries with a high performance level. This also indicates that respondents have not been inclined to assign a high score with the ulterior motive of boosting their country's overall score. In short, we believe that respondents have been sincere in their answers.

Most noticeable about this group is its diversity. It includes one of the poorest countries in Africa (Tanzania), a newly industrialized country in Southeast Asia (Thailand), a middle-income country in Latin America (Chile), a former communist state (Mongolia), an Islamic kingdom in the Middle East (Jordan), and the largest democracy in the world (India). Apart from India and Chile, which have a long history of building democracy, these countries have more recently shifted toward democratic systems of governance. This leads us to two important observations about governance. First, better governance is not a luxury of the rich or confined to certain regions. Second, our measure of governance, which focuses on the stewardship of the rules of the political game, calls into question the oft-stated proposition that there are certain economic and social requisites associated with a move toward democracy.[6] It is an important point to make at a time in the study of democratization when there is growing uncertainty about the extent to which specific measures of liberal democracy really are the most useful.[7] Governance may not tell us much—if anything—about democratic consolidation, but it does tell us something about the level of regime stability. It suggests that assessment of governance performance is independent of assessment of liberal democracy. Good governance is possible even where regimes may display features of what some call illiberal democracy.[8] A probable reason is that respondents do not assess the stewardship of rules in isolation of what the political system delivers in terms of tangible goods. As we turn to a brief discussion of each country, this becomes clearer.

*Thailand* is a good case in point. It is a country that has gradually democratized but where the military still holds power and may threaten civilian rule. It is also a monarchy that has allowed greater pluralism, but the king retains more than just symbolic power.

Our study suggests that the most interesting thing about Thailand may not be its level of consolidation as a liberal democracy but the fact that when assessing all six arenas together its overall score is one of the highest in this sample. Its ability to engage in constitutional reform as a way of finding a new balance between the executive and legislative branches of government, as well as between rights and obligations of Thai citizens, is an indication that it has reached a level of regime stability that expresses itself in overall high governance scores. Also important is that civil service is held in high regard and that state-market relations are seen as functioning (in spite of the financial crisis that afflicted the country in 1997). Thailand has charted its own path toward good governance, allowing indigenous institutions rather than imported ideas to constitute the main basis for reform.[9] The fact that Thailand is in this category is no surprise.

Neither is *India* a surprise high scorer. It has had a long experience of democracy and regime stability. The secular nature of the Indian state has been a guarantee that this multiethnic and multireligious country can be held together. Even though communal clashes have increased, especially between Hindus and Muslims, there is no evidence that they threaten the regime. Above all, India has retained a vibrant civil society with a high density of local associations. It is confirmed in our survey, which indicates a high score for civil society. The same applies to the judiciary and the bureaucracy, although there are also blemishes. Foremost is the widespread sense that it is difficult to get anything done without bribery. As one of our respondents dejectedly put it: "Right from birth to death nothing happens without bribery and corruption. People can neither live nor die with dignity."

*Chile* is a contender for the highest governance score among all those included in this study. Although it saw a tumultuous period of rule during the beginning of the 1970s, and the ensuing military dictatorship under General Augusto Pinochet prevented a return to liberal democracy, Chile since 1988 has made strides toward democracy. Of all the countries, Chile may be the case where the scores for civil liberties and political freedoms—per the Freedom House Index—and our governance measures have the closest association. Thus we find that Chile enjoys regime stability while also making headway toward consolidation of its democracy. It may be worth noting here that Chile scores higher than its neighbor, Argentina, which began democratizing earlier but has been bogged down by problems of governance, notably the relationship between key institutional actors (e.g., between federal state and provinces and between the executive and legislative branches).

We now turn to a more surprising case among high-scoring countries: *Jordan*. Given the low scores that virtually all of the Arab countries have on the Freedom House Index, it is easy to dismiss them as being afflicted by poor governance. However, the score on the liberal democracy scale is not identical to the score on the governance scale. Jordan is an exception to the trend in this region, which, according to the Freedom House Index, has been deteriorating. Jordan has cautiously introduced multiparty democracy since 1989. Progress has not necessarily been easy. Between 1991 and 1993, for instance, the king dissolved parliament and ruled by decree. Since then, elections have been held. On the whole, political rights are less restrictive than in most other Middle East countries. Perceptions of governance in Jordan must also be seen in light of regional volatility. Jordan, for instance, has a sizable Palestinian population, so the Israel-Palestinian conflict has a bearing on trends in Jordan. The monarchy is seen as a stabilizing force. The adjustments to changes in the world and the region, in particular, that the kings of Jordan—first King Hussein and later his successor, Abdullah II—have encouraged are important for understanding why respondents give the country a high overall score.

*Mongolia* is another country whose high governance scores reflect relative success in the transition to democracy. Like other communist countries it went through a double transition: from totalitarian communist rule to multiparty democracy, as well as from central planning to a market economy. A unique feature of the Mongolian transition is that the communist system collapsed under its own weight when party leadership voluntarily resigned. Its relative isolation may have facilitated this outcome. The reform process went on without outside pressures. At the same time, in a country where the vast majority is nomadic, citizen pressures in one direction or the other have been faint. In short, autonomy seems to have helped Mongolia successfully make the double transitions, which culminated in the adoption of a new constitution in 1992. The first election brought a new generation of leaders to power, but in the most recent election the former communist leaders were returned to office. Although the party now has a different name, their personal reputations are such that they have been able to return to power in a competitive political process. Although Mongolian respondents spotted several weaknesses, they are also appreciative of the progress the country has made without violence. That political leaders have managed the sensitive relationship with China, with its sizable Mongolian minority, also figures in the comments our respondents made.

*Tanzania* is the final high-scoring country, where regime stability— since independence 1961—features prominently. In spite of severe economic problems, it has moved forward and remained peaceful. Unlike many neighbors, it is not afflicted by ethnic conflict. Governance in Tanzania may be defective in some aspects, but in the more comprehensive perspective many positive aspects make a difference for the better. For example, Tanzania is far from being a liberal democracy, but it has made progress toward an institutionalized form of electoral democracy. Neither is its bureaucracy free from corruption, but even there steps to curb it have been taken. The Tanzanian case illustrates that governance, when assessed by local stakeholders as opposed to outside observers, registers the difference that political leadership can make at points in time. Our respondents give credit to the fact that Tanzania is seen as moving upward and forward after a long period of decline. This is especially true for the insiders—those associated with the incumbent government—because they are well placed to see the difference that has been brought to government operations since 1995.

### Medium-Scoring Countries

This group includes five countries: Indonesia, China, Peru, Argentina and Bulgaria; all have scores in the low eighties (see Figure 2.3). Again, this is a diverse set of countries. Particularly interesting is that all are involved in processes of transition. Bulgaria has been moving away from a communist dictatorship, and Indonesia and Peru came out of authoritarian rule during the period of the survey. Argentina is gripped by crisis. China remains autocratic but is involved in a process of market reform and, to a much lesser degree, political reform.

　　Because political and economic reforms form such an important part of recent history in these countries, this middle category reflects another feature of governance measures: perceptions of how the rules of the political game are handled can change quickly and dramatically. There is enough evidence to suggest that a shift in perceptions may lift a country in its propensity and ability to develop resources, whether financial, human, or

**Figure 2.3　Countries with Medium Governance Scores, 1995 and 2000**

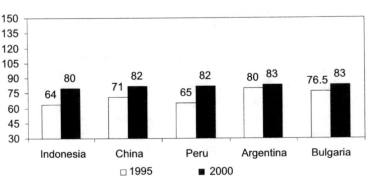

social. The way people—especially elites—feel about their country's politics is likely to have a bearing on events in society. This suggests that governance measures are more important when assessing prospects for social and economic development than merely measures of liberal democracy. The study of governance offers the prospect of providing important insights into how politics relates to development, something that the current debate about the relationship between development and democracy does not. Below we discuss the five individual countries in this group.

*Indonesia* offers interesting insights. It underwent a major political transition after the 1997 financial crisis that brought to an end the economic boom that had shielded an economic elite closely allied with President Suharto, no longer in office. Indonesian respondents reflecting on conditions could not escape noting the difference between 2000 and 1995. During the period when the military exercised close control of social and political life—via the New Order—civil liberties and political freedoms were denied citizens. By 2000, there was a sense of freedom and a growing respect for human rights—except in East Timor, where Indonesian soldiers battled freedom fighters. These changes gave respondents reason to provide a satisfactory yet cautious score, indicating hope for the future. However, this optimism was tempered by a sense that the principal beneficiaries of the new reforms would be people with money. For instance, individual comments suggested that many people were running for office because they were rich; whether they would attend to the interests of constituents once in office was suspect.

*China* is interesting because there is so little survey data available, especially on political issues. Notable is the fact that Chinese respondents recognized the shortcomings in the system of governance. It is no surprise that China scores highest on such measures as government effectiveness and state-market relations but scores much lower on civil society and political society. Chinese respondents point to the impressive results that the country has been able to achieve, especially during the 1990s. Although there is not much indication that Chinese respondents see democracy just around the corner, one interesting tidbit is that they acknowledge the increasing role that the People's Assembly—the legislature—has been allowed to play. Even if that body is far from resembling any parliament in a liberal democracy, its influence is growing, and Chinese respondents register it as an important change in governance.

The case of *Bulgaria* is less dramatic. Like neighbors in Eastern Europe, it has been struggling toward democracy; it trails neighbors to the north—except Romania—in meeting criteria for membership in the European Union. This lack of political progress is reflected in its modest scores on the governance measures in our survey. These reveal a certain disappointment, if not disillusion, among respondents that the transition from communism has not proceeded fast enough or produced better results. Getting new rules in place and enforcing them has, as in so many transitional societies, been difficult. New institutions take time to build.

*Peru* is seen in light of a stormy political period during the rule of President Alberto Fujimori. In 1980, after twelve years of military rule, Peru was the first country in Latin America to shift to a democratic regime. Over time, the democratic situation slowly deteriorated despite competitive elections, and the Fujimori regime was characterized by increasing authoritarianism. Fujimori was proclaimed winner of the 2000 election despite accusations of irregularities that led to the withdrawal of international observers. The collapse of his rule came with the disclosure of a videotape (the first of many) showing Fujimori's intelligence adviser, Valdimiro Montesinos, bribing an opposition congressman to join the government's parliamentary group. Although Fujimori tried to blame the scandal on Montesinos, there was massive public outrage and Fujimori fled the country. After winning a legitimate election, Alejandro Toledo was chosen as president. The survey, carried out after Fujimori fled, reflects this situation. The survey scores are indicating a certain degree of optimism, but there is also a sense of caution among most respondents given previous experiences.

The case of *Argentina* deserves a bit more discussion. One may say that at a first glance its governance scores are much lower than expected given that the survey was conducted in 2000, before the latest economic crisis set in. Our survey, however, indicates a well-founded and widespread skepticism toward the rules that regulated the political system. More specifically, our respondents indicated that public input into policy was limited. The government did not provide an environment in which input was facilitated and continued to set the policy agenda on its own. Most respondents, in their qualitative comments, argued that there is an important gap between citizens and representatives. Individual or institutional views outside the government's agenda very rarely become inputs in the political process. Moreover, the mechanism of party candidate lists (*listas sabanas*) makes representation even more difficult because citizens do not know whom they are voting for. As one of the respondents observed, there is formal competition for political power, but in reality electoral mechanisms are not effective. Third, respondents in Argentina were also frustrated by the degree of corruption and bureaucratic inefficiency. People were inclined to blame civil servants' inefficiency for most of the country's problems. Thus, despite the existence of political rights and civil liberties, governance scores are rather low. Democracy is no guarantee of more effective development.

At the same time, it is important to note Argentina's ability to withstand a return to military rule. One reason is that the military in Argentina was weakened considerably after civilian rule was reintroduced in the 1980s. It also indicates the costs that the military itself associates with a return to power. Most officers would probably not consider it worthwhile, economically or politically. This means that even a serious economic crisis, like the one that has plagued the country since 2001, does not necessarily translate into a change in regime. Instead, the country continues to barely stay afloat, at high cost to citizens.

### Low-Scoring Countries

The low-scoring group consists of Togo, Pakistan, Russia, Kyrgyzstan, and the Philippines. The first two have the lowest scores in the whole survey—only in the mid-60s—while the other three score in the low to mid-70s. This is the group where decline is more common than improvement in governance scores. Only Russia records a higher score than in 1995, although it is by no means a significant increase (see Figure 2.4).

This group confirms our proposition that who makes what rules, when, and how? often matters more these days than the issue of who gets what, when, and how? These countries have all scored low on an index that measures the significance of rules. When rulers abuse their power, and especially if they ignore rights of their citizens, governance scores go down. In short, people care about how they are being governed. This comes out in the account we provide of these five countries.

*Togo* has the lowest overall score for both periods. The low scores are no surprise to those who follow Togolese politics. The incumbent president, Gnassingbé Eyadema, the longest-serving ruler in sub-Saharan Africa, has fought to stay in power at any cost, interfering with the electoral rules and harassing members of the opposition. He has even gone to the extent of try-

**Figure 2.4   Countries with Low Governance Scores, 1995 and 2000**

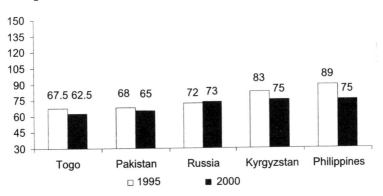

ing to assassinate his most powerful rival. It is also a country in which the economy has stagnated and living standards for the elite and masses have deteriorated because of misrule.

*Kyrgyzstan* has suffered from ongoing political instability since it became independent after the breakup of the Soviet Union. Like its neighbors in the region, much of Kyrgyz politics centers on managing patron-client relations and ensuring that all the patrons have a stake in the system. There have been several incidents indicating that managing these informal institutions is difficult. Political instability always looms at the horizon. Although Kyrgyzstan has not been as hard-hit as Afghanistan, it is clear that in Central Asia the main issue is not how to become democratic in a liberal sense but how to maintain political stability without causing harmful civil conflicts. The low scores demonstrate the extent to which this concern is real.

The low score for *Pakistan* is hardly a surprise given that it recently reverted to military rule. It is perhaps even a little surprising that the military coup in Pakistan did not have a greater impact on the respondents in that country. It is possible that for many Pakistanis, despite the curtailment of political freedoms, there was a sense of relief because of the high levels of corruption associated with the civilian regime that was ousted. In spite of possibly giving the military the benefit of the doubt when it comes to commitment to improved governance, respondents are generally critical or skeptical, something that seems to have been further fomented after the events of September 11, 2001.

*Russia* provides an interesting case of transition. Although the overall political situation has stabilized in the country since the early years of the transition 1989–1991, evidence suggests that uncertainty still reigns with regard to the country's destination. The perception of our respondents (as well as external ratings[10]) is that government effectiveness has improved in Russia. However, the same sources also point to a decline in the rating for political participation. One concern is freedom of expression. Our WIPs suggested that authorities and oligarchic clans increasingly control the mass media. One of the clearest findings of our survey in Russia was the perception about the weakening of political society, particularly the legislature. Experts perceive that the legislature's already limited influence has deteriorated due to subjugation by the executive and that the accountability of legislators to the electorate has remained low.

The most serious decline is recorded for *the Philippines*—putting it in this bottom group. Because our survey was conducted about the same time as President Joseph Estrada was going to be impeached, it is clear that the perceptions of our respondents were colored by events surrounding that process. Many people in the Philippines had grown weary of Estrada's corruption, cronyism, and incompetence. After the collapse of the impeachment hearings, people took to the streets and swept Estrada out in another showing of people's power. Most people breathed a sigh of relief as Gloria Macapagal-Arroyo was sworn in as the new president soon thereafter.

The Philippines provides an interesting example of advances as well as setbacks. Some commentators have argued that the role of the military—in allowing removal of an elected president—essentially made the exercise of people's power a reality. In that sense, what happened was a de facto coup.[11] Many feel it would have been preferable if Estrada had been removed through the constitutional processes of impeachment and conviction. But how does such an issue get resolved when normal constitutional means and due process are seen as so corrupt? The situation in the Philippines illustrates again the value of taking a governance approach to measuring political progress, because it allows for an assessment of a broader range of variables that are important to local people than efforts at assessing democratic consolidation do.

## Changes over Time

We have already referred to the comparisons that we asked our respondents to make between the situation in year 2000 and that of five years earlier. There are always problems associated with assessing the past. For instance, respondents may not be immune to exaggerating their impression of the past, especially if it varies considerably in either positive or negative terms. An element of nostalgia may enter into their assessment (or the opposite may be true, if the present looks so much better). The point is that we are not attempting to provide an accurate account of each country's history. All we suggest is that perceptions are important for understanding the dynamics of governance. The sense of whether the rules in use are legitimate stems from a comparison, not only in the present but also with the past. Our findings reflect the reality in which respondents live and work. As in the case of the Philippines, single events that bear on the nature or quality of the regime tend to translate into a major dent in the ratings. Trends in each country differ. Some record progress, others decline. Some show marked difference over the five-year period, others very little. We divide the countries into three groups, along the country composite ranking for the present and five years ago: (1) those that record improvements, (2) those that have no or little change,[12] and (3) those that have slid backward. Out of the sixteen countries analyzed here, ten recorded an improvement over time in quality of governance; three countries report no real change; and three have experienced a decline.

As can be seen from Figure 2.5, Indonesia and Peru record the most impressive improvements. The difference in scores in Indonesia is 25 per-

**Figure 2.5    Change in Overall (Median) Governance Scores, 1995–2000**

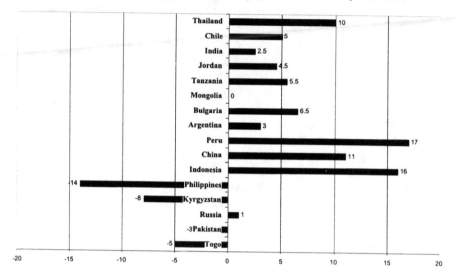

cent, and Peru is not far behind at 22 percent. Other countries such as China, Bulgaria, and Thailand have also registered 10 percent or more improvement in their governance scores. More modest gains are recorded for Chile, Tanzania, Jordan, Russia, and India.

Only three countries fall into the category of *no or little change*— Mongolia, Pakistan, and Russia. Although there is some variation in scores among the arenas in these three countries, they are small and they even out on an aggregate level. Three countries experienced a decline in perceptions of governance—the Philippines, Pakistan, Kyrgyzstan, and Togo. The decline is noticeable but not dramatic in the latter two countries but significant—more than 10 percentage points—in the Philippines. It suggests to us that perceptions of governance do change over time, often in response to events that affect regime stability. It also tells us, however, that perceptions remain relatively stable, since not all events strike at the meta level of governance. Much of what affects people's lives takes place at the policy or administration levels. These things only occasionally spill over into the governance realm.

### Changes in the Six Governance Arenas, 1995–2000

Much discussion has taken place in the literature on democratization about what factors cause the process to move forward. Some have focused on structural explanations. They argue that democracy is only possible—or democracy can only survive—under certain socioeconomic conditions. We are excluding them from further consideration here. We focus instead on those who have looked at what institutional aspects are most important. Some would focus on civil society or associational life as important explanatory variables. They would argue that the presence of vibrant associations is a key ingredient in any move toward democracy.[13] Others would emphasize political culture. Without a civic type of political culture, democracy is unlikely, if not impossible.[14] There are also those who focus primarily on the electoral rules and regulations because they are the most powerful instruments of changing political behavior.[15] All these approaches contribute important insights to our understanding of democratic consolidation.

Drawing on our own design for the study of governance, we recognize the significance of all six arenas to regime stability. We are interested here in identifying what the most important changes have been among the six before we detail the specific changes that have occurred within each (with illustrations from the more interesting country cases). The details of the changes over time by country and arena are summarized in Table 2.1.

What interests us first in this table are the totals for each arena 1995 and 2000 and how these compare when applied to the three categories of governance performers: high, medium, and low. We are focusing here on the more important differences over time.[16]

The first point to note is that the scores are more stable in each arena among the high performers than they are among the others. In no single arena does the difference over time exceed 10 percent. Moreover, in all cases the differences are upward. The second point is that the medium performers display the greatest fluctuations. In all but one arena—civil society—has there been a change, again to the better, exceeding 10 percent or more. Especially noteworthy are the improvements in political society, economic society, and the judiciary. This suggests to us that both political and economic reforms have been effective; and that both political democratization and economic liberalization have left behind a positive legacy, at least as far as the rules of the game are concerned. The third point is that all changes among the low performers have been downward. These countries have suffered deterioration in governance. Our respondents point to both civil and political society as the two arenas where this decline has been especially noticeable. The score for political society in year 2000 among this group of countries is the lowest arena score overall.

The next step is to offer the summary scores of each arena for both years. They are contained in Figure 2.6. It may be important to remind the reader that our respondents represent a cross section of well-informed persons in each country. They include religious leaders, government officials, politically elected leaders, businesspersons, members of the media, lawyers, academics, and leaders of national and international nongovern-

**Table 2.1  Comparative Analysis of the Six Arenas of Governance, 1995 and 2000**

| Country | Civil Society 1995 | Civil Society 2000 | Political Society 1995 | Political Society 2000 | Government 1995 | Government 2000 | Bureaucracy 1995 | Bureaucracy 2000 | Economic Society 1995 | Economic Society 2000 | Judiciary 1995 | Judiciary 2000 |
|---|---|---|---|---|---|---|---|---|---|---|---|---|
| **Low-scoring Countries** | | | | | | | | | | | | |
| Togo | 13 | 12 | 10.5 | 7 | 10 | 9.5 | 10.5 | 11 | 13 | 12.5 | 12 | 11 |
| Pakistan | 14 | 11 | 12 | 7 | 10 | 10 | 13 | 14 | 12 | 13 | 10 | 11 |
| Russia | 14 | 15 | 13 | 12 | 12 | 14 | 13 | 13 | 11 | 12 | 11 | 11.5 |
| Kyrgyzstan | 16 | 13 | 14 | 12 | 17 | 15 | 12 | 11 | 14 | 14 | 12 | 12 |
| Philippines | 17 | 15 | 13 | 12 | 16 | 12 | 14 | 11 | 16 | 13 | 13 | 12 |
| Total | 74 | 66 | 62.5 | 50 | 65 | 60.5 | 62.5 | 60 | 66 | 64.5 | 58 | 57.5 |
| **Medium-scoring Countries** | | | | | | | | | | | | |
| Indonesia | 12 | 17 | 7 | 15 | 11 | 12 | 10 | 11 | 11 | 13 | 10 | 13 |
| China | 11 | 13 | 11 | 13 | 14 | 15 | 11 | 12 | 11 | 14 | 12 | 13 |
| Peru | 12 | 15 | 9 | 14 | 11 | 14 | 11 | 13 | 13 | 14 | 8 | 12 |
| Argentina | 15 | 16 | 12 | 12 | 15 | 15 | 11 | 12 | 14 | 14 | 12 | 13 |
| Bulgaria | 15 | 15 | 13 | 13 | 13 | 15 | 12 | 13 | 12 | 15 | 12 | 13 |
| Total | 65 | 76 | 52 | 67 | 64 | 71 | 55 | 61 | 61 | 70 | 54 | 64 |
| **High-scoring Countries** | | | | | | | | | | | | |
| Mongolia | 15 | 15 | 15 | 16 | 15 | 15 | 14 | 14 | 14 | 14 | 13 | 13 |
| Tanzania | 15 | 15 | 14 | 15 | 17 | 16 | 14 | 16 | 14 | 16 | 13 | 14 |
| Jordan | 16 | 16 | 13 | 13.5 | 18 | 18.5 | 14 | 15 | 17 | 18 | 16 | 17 |
| India | 16 | 17 | 16 | 16 | 17 | 16 | 17 | 17 | 15 | 16 | 14 | 16.5 |
| Chile | 17 | 18 | 14.25 | 15.5 | 15 | 18 | 14 | 15 | 18 | 19 | 13 | 15 |
| Thailand | 15 | 19 | 13.5 | 16 | 15 | 16 | 15 | 16 | 15 | 16 | 16 | 17 |
| Total | 94 | 100 | 85.75 | 92 | 97 | 99.5 | 88 | 93 | 93 | 99 | 85 | 92.5 |

*Notes:* We provide the absolute numbers in this table in order to give the reader a sense of the actual scores per arena. The percentages provided in the text are derived from these absolute numbers.

**Figure 2.6   Summed Governance Arena Scores, 1995–2000**

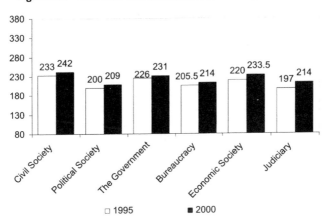

mental organizations. The highest overall score for both occasions is for civil society, indicating that this arena is reasonably well governed. This is also another indication that reforms aimed at enhancing civil liberties and political freedoms have yielded meaningful results. Scores for economic society are also high, as are those for the government arena. The latter is more of surprise than the former but does indicate that how governments operate is appreciated and presumably as important as what they do. The lowest arena scores overall are for the judiciary and for political society, whereas bureaucracy falls somewhere in between the other five. However, we should note that the judicial arena did experience the largest percentage gain of any arena from 1995 to 2000. This suggests that both political society and judiciary are more problematic than the other arenas. We assume that reforming institutions in these two places is politically more controversial and therefore more difficult to achieve. For instance, political society, as we all know, is a highly contested arena because it focuses not only on making policy but also on who should have the right to make policy. Before proceeding to an analysis of each arena, we look more closely at some crosscutting issues.

One such issue of interest is the relatively high score for civil society and the low score for political society. At a first glance, it may look like a contradiction. The assumption is that a stronger civil society would increase pressures on public officials and that political society would respond to such pressures. It may be that this finding is in fact a reflection of the time lag between identifying a problem (or the public institutions experiencing pressure from the civil society) and finding a solution to it (or the public institutions responding to the pressure from civil society). It may also be possible that civil society is stronger and yet remains somewhat separate from the state. Our findings, however, also point in another direction: civil society may have grown in strength but it has done so largely because of the inadequate performance of the state. This finding is in line with the argument[17] that civil society is a sphere that evolves largely in response to the inability or failure of the state to meet needs or demands of its citizens. The results of the survey, therefore, support the increasing literature that people engage in collective action on their own—whether to strengthen political and civil liberties, promote economic prosperity, or provide social services—because public institutions do not.[18]

The relatively low scores for the political society, bureaucracy, and judicial arenas indicate that people in the survey countries believe that public officials do not act with the public interest in mind. Although this may not be factually correct in all instances, it is nonetheless significant that scores and qualitative comments by our respondents confirm the existence of a relatively widespread belief that individuals in public office cannot necessarily be trusted to act as guardians of the public interest. Our study suggests that this common perception that public officials are not accountable can be explained both by a generalized suspicion toward these officials among the public and a more specific knowledge of the tendency among the latter to act in their private rather than the public interest.

Related to the issue of lack of trust is the common reference by respondents to the persistence of patronage and corruption in the public realm. Although there are exceptions, this phenomenon is reported in the data from countries in every region. Many respondents have personally experienced corruption in public transactions and can speak to it with some authority. Our data certainly confirm the widespread existence of corruption, not only in obtaining business licenses but also in other arenas where citizens engage the state to obtain permits, goods, and services. This reiterates a common finding in the literature that the way in which institutions function is important for a country's development.[19]

There is discontent about public institutions in many countries, and the state and civil society often do not seem to engage each other in win-win processes on a day-to-day basis. It is possible that the major explanation is the relative weakness of political society in many countries. The intermediate mechanisms between civic associations and interest groups, on the one hand, and government (e.g., political parties, electoral systems, and legislatures), on the other, are not very well institutionalized. This finding is similar to the conclusion that Linz and Stepan[20] draw in their overview of democratic transition and consolidation in Southern Europe, Latin America, and Eastern Europe.

Given the view that political society is weak, it is interesting that the government arena scores so well. Respondents across the board believe that governments generally act responsibly with regard to key concerns to citizens. Comments indicate that governments deal with conflicts without excessive harm or humiliation. They also suggest that governments demonstrate commitment to ensuring the personal security and basic needs of citizens and to resolving conflicts peacefully. This may imply that government is more directly responsive to increases in participation, whereas the political society, bureaucracy, and judiciary arenas are less directly responsive to pressure. Another explanation is that the public interacts more with institutions in political society, the bureaucracy, and the judiciary and thus tends to be especially critical of officials in these arenas. Nevertheless, this issue has not been emphasized in much of the recent literature on political transitions and is certainly worth investigating further.

Like the study by Linz and Stepan,[21] which draws attention to the state as a key variable in democratization, our study indicates that state performance is crucial to understanding the prospects for improved governance. The state has the ultimate responsibility to deliver public goods and services to citizens. The latter will often judge the state on the basis of how well it performs this responsibility rather than how well it conforms with principles of good governance. Bread matters more to them than beliefs. Although there is evidence that our respondents see improvements in government operations, their substantive comments also indicate that much remains to be desired from the way the state relates to society. The so-called soft state characteristics that Gunnar Myrdal[22] identified in his late-1960s review of developments in Asia are still very much present in the countries covered by this survey.

This leaves us with the conclusion that civil society and state cannot be treated as if one is the good guy, the other the bad guy. Since the end of the Cold War civil society has often been regarded as the hope for the future, especially where governments are weak and corrupt. And though it is often true that civil society has accomplished things that the state has failed to do, the assumption that it is a matter of either-or is mistaken. The two should be treated as interlinked. Experience tells us, and this study seems to confirm it, that the quality of the state reflects the quality of its societal base. Public officials are also members of society and carry the same values as other citizens. It is important, therefore, that efforts to improve governance tackle reforms of the state as part of strengthening civil society and the linkages between the two. Before concluding this chapter, we shall give a summary profile of each arena, although they will be subject to more detailed analysis in the following six chapters.

## Civil Society

This arena focuses on the rules that guide public involvement in the political process. It asks questions about the conditions under which citizens can express their opinions, organize themselves for collective action, compete for influence, have an input into policy, and fulfill their own obligations as citizens by adhering to the rules set for the conduct of public affairs. According to the WIP ratings, the lowest country averages are for Pakistan, Togo, and China, and highest is Thailand. Interestingly, Chinese respondents recognize that civil society is not as strong or vital as it may be in other places. This is the case regarding freedom of association, where the very low rating for China makes an interesting contrast with the high rating for India, the other population giant. Indeed the survey participants point to two activities that are currently banned in China that would enhance political involvement. There is the ban on newspapers and freedom of expression and the ban on freedom of establishing parties and mass organizations.

A general observation is that civil society is seen as being open in the survey countries. Respondents acknowledge that it is difficult for governments to sustain control over citizens, as was attempted before the recent efforts to introduce more democratic forms of governance. In this respect, democracy has scored a victory.

However, not everything is fine. Comments by respondents indicate that in many countries there is still a tendency for governments to arrest or intimidate citizens who propagate views different from those in power. It is also clear that in many places there is discrimination in the public arena. For instance, respondents in the Philippines report this as a problem.

### Political Society

This is the arena where public preferences and private interests are supposed to be reconciled and aggregated into policy. The focus here is on the representativeness, influence, and accountability of legislators, as well as the mechanisms for electing these persons and how fairly policies are put together.

As indicated above, the average score for this arena is significantly lower than that for civil society. In particular, a few country scores may raise eyebrows. Argentina, for example, scores lower than might be expected. This could reflect the problems governing institutions had in coping with the country's public finances even before the recent more systemic economic troubles.[23]

Another interesting score is the very low rating of political society in Togo. This is indicative of the dissatisfaction many Togolese have with the way elections have been administered and the lack of effectiveness of the country's National Assembly. The low rating for Pakistan is very much reflective of the assessment of military rule there.

*Government*

With regard to the government arena, we report on how the executive is assessed in terms of the stewardship of society. Included here are issues like the extent to which government is seen as being concerned about ensuring the personal security of citizens and their freedom from want, as well as how it may rise above narrower special interests to make tough decisions in defense of the public interest; how far the military is subordinate to civilian leadership; and how effective government is in resolving conflicts in a peaceful manner.

We have already suggested that respondents record a surprisingly high appreciation of how government performs with regard to respect for these rules. To be sure, as we will detail, respondents vary within countries. In India, for example, respondents most closely associated with the political establishment have a more favorable view than those outside it with regard to how effectively government deals with violence. The strongest comments about the lack of law and order come from Russia and the Philippines, no surprise given that both countries suffered serious internal violence at the time of our survey.

The low score for the Togo government is indicative of the dissatisfaction many people have with President Eyadema, especially in the capital, Lomé. To this day, he has refused subordination to a purely civilian leadership, and he has continued to harass members of the public instead of enhancing their security. This stands in contrast to Indonesia, where the assessment goes in the opposite direction. Respondents there believe governance has improved dramatically since the fall of the authoritarian regime of President Suharto in May 1998. In particular, the military has been pushed into concentrating on its original role of national defense. Most important, respondents firmly believed that the military has come to accept its subordination to a civilian government. As one of them noted: "It is clear that the military is more willing to accept civilian leadership now than before."

*Bureaucracy*

The framework for implementing policy is important. How the day-to-day management of government operations is structured affects popular perceptions of effectiveness. Here we are interested in assessing the quality of governance as it relates to rules applying to bureaucratic performance. What room is there for expert advice? On what grounds are civil servants recruited? How accountable are they, and is there any transparency in the way the civil service operates? Finally, are public services through the bureaucracy accessible to every person?

Among the individual country scores, it may be worth noting that the reputation of the elite of the Indian civil service as the backbone of the country's government is generally confirmed. Although the lower echelons tend to be corrupt and the image is not positive overall, our Indian respondents recognize the input into policy by the higher echelons of the service and its reliance on recruitment based on merit criteria. The Indian score contrasts with those of the countries in Latin America and Africa, where political patronage and red tape (administrative statutes being followed blindly) seem to be much more prevalent. It is also interesting to compare the scores for Thailand and Indonesia. In the former, respondents hold the civil service in high regard, whereas their Indonesian counterparts have serious doubts about the extent to which the civil service is really being recruited on grounds of merit.

### Economic Society

In this survey, we asked questions relating to the state's respect for property rights; how equally regulations are applied; how easy it is to obtain a business license without paying bribes; the extent to which private sector representatives are consulted on policy matters; and how well government is responding to the challenges of globalization with regard to liberalized trade, financial flows, and new technologies.

Some of the individual country scores deserve attention. For instance, it is interesting to compare Argentina and Chile with regard to the score on corrupt transactions. Qualitative comments by respondents in both countries very much support the ratings and suggest that Chile seems free from corruption while Argentina is much less so. The scores for consultation between government and private sector tend to be generally high. It appears to be no coincidence that these scores are lowest in less market-oriented countries such as Togo and China. However, there has been a marked improvement in China. This does not necessarily mean that these consultations are formalized and transparent. Comments by respondents suggest that in some countries these consultations tend to be informal and aimed at securing mutual favors of a private type.

An important observation beyond these comments on the country scores concerns the prevalence of soft state characteristics in many countries. With regard to the first, there are multiple comments of a general character to suggest that cronyism and bribery are common in the transactions between government and the private sector. Several respondents in countries like Argentina, Indonesia, Philippines, and Russia make reference to these problems. It is not difficult to buy influence. Government officials, especially politicians, do not hesitate to ask for a piece of the cake when business transactions are being negotiated.

## Judiciary

This is what is typically referred to as the third branch of government. Societies produce their own dispute or conflict-solving institutions, the most important being courts that resolve conflicts of both a civil (between private parties) and public nature. In this survey, we are interested in how easily members of the public have access to justice, how transparently justice is being administered, how accountable judges are, how open national rights regimes are to international legal norms, and what the scope is for nonjudicial forms of conflict resolution.

The first observation concerns the quality of the justice systems, which our respondents complained about in most countries. There are three main types of critical comments. One is that money buys justice. The rich have an easier access. Implied in this comment is also the assumption that judges can be bribed. The second comment refers to the slow processing of cases. "Justice delayed is justice denied" is a proposition that many of the respondents agree with.[24] The third comment deals with the fact that many poor and illiterate people fear to approach the courts. Respondents in both Argentina and Chile refer to the inefficiency of the judicial systems in their countries but express hope, at least in Chile, that some recent reforms will improve the administration of justice in the future. The average score for access to justice is the lowest of all questions in this arena and indicates that this issue deserves further attention.

The second, more positive observation is that most countries report that they have community justice institutions for resolving conflicts which are not necessarily suited for resolution by a formal court. This form of local justice works better in some countries than in others, but it is reported as being an important part of justice administration and dispute resolution in all countries except Argentina and Chile. For example, in the Philippines case, it was very clear that there is much higher trust in indigenous courts than the formal courts; the former were perceived to be very effective in settling disputes.

## Conclusion

Our study provides a way to combine systematic quantitative comparisons with qualitative data on specific issues. We have demonstrated that governance, as subjectively perceived by persons who are well placed to assess governance at the country level, offers a perspective on the political process in these places that transcends those provided in studies of democratization. Thus we find that some countries that would not qualify as representatives of good governance using specific measures of democratization actually fare well in our study. In short, if one studies governance empirically rather than in a normative perspective, it is no surprise that the findings are different.

This does not mean that our study rejects the relation between governance and democracy. What we have found is that good governance in the eyes of respondents is a combined measure of both regime stability and quality. Their assessments are inevitably influenced by the particular sociopolitical and temporal contexts in which they see their country. Although regime stability may be a common underlying factor in many countries, those that belong to the high- and medium-scoring categories tend to combine it with a sense of improvement in quality, typically interpreted as greater respect for properties associated with liberal democracy. Thus the latter matters, although not exclusively, in the ratings that our respondents have made in this study.

Our study also shows that perceptions of governance are sensitive to specific events and trends. Opinions change much more often and with greater effect than scores are capable of registering (e.g., those for civil liberties and political rights in the Freedom House Index) because they are provided by outsiders. The importance of our study is that it shows how changes in governance may provide honeymoon periods for progress in political as well as social and economic terms or, when governance deteriorates, the opposite (e.g., greater uncertainty about the future and less interest for people to make investments in the economy or any other aspect of the country's portfolio of resources). In short, how well a country attends to the rules that set the stage for its politics matters more than other studies of political changes tend to acknowledge.

Finally, there are significant differences in the scores for the six governance arenas. Some, like civil society, come across in a more favorable light than others. Political society and the judiciary are the arenas where scores not only vary significantly but also are generally lower than in the other four. Time has come to turn to a more detailed assessment of each arena and specific indicators associated with each.

## Notes

1. Robert Dahl, *Polyarchy* (New Haven, CT, and London: Yale University Press, 1971).

2. Dietrich Rueschemeyer, E. H. Stephens, and J. D. Stephens, *Capitalist Development and Democracy* (Cambridge, UK: Cambridge University Press, 1992).

3. Thirty points marks the lowest possible, 150 the highest possible from using the 5-point scale in assessing each of the thirty variables. We realize, of course, that it is unlikely that respondents would assign the highest or lowest possible. Anything close to 150, for example, would be like an ideal type of governance.

Instead respondents would tend to congregate toward the middle of the scale. For these reasons, we decided on the following cutoff points: high = an aggregate score above 85 for the six arenas; medium = an aggregate score between 76 and 85; and low = an aggregate score below 75.

4. We are anxious to emphasize that each country report provided a very rich discussion of the situation in that country—usually linking analysis of the data and comments received as part of the survey process to the key findings in the literature and historical background of the situation.

5. We remind the reader that the total score per arena is 25 (i.e., five points scored on each of the five questions), the lowest being 5 (one point per question).

6. E.g., Seymour M. Lipset, "Some Social Requisites of Democracy," *American Political Science Review* 53 (1959): 69–105.

7. This finding should be compared with that of Przeworski and his colleagues, who argue that no democratic system has ever collapsed in a country where per-capita income exceeds U.S.$6,055 (1976 value). Apart from the fact that some countries with a higher per capita income level are not democracies, it is important to note that many regimes may survive at much lower levels of per capita income, if the measure is not a liberal form of democracy but a measure of governance. See Adam Przeworski, Michael Alvarez, Jose Antonio Cheibub, and Fernando Limongi, "What Makes Democracies Endure?" *Journal of Democracy* 7, no. 1 (1996): 39–55.

8. Cf. Fareed Zakaria, "The Rise of Illiberal Democracy," *Foreign Affairs* 76 (November–December 1997): 22–43.

9. This is also the finding of the Governance in Asia Revisited project, led by professor Yasutami Shimomura, Hosei University, Tokyo.

10. D. Kaufmann, A. Kraay, and P. Zoido-Lobaton, "Aggregating Governance Indicators," *Policy Research Working Paper No. 2195* (Washington, DC: World Bank, 1999).

11. This happened when a number of senators refused to admit key evidence in Estrada's trial and people out of protest responded by taking matters into their own hands.

12. In determining these three categories, we took the point difference between 1995 and 2000 as percentage of the composite aggregate score for year 2000. "Little or no change" applies when the percentage difference is 3 percent or less.

13. See, e.g., John Keane, *Democracy and Civil Society* (London: Verso, 1988); and Robert Putnam, *Making Democracy Work: Civic Traditions in Modern Italy* (Princeton, NJ: Princeton University Press, 1993).

14. Notably the work of Gabriel Almond and Sidney Verba, *Civic Culture* (Princeton, NJ: Princeton University Press, 1963). The importance of culture is also reflected in the work of Ronald Inglehart, *Silent Revolution* (Princeton, NJ: Princeton University Press, 1977).

15. Giovanni Sartori, "Political Development and Political Engineering," in J. D. Montgomery and A. O. Hirschman (eds.), *Public Policy* (Cambridge, UK: Cambridge University Press, 1968).

16. We regard any difference in scores amounting to 10 percent or more to be important and interesting to discuss here.

17. John Dryzek, "Political Inclusion and the Dynamics of Democratization," *American Political Science Review* 90, no. 1: 475–487.

18. See, among others, Ernest Gellner, *Conditions of Freedom: Civil Society and Its Rivals* (London: Penguin Press, 1994); Larry Diamond, *Developing Democracy: Towards Consolidation* (Baltimore: Johns Hopkins University Press, 1999).

19. E.g., Susan Rose-Ackerman, *Corruption and Government: Causes, Consequences, and Reform* (New York: Cambridge University Press, 1999).

20. Juan Linz and Alfred Stepan, *Problems of Democratic Transition and Consolidation: Southern Europe, South America, and Post-Communist Europe* (Baltimore: Johns Hopkins University Press, 1996).

21. Ibid.

22. Gunnar Myrdal, *Asian Drama* (New York: Pantheon, 1968).

23. It is important to remind the reader that the survey was carried out before the economic crisis hit Argentina in late 2001.

24. India provides a fascinating illustration of the effects of slow processing of cases. The country coordinator noted that while the higher courts are seen as exemplary, there is a huge backlog of cases.

# 3

# Civil Society

Civil society has emerged as one of the key concepts in the study of comparative politics. Its rise to prominence marks a big shift in both academic and political discourse on development. For most of the latter twentieth century, the development debate focused on the state or on the economic forces underlying a country's aspirations for progress. This is as true for the modernization theorists of the 1960s as it is for the neo-Marxist and neoliberal students of political economy of the 1970s and 1980s. With a growing interest since those days in participatory forms of development and the idea that institutions outside the state are also important contributors to social and economic advancement, civil society has acquired new significance.

There is no consensus as to what constitutes civil society. In this respect, the concept resembles governance. For instance, in international development circles, civil society tends to be the equivalent of NGOs that handle donor money. For the purpose of this study, we want to make the following introductory observations. Civil society sits between the family and the state. It is made up of associational life that reflects the extent to which citizens share their personal grievances and demands with others. It is the arena where the private becomes public, the social becomes political. In the political-process perspective adopted in this study, it is where values are formed and expressed. It is also where interests are articulated in public. It is the first station in a political input-output scenario. We accept the argument that not everything that happens in civil society creates responses by state institutions; nor do we rule out the possibility that policies may be initiated within the latter rather than in civil society. The extent to which civil society is an integral part of policymaking, however, is an important factor in national development. How it relates to state institutions matters.

This chapter and Chapters 4–8 are organized in the same way, each dealing with one of the six governance arenas. The first section reviews the literature relevant to the chapter. The second analyzes the aggregate findings of the World Governance Survey as they pertain to civil society, first by country category (high, medium, and low scorers), then by major changes over time. The third section is a more detailed analysis of the country scores for each individual indicator. The fourth and final section in the chapters focuses on the implications for research and practice in the governance field.

## Governance Issues in Civil Society

The range of issues of potential interest is broad. It is impossible to do justice to all facets of the literature on civil society. We have decided to divide it into three subsections. The first deals with the origins of the concept, the second with its meaning, and the third with its roles.

### Origins

It is necessary to outline the origins of the notion of civil society, if for no other reason that it is currently being used in such an ahistorical manner. Civil society can be traced back to the period when modern ideas of democracy were beginning to take root. Historically, it is also connected with the rise of capitalism and the evolution of a modern state in the Weberian sense of rational-legal structures of governance. Civil society is as much an integral part of the development of the West as is either market or state. However, theorists differ in terms of what they consider the nature of civil society to be and how it relates to the state.

John Locke argued, very much like Thomas Hobbes, that the state arises from society and is needed to restrain conflict between individuals. The state cannot be given unlimited sovereignty because that would pose a threat to individual freedoms derived from *natural law*. Thus there must be a social contract between rulers and ruled that guarantees rights but also gives the state authority to protect civil society from destructive conflict. A constitutional arrangement that both state and civil society respect is, according to Locke, the cornerstone of liberal democracy.

Thomas Paine's view is different. Drawing on the traditions of the Scottish Enlightenment—David Hume and Adam Smith—his position was considerably more *antistatist*. Any expansion of state power poses a threat to the liberties that keep civil society alive. In his libertarian view, it is the market rather than the state that allows civil society to grow. The latter happens whenever individuals are free to exercise their natural rights. State and civil society, therefore, cannot be viewed as reinforcing each other. Their relation is reflective of a zero-sum game.

Alexis de Tocqueville was alarmed not only by the prospect of a powerful state but also by the tyranny of the majority. Associations, in his view, constituted the strongest bulwark against an unmediated popular will. Self-governing associations educate citizens and scrutinize state actions. They encourage distribution of power and provide opportunities for direct citizen participation in public affairs. Without taking such a strong promarket view as Paine, de Tocqueville still adopts a *voluntarist view* of civil society. It is capable of protecting and promoting the interest of individuals regardless of their socioeconomic position.

Georg Hegel breaks with the tradition of civil society as a natural phenomenon and instead regards it as a product of specific historical processes. Division of labor creates stratification within society and increases conflict between strata. Civil society, in his account, is made up of the various associations, corporations, and estates that exist among the strata. The form and nature of the state are a result of the way civil society is represented and organized. In Hegel's *organic perspective*, the state exists to protect common interests as it defines them by intervening in the activities of civil society. Karl Marx picks up on this notion and argues that the economic dominance of the bourgeoisie gives it control of civil society via the state. Antonio Gramsci, the foremost Marxist analyst of civil society, bypasses the economic determinism of Marx by arguing that *associations* are the mechanisms for exercising control in society. By transferring the focus from the state to civil society as the key arena of conflict, Gramsci concludes that civil society harbors the resources needed to develop counterhegemonic norms to those prevailing at the state level.

We are including this brief review of the origins of the concept because it has its own implications for how members of the international development community tend to look at the role of civil society. It is evident, for instance, that the Europeans have followed in the footsteps of Locke and Hegel, whereas the United States has followed a path closer to Paine and de Tocqueville. This is reflected in the way they approach support for democratization in other parts of the world. The U.S. Agency for International Development (USAID) focuses on privatization and economic liberalization to a greater extent than its European counterparts. Similarly, when it comes to support of civil society, the former tends to act on the premise that associational life is independent of the state. Many Europeans, in contrast, stress the interconnectedness between state, market, and civil society (e.g., in the way that they see the role of governance in development). For the purpose of studying governance, one could ask what difference it makes if the emphasis to improve it is laid more on civil society than on the state.

*Meanings*

How well the concept of civil society—with its Western baggage—travels across cultural and national boundaries depends very much on the way it is being used and operationalized in research and practice. It is common, especially among practitioners (e.g., analysts in international development agencies and activists in the nongovernmental community), to ignore the issue of what civil society really is. For a study of civil society, however, it is necessary to provide some stricter definitional guidelines for how the term is being used. There are at least two issues that are important for understanding governance as it relates to civil society. The first is whether the emphasis is on *civil* or on *society*; the second, what goes into the notion of *civil*.

It makes a difference if the emphasis is laid on civil as opposed to society. The former has a definite normative connotation that is associated with its Western origin. *Civil* refers to a citizen who respects his rights and obligations as a member of society and thus is ready to play by the rules. The long historical evolution of this notion in Western societies means that it is well embedded there (even if some, like Putnam, might argue that it is on the decline).[1] The combination of both rights and obligations is the essence of *civil*, although the connotation in Western societies is often more on rights than on obligations.[2] Especially in the United States, civil is associated with the so-called negative freedoms (i.e., freedom *from* oppression or freedom *from* interference by the state). Obligations typically feature more prominently in European societies (cf. U.S. and European attitudes toward paying taxes), but the package is even more loaded toward obligations in many other societies. In Asia, it is the long history of strong and centralized government that best explains the prevalence of obligations over rights.[3] In African societies, it is the prevalence of communal obligations at the level of community rather than the state that is cited as the big difference.[4] Authors vary in terms of explaining this orientation. Peter Ekeh sees the origin of loyalty to a "primordial" public realm—as compared to a "civic" public realm—as stemming from the precolonial days of the slave trade; Africans turned to their own communities for protection and help.[5] Mahmood Mamdani, by contrast, blames the weakness of civil rights in African countries on the legacy of late colonialism (i.e., the period when the colonial powers were involved in giving power to African nationalists).[6] In the countries of the former Soviet Union, or in its former satellites in Eastern Europe, the issue has largely been that the postcommunist period is characterized by privatization without liberalization.[7] In Latin America, the issue of civicness has been very much determined by two factors: the legacy of military rule and the economic liberalization that has been widely carried out by governments in the region.[8] Given the differences in historical legacy from one region to another, finding a set of indicators that every one can accept is not easy.

If there is scope for different interpretation of what constitutes *civil*, the problem with *society* is that it is usually ignored. Its definition is taken for granted, although we know that societies differ in terms of how they are constituted and structured in socioeconomic terms as well as in terms of race, ethnicity, and religion. For instance, poverty is widespread in many countries. Social stratification leaves some individuals better placed than others to participate in civic activities and thus enhance their chances of improved living conditions.[9] In short, society matters. Even where individuals have formal rights, they find it difficult to exercise them because of their vulnerable status. In order to fully understand how civil society operates or is governed, therefore, one needs to look at the extent to which social and economic rights are protected. Amartya Sen has argued that famines do not occur wherever the media are free to express critical opinions of government policy,[10] and Zehra Arat found that the distributive impact of economic policies is important for the fate of democracy.[11] If elected governments cannot reinforce socioeconomic rights at levels comparable to those of civil-political rights, democracy is in danger. We return to this important issue in Chapter 9.

Discussing the meaning of civil society suggests that the historical context cannot be ignored. Although many of the civil and political rights are widely embraced across cultures, the extent to which they are practiced, and how they relate to duties vis-à-vis the state or community (or both), will vary from region to region. In short, we are sensitive to the existence of universal values for a civil society as well as their embeddedness in specific historical and social contexts. Our choice of indicators is meant to reflect the need for such a balance between universalism and contextualism.

## Roles

The political-process approach adopted in this study assumes that each arena plays a particular role in it. Governance determines the way issues are handled in each arena. This implies human agency. Civil society is not a given but rather a product of desires and demands that people have. Seen through the lenses of individual citizens, civil society has at least three main roles: (1) political socialization, (2) fostering associational growth, and (3) creating an enabling environment for policy input.

Political socialization is a key aspect of civil society. How this socialization is carried out matters. As Mancur Olson argued long ago, collective action comes about as a product of individuals combining their private interests in pursuit of a common good.[12] As they interact with others, their views on what is going on around them is likely to be affected. Olson's idea that individuals get together only to enhance their personal interest may not always apply. Certainly it is not the only type of setting in which political socialization takes place. Every human being is born into a family and a lineage to which he or she has an ascriptive relation. The extent to which lineage relations bear on a person's views varies from one society to another. The stronger this pressure is on the individual, the more confined his views are likely to be. Even so, it would be wrong to assume that individuals have no alternative in societies with strong communitarian values. For instance, there is often much more flexibility and choice in the way social relations are organized in African societies than is evident from those studies that assume these relations to be predominantly ascriptive or traditional.[13] For the purpose of this study, it is important to acknowledge that how rules for the civil society arena are constituted and managed is a determining factor in how it plays its role in the political process.

The more such rules permit the growth of associations, the more likely it is to have some influence on policy. This is an assumption that is justifiably made not only here but also by those who are interested in strengthening civil society. Where rules permit the freedom to create organizations, they are likely to flourish. These organizations do not necessarily have to be officially political in nature to contribute to political socialization. For instance, in the period of decolonization in Africa, when the local population was still prevented from legally organizing political groups, other types of organized activities, such as sports clubs, churches, and trade unions, served to generate a new political consciousness.[14] More recently, Robert Putnam has demonstrated the same phenomenon with reference to how civic traditions developed in Italy.[15] What is important for this study is that the rules that permit the growth of associations are designed and managed such that they reduce discrimination of certain groups. Thus it is important to find out not only what the legal rights of citizens are but also how effectively they apply to everyone regardless of social background.

These differences explain why the third role of civil society—creating an enabling environment for policy input—is important. Civil society is the place where interests and demands are initially articulated, but its ability to effectively serve this purpose also varies.[16] Civil society does not necessarily engage the state and vice versa. For instance, in many countries the state sees itself as primarily, if not exclusively, responsible for national development. The legacy of the development state has lingered on in many countries around the world despite liberalization.[17] In some countries, frustration with government has led to civil society being perceived as an alternative to the state.[18] The extent to which civil society is likely to be a functioning platform for citizen demands and input into policy, therefore, is bound to vary. It is most probably the greatest in two different scenarios. The first is where rules are institutionalized along democratic lines and civil society actors are respected and recognized as legitimate contributors to policy. The second is where the state is weak or failing and civil society is important not by design but by default (i.e., because the state is unable to play its role in fostering development).

## Civil Society: Aggregate WGS Findings

Much of this has guided us in choosing indicators for the civil society arena. They focus on the extent to which state actors allow an open civil society, how far groups themselves are tolerant and respectful of each other, and how far they are ready to accept the rules that guide their involvement in the political process. Our five specific indicators are (for full details, see Appendix 2):

1. *Freedom of expression.* This indicator is meant to capture how rules affect people's opportunities to seek, receive, and impart information in public.
2. *Freedom of assembly.* This indicator is meant to show the extent to which citizens can form and belong to associations of their choice.
3. *Freedom from discrimination.* This indicator is meant to assess the level of tolerance between individuals and groups in society.
4. *Input into policymaking.* This indicator is meant to assess the extent to which government engages in consultation with citizens on public issues.
5. *Respect for rules.* This indicator is meant to capture the extent to which citizens respect the rules that are necessary for the achievement of public order and stable government.

We recognize that there is more to civil society than we are able to capture with our five indicators, but we also believe that they capture crucial dimensions of civil society that relate to quality of governance. The first indicator refers to the *decency* by which citizens are treated by the state; the second to citizen *participation* in public life; the third to *fairness* in state-society relations; the fourth to the *efficiency* of civil society in articulating interests and demands; and the fifth to the perceived level of *accountability* that citizens perceive in relation to others and the state. By disaggregating civil society in this way, we expect to get a better sense of what the more critical or controversial dimensions of civil society are overall and in each country. However, before we proceed to a discussion of each indicator, we examine the aggregate score for each country. For consistency, we divide the countries into the same groups—high, medium, and low—based on their overall 2000 WGS scores (Table 3.1).

## General Observations

Our findings lead us to four general observations. The first is that civil society is generally considered open in most all the countries surveyed here. Respondents acknowledge that it is more difficult for governments to sustain control over citizens than before the recent introduction of more democratic forms of governance. In this respect, democracy has scored a victory. One might also note that investments made by donors in the civil society arena appear to be paying off. Not everything, however, is fine. Comments by respondents indicate that in many countries there is still a tendency for governments to arrest or intimidate citizens who propagate views different from those in power. It is also clear that in many countries there is discrimination in the public arena. For instance, respondents in the Philippines reported discrimination as a problem. China had one of the lowest civil society scores, as is evident from Table 3.1. Respondents recognized that Chinese civil society is not as strong or vital as it may be in

**Table 3.1    Aggregate Civil Society Scores by Country, 2000**

| Country | Decency | Participation | Fairness | Efficiency | Accountability | Average |
|---|---|---|---|---|---|---|
| **High-scoring countries** | | | | | | |
| Chile | 3.70 | 4.27 | 3.43 | 2.87 | 3.60 | 3.57 |
| India | 4.11 | 4.39 | 3.06 | 2.61 | 2.50 | 3.33 |
| Jordan | 3.33 | 3.45 | 3.05 | 2.90 | 3.30 | 3.21 |
| Mongolia | 3.33 | 3.85 | 2.95 | 2.38 | 2.97 | 3.10 |
| Tanzania | 3.45 | 2.97 | 2.58 | 2.73 | 3.03 | 2.95 |
| Thailand | 4.22 | 4.32 | 3.41 | 3.59 | 3.00 | 3.71 |
| **Medium-scoring countries** | | | | | | |
| Argentina | 3.97 | 4.49 | 2.77 | 1.86 | 2.43 | 3.10 |
| Bulgaria | 3.37 | 3.76 | 2.66 | 2.37 | 2.56 | 2.94 |
| China | 2.76 | 1.82 | 2.76 | 2.45 | 2.45 | 2.45 |
| Indonesia | 4.26 | 4.29 | 2.94 | 3.23 | 2.31 | 3.41 |
| Peru | 3.43 | 4.05 | 3.19 | 2.81 | 1.97 | 3.09 |
| **Low-scoring countries** | | | | | | |
| Kyrgyzstan | 3.00 | 3.15 | 3.12 | 2.74 | 2.36 | 2.87 |
| Pakistan | 2.94 | 2.03 | 2.45 | 1.91 | 1.97 | 2.26 |
| Philippines | 4.00 | 4.00 | 2.60 | 2.49 | 2.46 | 3.11 |
| Russia | 2.84 | 3.76 | 3.26 | 2.34 | 2.42 | 2.93 |
| Togo | 2.55 | 3.02 | 2.86 | 1.79 | 2.43 | 2.53 |
| Average, all countries | 3.45 | 3.60 | 2.94 | 2.57 | 2.61 | 3.04 |

other places. This is particularly the case regarding the indicator for participation, where the very low rating for China makes an interesting contrast with the high rating for India, the other population giant in our survey.

Second, not only does the civil society arena get the highest governance score; it also records a solid improvement of 8 percent between 1995 and 2000. A closer look indicates that the improvements in decency and participation are relatively constant across countries and among the highest scores obtained in the entire survey. This evidence reflects the situation on the ground in many countries: for example, the number of NGOs in Mongolia increased from only thirty in 1989 to around 1,700 in 2000—particularly in the area of service delivery.

Third, civil society may be vital, yet there is a general impression that public input into policy is still limited. Its efficiency level is generally on the low side. Many governments simply do not provide an environment in which such input is facilitated. This suggests that civil society and state live separate lives, with governments continuing to set the policy agenda on their own. This is the case not only in countries such as Togo but also in Argentina, where respondents rate government attitude to facilitating public input as low. This indicator received the lowest average rating for the civil society arena in the countries included and perhaps deserves further consideration.

Fourth, high scores on accountability do not come from democratic countries only. We differ from studies of democratic consolidation in that we include other types of countries as well. We also differ from the international discourse on good governance, which has a very distinct bias in favor of liberal democracy. Our study confirms that high civil society governance scores are also obtainable in countries with something other than a liberal political dispensation. Jordan is the most obvious case, with the fifth highest score. Its civil society may not be as pluralist or open as in other countries, but it functions satisfactorily in terms of efficiency and accountability. It confirms to us that any assessment of good governance is more complicated than merely taking the qualities associated with liberal democracy.

## Differences Among Countries

Because we are looking at civil society in how it operates in relation to the state, the aggregate score for each country includes more than what is typically part of an assessment of the role that it plays in development. We provide a more holistic view of civil society that is differentiated to register the qualitative differences between countries and among variables specific to the arena. Ours is a tougher test for each country than those assessments, like the Freedom House Index, that only measure civil liberties and political rights.

There are no real surprises in our country findings. There are some outliers that we discuss below, but by and large the high scorers come out on
top on most indicators, the low scorers at the bottom across the board. We
discern that countries with a tradition of democratic governance (e.g.,
Chile, India, Argentina, and the Philippines) have a well-functioning civil
society. Associations know their role and are less tentative or timid, as
comments by our respondents indicate. There is also evidence to suggest
that countries that are socially homogeneous (e.g., Thailand, Jordan, and
Mongolia) tend to score higher than countries that have no democratic tradition and are more socially divided either by ethnicity or by religion.

Some variations in scores within the same country are worth a brief
discussion. Although Argentina's overall score is on the high side, there is
a noticeable difference between its scores on decency and participation,
on the one hand, and efficiency, on the other. In other words, the influence that civil society has on policy, according to our Argentinean respondents, is low. They suggested that government is not really interested in
public debates on policy choices. It prefers to act on its own, responding
to the demands for specific economic policies by international finance
institutions. It is important to note that these views were expressed almost
a year before the financial crisis hit the country in December 2001. A
similar variation in scores can be found also in the Indian and Philippine
data.

The case of Indonesia also warrants additional remarks. Comments by
respondents confirm that the important role that voluntary associations
played in the transition from President Suharto is also part of the explanation of this score. It is definitely one reason why Indonesia scored higher
than other medium scorers. Indonesia, the second highest scorer on efficiency—or policy input—had one of the lowest scores on the accountability indicator. In Indonesia, between 1995 and 2000 the accountability score
fell slightly (.29, or about 7 percent), and the efficiency went up significantly (1.6 points, or more than 30 percent, a considerable jump on a five-
point scale). This suggests to us that the fall of Suharto created new political opportunities for civil society, but what happened may be best described
as a mad rush to fill the vacuum (hence the decline in accountability). Civil
society groups and organizations simply did not respect each other or the
state. The narrative comments by our respondents in Indonesia confirmed
that with the change in regime came decreased respect for the law and a
lack of enforcement.

China is another case that deserves comment. Its average score for civil
society is the second lowest of all. Even with economic liberalization and
cautious political reforms, such as the introduction of elections for government leaders at the village and parish levels, China still has a long way to
go in developing civil society. Its score on decency is low, considerably

below other countries with an autocratic regime such as Pakistan and Togo. At the same time, there is evidence that the voice of the public is not completely silent. The score for efficiency in handling demands and interests is somewhat higher, indicating that there is scope for consultation between government and citizens.

The case of Jordan is interesting. It is not known for being democratic, but it confirms our view that governance may be legitimate even given circumstances that do not resemble Western democracy. In Islamic societies where religion is a dominant factor in all walks of life, groups and organizations are more closely tied to the rulers. The issue that arises here is the extent to which they are voluntary. Muslims have definite obligations to the welfare of others. The line between duty and right, therefore, is more difficult to establish. The high score on accountability confirms this. It suggests to us that comparative studies of governance that incorporate Islamic societies have to be especially attuned to the different interpretation of the relationships between rights and duties that apply in such countries.

The Philippines has a high average score for civil society compared to the other arenas and to other low scorers. This reflects a legacy of strong public participation in politics and development. But it is also indicative of the experience with President Estrada's demise and impeachment. The opposition to his way of ruling the country was very much driven by popular organizations. Demands were articulated as much in the streets as in the legislature. Thus it is not surprising that the Philippine score for this arena is relatively high.

The mean scores for each category of countries, finally, confirm what we have stated about the overall picture for this arena: in spite of some exceptions, the mean for each category differs significantly, as indicated in Table 3.2.

There is an almost equal amount of difference between the high, medium, and low scoring groups: approximately .30. The fact that the Philippines scores so much higher on this set of indicators does not help to elevate the low-scoring countries in any significant way. To fully appreciate the governance situation in 2000, however, it is also important to examine what changes have taken place over time and where.

**Table 3.2   Mean Scores on Civil Society Indicators by Groups of Countries**

| Category of Countries | Mean Score |
| --- | --- |
| High scoring | 3.31 |
| Medium scoring | 3.00 |
| Low scoring | 2.74 |

## Changes over Time

Overall, there was a very slight improvement in the civil society arena between 1995 and 2000. This average, however, hides some dramatic changes both upward and downward in individual countries. Figure 3.1 illustrates changes over time by country for the civil society arena.

The overall pattern suggests that high- and medium-scoring countries have registered improvement, whereas low-scoring countries have declined. The medium category contains some of the greatest improvements. The significant shifts in Indonesia and Peru are indicative of the regime change that has taken place and in which civil society played an important role. Greater freedom and a stronger role for voluntary associations were not given to the people of these countries on a golden plate. They were the outcome of struggles in which groups of citizens risked their lives. The impact the events had in these countries as they emancipated themselves from military or civilian autocracy was high.

The decline was noticeable in Pakistan, the Philippines, and to a lesser extent Kyrgyzstan. In each case there is a clear explanation. In Pakistan, it has to do with the military takeover and the limitations on freedom of association that resulted. In the Philippines, the main drop was in regard to citizen compliance with rules for accountability. Respondents identified a breakdown in order, and the increased challenges to the regime by Muslim separatists, as evidence that things had become worse. Finally, in Kyrgyzstan the decline is with regard to decency and participation.

**Figure 3.1   Changes over Time in Civil Society, 1995–2000**

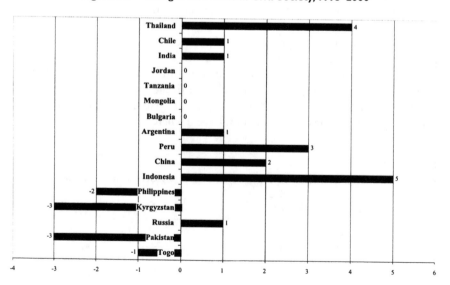

Deterioration took place after 1999, when extremist Islamic groups engaged in aggressive acts within the country that led the government to become more oppressive.

In sum the improvements exceed declines, an indication that civil society is an arena where progress has been made. In order to better understand what is going on, however, it is necessary to examine the performance with regard to each individual indicator.

## Analysis of Each Individual Indicator

Since the mid-1980s there has been a wave of democratization around the world. In addition, more than 170 countries have ratified international human rights treaties, and many have rewritten their constitutions. Many revised constitutions contain guarantees protecting freedom of expression and of assembly. Moreover, donors have made the development of civil society a major priority, and some conditioned aid on improvements in this arena. Therefore, we should expect to see a general improvement in at least the conditions that exist for group formation—freedom of expression and of the right to assemble peacefully. In addition, we are interested in trying to judge how the rules for the civil society arena operate with regard to policymaking input, preventing discrimination, and fostering respect for rules of governance. Our focus on each indicator provides some insights into these propositions.

### Decency

Article 19 of the Universal Declaration of Human Rights states that "everyone has the right to freedom of opinion and expression; this right includes freedom to hold opinions without interference and to seek, receive and impart information and ideas through any media and regardless of frontiers." Respect by state actors for freedom of speech is important for political socialization as well as the prospect that organizations will engage in lobbying and similar activities to influence policymaking. It relates to how decently these actors treat citizens. There has been an explosion of newspapers and other forms of media around the world, especially in developing societies. The increase in the number and amount of information resulted from changes in constitutions, as well as from pressure by donors.

With an increase in the sources of information, civil society groups have found expanded opportunities to take a more visible role in many countries. Many groups, which include women, labor unions, trade organizations, ethnic and religious minorities, and indigenous people, have voice and influence for the first time. In addition to the explosion of media, there has been a dramatic increase in the formation of political parties. Taken together, opportunities for groups to publicize concerns and policy needs increased dramatically. Of course, change takes time, and levels of free expression varied considerably across our sample of sixteen countries. It was particularly high in India, Indonesia, Philippines and Thailand. At the lower end, not surprisingly, were China, Pakistan, Russia, and Togo.

Increased freedom of expression leads to a greater sense of decency—a key element of governance. People become more aware of the value of tolerating the views of others and, by extension, treating them like they themselves want to be treated. By guaranteeing people a protected forum in which to voice concerns, the potential for good governance increases. Without this key ingredient, civil society lacks voice, and without voice peaceful change becomes more difficult.

### Participation

The cornerstone of a strong civil society is freedom of association. This indicator is a measure of how easy people find it to participate in public affairs. Our indicator reflects UDHR Article 20, which states that "everyone has the right to freedom of peaceful assembly and association. No one may be compelled to belong to an association, [and] as such it also includes the right that no one is compelled to belong to an association." Being able to organize into groups is a natural complement to having the right to freely express grievances and policy alternatives, draw attention to discrimination, and pursue other policy objectives.

There has been a dynamic growth in the number of civil society groups in almost all countries around the world.[19] This is especially true in many of the developing societies that have been caught up in the wave of democratization. One of the characteristics of modern democracies is the presence of groups seeking change. Backed by development projects designed to fund and promote group formation, the numbers of groups formed in many of the survey countries grew geometrically. In addition, many donors made financial aid conditional on states making room for civil society groups.

Scoring on this indicator is among the highest of all in the survey. The notable exceptions are China and Pakistan. Participation remains very limited in China in spite of economic liberalization. In Pakistan, control of associations grew after the military took power and extremist religious groups began to cause violence. The most important thing to register about this and the first indicator is that they confirm the extent to which this arena is now being recognized as important. Citizens have more scope to engage in public life than before. The improvement that has taken place, just between 1995 and 2000, is significant.

*Fairness*

This indicator is aimed at measuring the extent of fairness that exists in relations between individuals and groups in politics, a quality that is especially indicative of how *civil* society is in its constitution. As a governance issue, this is an important indicator of the potential for different groups to enter and compete in the political process. It reflects UDHR Article 2, which states that

> everyone is entitled to all the rights and freedoms set forth in this Declaration, without distinction of any kind, such as race, colour, sex, language, religion, political or other opinion, national or social origin, property, birth or other status. Furthermore, no distinction shall be made on the basis of the political, jurisdictional or international status of the country or territory to which a person belongs, whether it be independent, trust, non-self-governing or under any other limitation of sovereignty.

However, the interpretation of this variable requires a more in-depth look into each country. It is possible that the existence of discrimination can stimulate the growth of civil society, as those facing discrimination organize to fight it. Yet a country with low discrimination may score low on other indicators in the civil society arena for other reasons.

Tanzania, which generally did not record significant changes on most indicators between 1995 and 2000, suffered a significant loss here (1.2 points, or almost 25 percent on the five-point scale). This decrease reflects an increased tension between the Muslim and Christian communities, as well as the decline in fairness that our respondents saw following from that conflict. Other countries that noted a decline in fairness include Bulgaria, China, Pakistan, and Togo. There are two factors that seem to have caused this decline. One is the growing importance of religious identification in society, a factor that respondents refer to in Pakistan. Another is the increased tension that follows from a more competitive form of life as a result of economic liberalization, a factor in China, and political democratization, cited in Bulgaria and Togo.

*Efficiency*

The ability to influence policy is a key measure of success for organized activities in the civil society arena, and it relates to how efficient it is in performing its role of articulating interests and demands. For governments to effectively formulate policy, there need to be mechanisms for consultation with different groups in society. The extent and nature of these interactions are likely to have implications for the nature of policy and the legitimacy of the system. Although the first three indicators in the civil society arena gauge the conditions for its formation, this indicator attempts to gauge its capacity to produce results. Because of the wave of democratization and the conditionality of foreign aid, we are not surprised to see high scores on the decency and participation indicators. However, the low scores on influencing policy—the lowest of the five civil society indicators—suggest that with regard to efficiency many come up short. There are a variety of possible reasons. Some states want to look democratic and free in order to meet donor conditions for aid, but they still manage to mute the voice of civil society in the policymaking process. Another is that it takes time for groups to learn the skills to successfully lobby and influence policy change. Thailand seems to be an exception. Respondents there see civil society as playing an important role in policymaking. Associations are relatively strong and experienced especially in the social sector, and interaction with government is smooth. At the other extreme is Argentina, a country with a democratic tradition but where policy input is seen as very low. This reflects a widespread feeling, prior to the country's economic meltdown at the end of 2001, that policy was made more in response to narrow interests and to demands by the international finance institutions than by organized groups in society. The Argentinean case contrasts with that of Indonesia, where the fall of Suharto created a windfall opportunity for civil society to exercise influence on public policy.

### Accountability

The last indicator, which garnered the second lowest score, is a way to better understand the levels of respect citizens have for the fact that civil society not only provides rights but also demands duties in relation to other people and the state. Like the amount of influence groups or citizens have in the policy process, adhering to rules tells us whether people are vested or have a sense of ownership in the political system. Rights always imply correlative duties and responsibilities, and rights make no sense if seen in isolation from the responsibilities and duties that citizens have toward each other and the common good. It relates to the sense of obligation to the public realm that citizens have and, therefore, their accountability to each other and the state.

The theory is that once civil society is functioning well, respect for rules should increase as citizens and civil society groups influence policy and rules. Increased voice and policy influence should encourage respect for the system. The extent to which citizens respect rules governing the public realm, however, is not a given, even if civil society grows in other respects.

Following rules is about accountability. To make a claim of good governance, accountability must be present, not only for government officials.

Citizens must be accountable to the state and its rules. In many countries citizens have yet to develop such a sense of accountability. The problem of citizen accountability is especially evident in Peru and Pakistan. Both have a history of upheavals and military government, at least in part due to a lack of rule compliance among citizens. No country scores particularly high, and there have been only incremental shifts between 1995 and 2000. Chile and Jordan, for very different reasons, are the only countries where our respondents believe that respect for rules is reasonably high. In the former case, it reflects satisfaction with the way citizens have settled in to the new democratic regime that came about in the late 1980s. In Jordan, judging from qualitative comments by our respondents, the key factor is the deference that citizens show in response to the benevolence of the monarchy. They do not want to cause upheavals that would be interpreted as a protest against the king.

## Implications for Research and Practice

We conclude by discussing the implications that follow from the findings reported here. The first set of issues relates to how we can better understand specific governance challenges inherent in the civil society arena. The second set focuses on what our findings mean for practitioners working on improving civil society governance around the world.

We like to mention three important implications for future research. The first is that contextual factors matter. If state and civil society do not engage in win-win types of processes, there may be a possible lag between feelings of efficacy in policymaking and support for the system of rules. But it could also be that the strength of political society varies from one country to another. The intermediate mechanisms between civic associations and interest groups, on the one hand, and government (e.g., political parties, electoral systems, and legislatures), on the other, are not very well institutionalized in many of the sixteen countries. This finding is in line with the conclusion that Juan Linz and Alfred Stepan[20] draw in their overview of democratic transition and consolidation in Southern Europe, Latin America, and Eastern Europe.

The other implication is that the nature of associational life varies across countries because different types of social capital prevail. The assumption that Putnam's distinction between "bonding" and "bridging" types are enough to classify social capital is being challenged by our study, which indicates that the variation in form is greater. For instance, the relative strength of civil society in Jordan is not adequately explained by these categories alone. Nor is the associational life in countries like Tanzania, where interethnic ties are strong without being bridging in a *civic* sense. We believe that this issue—like relations between civil and political society—deserves more attention by the research community.

The third implication relates to the accountability issue. This is an overlooked aspect of civil society, but one that is increasingly important. Civil society is about more than rights. If it is going to develop to become a meaningful platform for all citizens, there is a need to respect responsibilities and duties also. This aspect of civil society can be explored along different lines; one might be to assess how far citizens are ready to pay taxes, to vote, and to avoid committing crimes.

There are several ways our study sheds light on challenges for the practitioners in the governance field. The first is the scope of concern under the rubric of civil society. We show that there is much more to the relationship between state and civil society than is captured by the concepts of participation or accountability alone. By recognizing the dual function of civil society as an arena for both political socialization and interest articulation, we are able to capture more of both strengths and weaknesses than those approaches that assume governance is linked more specifically only with qualities associated with liberal democracy.

The second is that we cannot continue treating civil society and state as if one is the good guy, the other the bad guy. Civil society has often been regarded as the hope for the future, especially where governments are weak and corrupt. Although it is sometimes true that civil society has accomplished things that the state has failed to do, the assumption that it is a matter of either-or is mistaken. The two should be treated as interlinked. Experience tells us, and this survey seems to confirm it, that the quality of the state reflects the quality of its societal base. Public officials are also members of society and carry the same values as other citizens. It is important, therefore, that efforts to improve governance tackle reforms of the state as part of strengthening civil society and the linkages between the two.

The third is that many of the countries included in our sample are newcomers to a system in which civil society is meant to play an important part in the political process. Institutions are only now being introduced or put into place. With regard to such key functions as adopting views from the public and transforming them into policy, our survey confirms that individual actors and organizations are still learning. They make mistakes, and there is reason in some places to consider whether the rules adopted so far really are the most suitable for the country's continued development.

The fourth is that many of the shortcomings of civil society are directly attributable to the behavior of individual members of the legislature. They do not necessarily live up to the expectations associated with the rules or, even worse, they outright violate these rules. We came across frequent references to elected representatives abandoning constituents or engaging in corrupt behavior. These breaches of expected norms contributed to lowering the legitimacy of civil society at large in some countries covered by this survey.

In conclusion, development programs sometimes leave much to be desired, but the investments made since the late 1980s are beginning to pay off as far as civil society is concerned. Not only do our respondents feel that they increasingly can speak out and form groups; in a good number of the countries in our sample there is a positive relationship between exercising these rights and influencing the policymaking process.

## Notes

1. Robert Putnam, *Bowling Alone: The Decline of Social Capital in America* (New York: W. W. Norton, 2001).
2. For a discussion of how human rights relate to the issues discussed in this chapter, see, e.g., David Beetham, *Democracy and Human Rights* (Cambridge, UK: Polity, 1999).
3. Joanne R. Bauer and Daniel A. Bell (eds.), *The East Asian Challenge for Human Rights* (Cambridge, UK: Cambridge University Press, 1999).
4. For a discussion of human rights issues in African societies, see, e.g., Abdullahi Ahmed An-Naim and Francis M. Deng (eds.), *Human Rights in Africa: Cross-Cultural Perspectives* (Washington, DC: Brookings Institution, 1990); Ronald Cohen, Goran Hyden, and Winston Nagan (eds.), *Human Rights and Governance in Africa* (Gainesville: University Press of Florida, 1993); John W. Harbeson, Donald Rothchild, and Naomi Chazan (eds.), *Civil Society and the State in Africa* (Boulder, CO: Lynne Rienner Publishers 1994); and Goran Hyden, Dele Olowu, and H. W. O. Okoth Ogendo (eds.), *African Perspectives on Governance* (Trenton NJ: Africa World Press, 2000).
5. Peter Ekeh, "Colonialism and the Two Publics: A Theoretical Statement," *Comparative Studies in Society and History* 17, no. 1 (1975): 91–117.
6. Mahmood Mamdani, *Citizen and Subject: Contemporary Africa and the Legacy of Late Colonialism* (Princeton, NJ: Princeton University Press, 1996).
7. See, e.g., Richard Rose, "Postcommunism and the Problem of Trust," *Journal of Democracy* 5, no. 3 (July 1994): 18–30.
8. See, e.g., Guillermo O'Donnell and Philippe C. Schmitter, *Transition from Authoritarian Rule: Some Tentative Conclusions*, vol. 4 (Baltimore: Johns Hopkins University Press, 1986); also M. A. Garreton, "Human Rights in the Processes of Democratization," *Journal of Latin American Studies* 26 (1994): 221–234.
9. Nelson Kasfir (ed.), *Civil Society and Democracy in Africa* (London and Portland, OR: Frank Cass, 1998).
10. Amartya Sen, *Development as Freedom* (New York: Anchor Books, 1999).
11. Zehra F. Arat, *Democracy and Human Rights in Developing Countries* (Boulder, CO: Lynne Rienner Publishers, 1991).
12. Mancur Olson, *The Logic of Collective Action* (Cambridge, MA: Harvard University Press, 1965).
13. See, e.g., Igor Kopytoff, *The African Frontier* (Bloomington: Indiana University Press, 1987).

14. See, e.g., Thomas Hodgkin, *Nationalism in Tropical Africa* (London: Frederick Muller, 1956).

15. Robert Putnam, *Making Democracy Work: Civic Traditions in Modern Italy* (Princeton, NJ: Princeton University Press, 1993).

16. For a discussion of this set of issues, see, e.g., John Dryzek, "Political Inclusion and the Dynamics of Democratization," *American Political Science Review* 90 (1996): 475–487.

17. For a discussion of this perspective, see the seminal work by Gunnar Myrdal, *Asian Drama: An Inquiry into the Poverty of Nations* (New York: Pantheon Books, 1968).

18. See Herman DeSoto, *The Other Path: The Invisible Revolution in the Third World* (New York: Harper & Row, 1989).

19. See Civicus, *Citizens Strengthening Global Civil Society* (Washington, DC: Civicus—World Alliance for Citizen Participation, 1994).

20. Juan Linz and Alfred Stepan, *Problems of Democratic Transition and Consolidation: Southern Europe, South America, and Post-Communist Europe* (Baltimore: Johns Hopkins University Press, 1996).

# 4

# Political Society

I n the political-process perspective underlying our approach, political
society is perhaps the most critical link in the governance chain. It is the
arena where citizens are represented and their views are aggregated and
packaged into specific policy demands and proposals. In this respect, it is
functionally different from civil society, where individual groups articulate
their interests.[1] Political society is where much of the political agenda is set
or at least *should* be set. The result is that it is also the arena that tends to be
the most intensely contested. Because power features so prominently in
political society, it is no surprise that this arena is also one of the toughest
to govern. Formal rules matter particularly much here. Managing them in a
manner that enhances the legitimacy of the political process is critical for
the stability of the political system at large. As students of democratic transition and consolidation studies have noted,[2] democracy becomes the only
game in town when political conflicts are habitually resolved according to
established norms and when costs are too high for violating these norms.
But governing political society becomes a critical issue in other contexts,
notably in societies divided by ethnicity, race, and/or religion. How political society is structured and how its rules are the subject of collective stewardship become of utmost importance in countries characterized by multiple cultures and/or nationalities.[3]

What specifically is political society made of? It is not a single institution but rather a series of them, all of which are important for the policy-
aggregating function. The first are political parties. Autocracies tend to
have only one, democracies many. The number of political parties in any
given polity is to a considerable extent determined by the electoral system
in place. There is great variation around the world, although the main distinctions are *plurality*, *majority*, and *proportional systems of representation*. Each has specific rules with implications for who gains elective office.
Presidential and parliamentary elections are common, though elections of

representatives to subnational or local authorities are also significant. For instance, elections of governors in Russia tend to have national significance, as in the United States. The remaining institution in political society is the legislature. Political parties compete in elections in order to get seats in the legislature. How the latter is constituted tends to be less politically significant than how it works.[4] The legitimacy of political society rests to a great extent on the credibility of individual legislators. How well they live up to the norms associated with representative government is definitely important.

This chapter first looks at existing literature and some of the main issues in political society. It provides the aggregate findings of the World Governance Survey for the political society arena, looking at how the three categories of countries—high, medium, and low—compare. The third section details the answers for each of the five indicators used in the survey. The conclusion discusses the implications of the findings for research and practice in the field of governance.

## Governance Issues in Political Society

It is impossible to discuss all issues that fall within the political society rubric. We focus on important ones that are also relevant to the analysis of the WGS data. The first relates to the issue of establishing a durable party system. The second concerns the extent to which elections help produce legitimate legislatures. The third refers to how well the policy aggregating function is performed by the legislature. We briefly discuss each.

### The Party System

The role of political society is to aggregate demands into policy. As such, it requires a manageable and functioning party system. A large number of parties is not necessarily better for political society and its functions. Effectiveness is typically easier when the number is not too high. In practice, countries tend to vary according to how they strike a balance between durability and adaptability. Larry Diamond, borrowing a conceptualization from Andreas Schedler, notes that the problem in some places is an under-institutionalized party system, in others an overinstitutionalized one.[5]

The more common pattern, especially in transitional societies, is one of underinstitutionalization. Political parties are often weak and fragmented, dependent on a single charismatic individual for leadership and guidance. These parties are weak in the sense of not being able to penetrate society. In the absence of true membership, their electoral support is volatile. Brazil is often raised as an example of the weak party system. According to the scale of effective political parties, Brazil had a considerably higher number than other countries not only in Latin America but also elsewhere.[6] For instance, in 1992 it had 8.5 parties in the lower house, making it much more fragmented than other consolidated democracies, both presidential and parliamentary.[7] The party systems of African countries are, if anything, even more fragmented. Parties tend to proliferate along ethnic lines, because each group constitutes a natural political constituency for hopeful candidates. In addition, because there is a lack of experience with multiparty politics, each candidate tends to assume that his party is going to become a viable entity. The result is a high level of volatility. Political parties come and go and institutionalization is hampered.[8]

Although underinstitutionalized party systems are more common, there are examples of the opposite. Wherever political parties become rigid and unable to accommodate changes in the economy or society, the party system may prove a hindrance to renewal and thus threaten political stability. Venezuela is a case in point. Political parties were capable of monopolizing the political process for a long time, robbing institutions of autonomy and alienating large groups of citizens.[9] This overinstitutionalization was a factor in the change that brought Hugo Chavez, a former military officer, into power in the late 1990s and allowed him to gain legitimacy at the expense of the established political parties.

Parties are vital to political society, and how the party system is constituted and institutionalized matters. Parties are important to mediating between citizens and government and tend to be indispensable in forming government as well as constituting an effective opposition.[10] Rules that determine how the party system works are significant because they also bear on how legislatures operate and how they are perceived.

### The Electoral System

Electoral systems have influence on political behavior and choice. The electoral system is the most powerful instrument available in constitutional engineering.[11] It is virtually a given that one-seat districts with a plurality rule will reduce the number of parties to two and that multiseat districts with proportional representation are associated with more than two parties.[12]

Many political scientists have considered this proposition as law, but it remains a hypothesis to be tested. One reason for caution is that plurality and proportional systems of representation are not monolithic. There are variations, especially on the proportional side. Some countries, like Germany, have adopted a mixture (i.e., approximately half the members of the Bundestag are elected in single-member districts, the rest through a proportional formula within one national constituency, tied to the outcome in the single-member districts).

There are two paramount considerations: fairness and accountability. Proportional representation satisfies the first of these principles more effectively than the other systems because it establishes a close association between percentage of votes and percentage of seats in the legislature. Plurality systems foster accountability in the sense that the single-seat formula encourages closer links between the electorate and their representatives. Another distinction is that proportional representation tends to be inclusive (e.g., it provides more scope for minority representation), whereas the plurality system tends to create a clear majority on which governments can depend in order to carry out policies.

Although each system has advocates, it would be a mistake to assume that one model is always preferable to the other. Because it is impossible to maximize each principle that matters in choosing an electoral system, everything depends on historical circumstances and the issues at hand. For instance, there has been a debate in Africa whether the plurality system is preferable to the proportional system. Some have argued that in countries where political parties are weak, politics is driven more by patronage and policy, and people vote more on the basis of where they live, a plurality system is better suited than any alternative.[13] Others support the proportional system by arguing that inclusiveness is the most important principle in culturally plural societies. It is better placed to promote political consensus and stability.[14] Looking at Africa, we see that many countries with proportional representation have fewer parties than those with plurality systems. One reason for this anomaly is likely to be the neopatrimonialist nature of African politics, where person rather than party, patronage rather than policy, matters to the electorate. Another is that the new rules have yet to produce a stable party system.

The design of the electoral system sets the basic rules that apply to how political representatives are chosen and thus how they perform their task of aggregating demands from society into policy. The legitimacy of these representatives, however, is determined not only by the system but also by their own behavior. If electoral rules are violated and norms of fairness and freedom of choice are compromised by candidates, then the whole exercise loses legitimacy. A parliament that lacks credibility will undermine the principle of good governance. This response is shared across cultures and nations. The international community has devoted resources to monitoring elections in transitional societies on the premise that formative elections are important to improve governance. What makes an election free and fair has not always been easy to determine, and many election observations have raised as many questions as answers.[15]

Forming and managing rules for the election of representatives to the legislature is important in two respects. The design of the electoral system itself has great impact on political outcomes. Without agreement on this fundamental issue, the regime is at risk, because electoral-systems design is such a prominent part of any effort to change a political system. Whenever such designs are associated with a transition from autocracy to democracy, they are likely to be especially vulnerable, because so many other issues are unsettled at that time. It may be somewhat less threatening if a shift in the electoral system is made when no other significant change occurs. Shifts under such circumstances, however, are not very common, because when there is no real challenge to the way the political system operates, political actors are not likely to call for electoral reform. Italy, Japan, and New Zealand are among the few countries where electoral system reforms have been approved without the system at large being under threat of collapse.

The second aspect refers to how well rules are followed and administered at election. Because of the significance of political society as the prime arena for contestation of power, any violation of the rules of the game is viewed as especially serious. Breach of such basic norms as fairness and freedom of choice becomes a potential threat to the regime at large. It certainly has a direct bearing on how the electorate views its representatives and their work.

### The Legislature

In every representative democracy, the legislature is expected to play an important role in formulating policy and in holding governments accountable for decisions and actions. What power these bodies possess varies according to how freely elected they are and their relationship to the executive branch. The tendency of legislatures since the fall of communism has been toward more formal power, at least relative to autocratic and totalitarian systems. Former communist countries have overwhelmingly chosen parliamentary systems for purposes of governance, whereas democratizing countries elsewhere in the world have preferred a strong executive via the presidential or semipresidential system. Thus the trend since the 1990s has been ambiguous: legislatures have, from a constitutional point of view, become more autonomous yet confined by official and unofficial executive powers.

There is a debate whether parliamentarianism or presidentialism is more suitable for transitional societies. The case is typically made with reference to existing systems and how they work. Some believe that presidentialism is in principle the best system for democracy because it guarantees checks and balances of power; the problem with the export of this system from the United States is that it has been considerably modified. Thus in Latin America, this modification has allowed for a considerable shift of power in favor of the president at the expense of the legislature.[16] Others believe that the issue of how well presidentialism works can only be fully understood in the context of the party system. The point is that wherever presidentialism is operating with a fragmented party system, as in Brazil, there is a tendency for ineffective policymaking.[17] Parliamentarianism, however, has also had its defendants, and some argue that in a historical perspective there has been more stability in parliamentary than in presidential systems.[18]

Constitutions alone, however, do not determine the role that legislatures play in developing societies. Because developing countries are undergoing political reform while the international community pushes for economic reform, the role of legislators is hampered. Governments typically negotiate major policy reforms with representatives of international finance institutions. For many reasons, legislators are overlooked. Time is of the essence, and involving legislators is seen as a complicating and delaying factor. Some argue that the strong influence that external actors exercise over domestic policy has created a situation of "delegative democracy."[19] Others have made a similar point in arguing that governments in developing countries undergoing simultaneous economic and political reforms have become more accountable to international agencies than to domestic electorates.[20]

In spite of the promise that political reforms present, legislatures have yet to prove themselves as important institutions in many developing societies. They have been held back by structural circumstances, but they also suffered setbacks because legislators have not necessarily lived up to the expectations of their electorates. Many have been more interested in their own personal political career and often managed to bribe their way back into office. For these reasons, it is clear that the role of legislatures remains controversial. With their legitimacy in question, this important component of the regime is threatening the legitimacy of the broader efforts to establish democracy.

With these background issues in mind, we now turn to an analysis of our own data and what we can learn from the survey findings.

## Political Society: The Aggregate WGS Findings

The five indicators used in the World Governance Survey reflect the issues that concern the literature and governance analysts in the international community. They have been constructed in order to minimize an explicit bias in favor of a particular regime or system. Countries in transition vary according to their degree of democracy, the system of government they have adopted, and the electoral system that is being used. The indicators used in the survey for the political society are listed below (for full details, see Appendix 2):

1. *Representativeness of legislature.* This indicator assesses the extent to which the legislature is representative of society at large.
2. *Political competition.* This indicator assesses the extent to which power can be contested without fear of retaliation.
3. *Aggregation of public preferences.* This indicator assesses how effectively and fairly public preferences are aggregated into public policy.
4. *Role of legislative function.* This indicator assesses the degree of influence that the legislature has on the making on public policy.
5. *Accountability of elected officials.* This indicator assesses how far elected officials are viewed as accountable to constituents.

These indicators capture five dimensions of political society that are crucial in any society. The first is how *representative* it is; the second how *competitive* it is; the third how *effective* it is; the fourth how *influential* it is; and the fifth how *accountable* political society is. By disaggregating the main variable—political society—this way, we expect to get a better sense of the more critical or controversial dimensions of political society. Before proceeding to a discussion of each indicator, however, we will provide the aggregate score for each country, divided in terms of overall score into three categories: high, medium, and low.

## Differences Among Countries

We will start our analysis by focusing on the overall pattern for each country and the variations among the countries included (see Table 4.1).

There is considerable difference in the average score for each indicator. The highest is for competitiveness, the lowest for accountability of legislators. Our survey tends to confirm that democratized countries have been able to institutionalize competitive party and electoral systems. Countries with a democratic tradition, like India, score especially high, but this is true also for countries that have turned to competitive elections more recently, such as Thailand and Indonesia. It is no surprise that China, with its one-party system, Pakistan, and Togo score lowest. For the latter two, one could have expected even lower scores given that opposition parties are not allowed to function freely. It may indicate that the situation in practice is perceived as not being completely authoritarian in nature.

The accountability of elected officials appears to be the most problematic aspect of political society. Even countries that otherwise score high have a lower-than-average score on this indicator. Newcomers tend to do better. Thailand and Mongolia are cases in point. China is interesting: it does well on this indicator in spite of its one-party system. The main reason is that the Chinese Communist Party has strict rules for ensuring that those

**Table 4.1  Aggregate Political Society Scores by Country, 2000**

| Country | Representativeness | Competitiveness | Effectiveness | Influence | Accountability | Average |
|---|---|---|---|---|---|---|
| **High-scoring countries** | | | | | | |
| Chile | 2.73 | 3.93 | 2.83 | 3.40 | 2.40 | 3.06 |
| India | 2.83 | 4.14 | 2.92 | 3.39 | 2.56 | 3.17 |
| Jordan | 2.63 | 2.63 | 2.83 | 2.68 | 2.25 | 2.60 |
| Mongolia | 2.79 | 3.82 | 2.49 | 3.08 | 2.74 | 2.98 |
| Tanzania | 3.15 | 3.24 | 2.76 | 2.76 | 2.67 | 2.92 |
| Thailand | 2.73 | 3.68 | 3.12 | 3.13 | 3.12 | 3.16 |
| **Medium-scoring countries** | | | | | | |
| Argentina | 2.17 | 3.51 | 2.33 | 2.77 | 2.20 | 2.60 |
| Bulgaria | 2.90 | 3.46 | 2.27 | 2.56 | 2.24 | 2.69 |
| China | 2.73 | 2.30 | 2.67 | 2.94 | 2.58 | 2.64 |
| Indonesia | 2.83 | 3.80 | 2.69 | 3.46 | 2.34 | 3.02 |
| Peru | 2.27 | 3.46 | 2.84 | 3.27 | 2.00 | 2.77 |
| **Low-scoring countries** | | | | | | |
| Kyrgyzstan | 2.46 | 2.95 | 2.67 | 2.51 | 1.87 | 2.49 |
| Pakistan | 1.60 | 2.12 | 1.70 | 1.23 | 1.61 | 1.65 |
| Philippines | 2.14 | 2.94 | 2.43 | 2.74 | 2.26 | 2.50 |
| Russia | 2.61 | 2.66 | 2.53 | 2.29 | 1.71 | 2.36 |
| Togo | 1.67 | 2.21 | 1.79 | 1.71 | 1.83 | 1.84 |
| Average, all countries | 2.51 | 3.18 | 2.55 | 2.74 | 2.27 | 2.65 |

elected to the People's Assembly actually work for constituents. Accountability among legislators is possible even when there is no competitive party system. The Chinese case stands in contrast to Argentina and Peru, which have seen multiparty politics off and on for a long time.

The representativeness of elected officials is also an important issue. One argument is that the electorate should have a legislator who actually represents their interests and preferences. Countries that use a plurality system with single-member seats, such as India and Tanzania, are among the top scorers. Tanzania is an especially interesting case because it is a multiethnic society. There are more than 100 different groups; the boundaries of electoral districts are drawn to give virtually all groups a chance to elect their own representatives to parliament. Moreover, Tanzania is not deeply divided by social class, another factor that reduces the extent to which the legislature is perceived as representative. For instance, it is worth comparing Tanzania with Argentina and Peru, where the scores are much lower because politics is seen as controlled by the elite at the expense of the poor and indigenous peoples.

Aggregating public preferences is used here to measure how effective political society is in performing its main function. There is little evidence that civil and political societies are at loggerheads. The aggregation of inputs from interest groups, social movements, NGOs, and any other organized activities is seen as functioning well in most countries, with the exception of those where the parliament is stymied by the military. It is no surprise that the older democracies like Chile and India score high due to a long tradition of institutions that facilitate it. Surprising is how well Thailand scored. Although it does not have formal separation of powers, its political society tends to function along the lines of checks and balances by virtue of the dominant factions in political society. It may be the best example of a functioning developmental state where the institutions—formal and informal—are already in place to make the state function effectively.

The fifth indicator refers to how influential the legislature is in helping to shape public policy. Again, we find that the older democracies do better, although newcomers like Indonesia and Mongolia also do well. The scores for the latter countries may reflect the fact that the parliaments under autocratic rule had a limited role. Respondents, therefore, are inclined to view the role of the legislature in the new political dispensation as vastly more important. We cannot rule out the euphoria factor in our data, and this is one place where it surfaces. The contrast with the past is so noticeable that it registers in the answers we obtained. On the whole, the average score for this indicator is higher than we expected given how the literature indicates that parliaments have lost the ability to shape public policy in many developing countries because of the influence of international finance institutions and donor communities.

If we compare the aggregate scores for each of the three groups of countries, there is no real surprise. As indicated in Table 4.2, there is a marked difference between the high- and low-scoring groups, with the middle group falling higher than the mean. Overall, scores for political society are lower than for other arenas, confirming that institutionalizing rules of governance in this arena is not easy. Still, our survey reflects scores that are better than expected given what the academic literature on democratic transition and consolidation holds. One reason may be that writers on Latin American countries, who have a critical, sometimes even cynical perspective on the issues, have dominated this literature.

How do the scores for 2000 compare with the perceptions of what prevailed five years earlier?

### Changes over Time

The most important observation is that all countries in the low-scoring group recorded a decline, but no country in the other categories did. In fact, among the latter, each country either recorded progress or at least retained the status quo. As Figure 4.1 illustrates, the decline has been especially marked in Kyrgyzstan, Pakistan, and Togo, the improvement most noticeable in Indonesia and Peru.

Pakistan is of special interest because it has practiced multiparty democracy off and on since independence in 1948. The record over those years has been checkered, but Pakistanis have by and large expected democracy and thereby sustain a viable political society. The sense of decline after the military takeover by General Pervez Musharaf, therefore, may have been strong. Togo, by contrast, has never had a tradition of multiparty democracy, but the sense of deprivation there seems to stem from the failure to transition to democracy like its neighbors Benin and Ghana. The abrogation of political rights in Kyrgyzstan due to the appearance of an Islamic fundamentalism is the main reason for a decline there.

With the possible exception of Thailand, the high-scoring group has not experienced much change in the political society arena since 1995. This is confirmation that these countries are stable and their institutions unchal-

**Table 4.2  Mean Scores on Political Society Indicators by Groups of Countries**

| Category of Countries | Mean Score |
| --- | --- |
| High scoring | 2.98 |
| Medium scoring | 2.70 |
| Low scoring | 2.17 |

**Figure 4.1 Changes over Time in Political Society, 1995–2000**

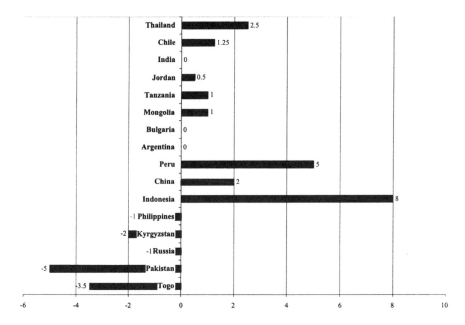

lenged. The improvement in Thailand reflects the resurrection of parliament after the military intervened in the mid-1990s. The most notable improvements are among the medium-scorers. Indonesia and Peru climbed up because the legislature has been able to regain power and relevance after a period of autocratic rule (in Indonesia for more than one generation, in Peru for a shorter time). In China the improvement is attributed primarily to a growing role for the People's Assembly in policymaking.

Even with improvements, scores in the political society arena are low for several reasons. We cover most below in our discussion of the five indicators.

## Analysis of Each Individual Indicator

Of the five measures of how political society is governed, each refers to an important aspect of the aggregating function sandwiched between civil society and the executive. Each also refers to a more specific or general principle contained in the UDHR, Article 21, which states that the authority of government should be based on the will of the people. In the discussion below, we draw on the statistical data as well as comments made by respondents and country coordinators.

*Representativeness*

Article 21(1) of the UDHR states that "everyone has the right to take part in the government of his country, directly or through freely chosen representatives." This sets the norm to which the vast majority of governments around the world have committed. There are more countries than ever that aspire to this norm, but countries undergoing democratic transition, even consolidation, have found that doing so fairly is difficult. There are at least three fairness issues that surface in our study.

The first is unequal representation for women. This is mentioned in several reports by country coordinators. Although some progress has been made since the 1995 Fourth World Conference on Women held in Beijing, women are not adequately represented. In the Philippines, for instance, women made up 12 percent of the lower house. In Mongolia, respondents claimed that neither government nor political parties could do anything to encourage female candidates. Traditional customs are alleged as the culprit.

The second issue concerns the poor. Politics continues to be seen by most as an elite activity. Citizens with little income or education do not have the means to compete for office. The gap between elected representatives and the electorate is large. In Indonesia, there is widespread belief that politics belongs to the capital, Jakarta. In Latin American countries, which tend to be characterized by deep social stratification, there is reference to the exclusive character of the political establishment. This may explain the strong reaction in favor of Lula da Silva's candidacy for president in Brazil in 2002. Coming out of the ranks of the poor, he mobilized low-income groups to support his party and did so without alienating the well-to-do.

The third issue concerns indigenous groups. The scheduled castes and tribes of India, as well as the native Indian population in countries like Peru, provide examples. They constitute significant groups within the population, but their voice is not represented in the legislature commensurately. In their view, the formal political process does not offer incentives or opportunities to participate.

Two institutional issues are important here. One is the electoral system. There are respondents in places like Indonesia who argue that the system of proportional representation is confusing. It leaves ordinary citizens without a sense of whom they are voting for. They don't see the connection between themselves and their elected representatives. The second issue concerns the extent to which political parties—as private organizations—make an effort to introduce fairness in the way they represent the electorate. For instance, in South Africa political parties have deliberately tried to make party lists in the elections more gender-equal and representative of everyone. Other respondents argue that the absence of such measures leaves the legislature representative of some but not all groups in society.

## Competitiveness

This indicator tries to capture the extent to which there is peaceful contestation for power in society. If divergent interests are to become part of official policy, the degree of competitiveness permitted becomes important. Competition is generally among political parties. Wherever parties are allowed to compete freely, the level of competitiveness should be high. There are countries where more modest forms of competition exist. Uganda, for example, has a no-party system, which allows for competition among individual candidates in single-member districts. China is an example that has only recently opened up, in an incrementalist fashion, introducing competitive elections at local levels.

Most countries, including the clear majority in our study, belong to the group that has attempted a wholesale transition from autocracy to democracy. This transition approach has raised public expectations and has not always been easy. Those countries that have fared well are in Latin America and Eastern Europe. The transition has remained more troublesome in Africa and Asia.

In our study, this is confirmed in the reports from various countries. In Togo, there has been political violence directed against the opposition. The government of President Eyadema, Africa's longest-serving head of state, has done its utmost to undermine the political opposition, including harassment and other interventions that have made the notion of free and fair elections a farce. There have been instances of political violence in Tanzania, though they have largely been confined to the islands of Zanzibar.[21] In Asia, the report from Pakistan indicates that while the military intervention put a lid on competitive politics, respondents were frank in stating that the civilian political leaders and their parties were all corrupt and manipulated political society to satisfy their own interests.[22]

Although these examples indicate problems in institutionalizing competitive elections that are free and fair, there is a broad sense among respondents that competitiveness has improved since 1995. Although the notion of competitiveness may vary in the minds of respondents, this improvement is an indication that as societies in transition are obliged to hold regular elections, actors as well as administrators learn the rules and become better at respecting them. This point is made in reference to elections in Africa.[23] Thailand may be a case where such learning has resulted in a more stable representative democracy with regular elections. The euphoria expressed by respondents in Indonesia reflects that people were allowed to participate in a free election for the first time in 1999. Our interviews were conducted while the honeymoon effect of these elections was strong.

The competitiveness score is probably the most encouraging comment on political society. It suggests that managing the rules actually matters. Even if elections are not all that matters in the context of democratization or good governance, they are a significant part of it. Institutionalizing the norm that elections must be free and fair is not easy, especially in societies with a neopatrimonialist political legacy, where patronage tends to dominate electoral politics. Thus, in our view, the competitiveness score recorded indicates, finally, that improving governance is possible.

## Effectiveness

There are typically more demands for public resources than can be afforded by government given limited public revenue. Priorities must be set. We are interested in the extent to which political society contributes to an aggregation of public preferences in an effective manner. By this we mean that the institutions in political society (e.g., political parties, elections, and legislatures) function in ways that allow them to process demands from civil society groups. Effectiveness, therefore, is an indicator of how capable political society is in adopting and processing political demands from civil society.

The party system is key. If fragmented, it will be difficult to create coalitions and alliances capable of agreement. Fragmentation does not primarily mean ideological cleavages. It is possible for policies to be developed even if the ideological divide between the main parties is gaping. But fragmentation due to too many parties is another matter. For instance, Denmark and Italy are countries with a considerable number of effective parties (i.e., actors that may have a bearing on how a cabinet is formed and coalitions established). Brazil, as suggested above, also stands out as a country with a large number of political parties. The point is that while parties are often closely tied to specific interest groups, and articulation may be effective, finding a compromise with other parties on specific policies is difficult.

Our study confirms that the party systems in many countries are weak. Judging from the comments, there are at least two reasons. One is the electoral system that encourages weak parties. For instance, in Argentina respondents complain that the *listas sabanas* (different lists of candidates sponsored by the same political party) cause not only confusion in the electorate but also a weakening of the party as a coherent actor in the legislature. Election laws are also blamed for the persistence of weak political parties in countries like Jordan. Because democratic rule is so new in many transitional societies, political parties have not yet coalesced as autonomous actors. Mongolia is a case in point: we see an inability of parties to act coherently and consistently.

The other reason is that political parties remain controlled by powerful and/or charismatic individuals. Voters often choose a party because of the personal appeal of the candidate. Although this is by no means unique to transitional societies, its consequences tend to be more dramatic. Respondents in the Philippines, for instance, made it clear that voters support parties because of the personal attributes of the candidate, including whether he or she is from their district.

It is no surprise that the highest scores on this variable can be found in countries that have been exposed to democracy for longer periods. Chile, India, and Peru have political societies that have worked well for a long time, albeit with some interruption in Chile and also Peru. A few others deserve special mention. Thailand, a relative newcomer to democratic rule, is seen as having a legislature that is capable of absorbing and processing political demands from below. Its institutions are also stable and functioning. The same may be said for China. As a mass organization, the Chinese Communist Party has a system in place for processing demands from cadres, if not directly from citizens. The former may not always represent the latter, but respondents indicate that when it comes to effectiveness, political society functions well and is effective enough to pick up on specific demands while not opening the floodgates to rising expectations.

## Influence

This indicator refers to how far the legislature is seen to bring public preferences to bear on policy. More specifically, it refers to political society's interaction with the executive branch of government. A legislature may be capable of responding to civil society demands but still not be influential in shaping policy. Public preferences may get lost because legislators are unwilling or unable to pursue them without watering them down. Influence depends on at least three major factors. One is the system of government. Differences in degree of influence may be a reflection of whether the system is presidential or parliamentary. A second factor is the extent to which political parties are centralized or decentralized. Whether a legislature is capable of influencing policy differs on the degree of party control. The third factor is the extent to which the legislature has a committee system that is not only exercising oversight but also working out specific compromises between the government and the opposition.

There is indication that parliamentary systems may score higher than presidential ones. India and Thailand, which function within the parliamentary tradition, score high. In both instances, the opposition is part of the policymaking process. It is treated as a loyal contender that can bring insights to the final bill. Other countries that score high include Chile and Peru in Latin America and Indonesia in Asia. All three have presidential systems, although the separation of powers is not as clear as it is in the U.S. Constitution. Judging from the comments of our respondents, the high scores are a reflection of recent gains made by the legislatures in relations with the executive. In Chile, for instance, the score reflects the ability of the legislature to free itself from a constitutional provision for the military to have reserved seats. In Peru, it was the enhanced influence that came in the wake of Fujimori's resignation. Much the same applies in Indonesia, where the parliament gained influence after Suharto's resignation. In other words, it is not clear that these scores can be attributed to institutional factors as much as cyclical variations in politics.

The influence score does not only reflect the variations in system of government. If political parties are strong and centralized, one would expect that legislators have less influence on policy than the executive. This comes out of the experience of consolidated democratic systems; our survey is more ambiguous. A country like Tanzania ranks lower. Yet Russia and Bulgaria, which do not have strong parties, also rank low. The most convincing evidence that decentralized parties give more influence to legislators is in India and the Philippines, both of which have decentralized political parties yet score high on influence. Furthermore, we find that the People's Assembly in China is perceived as having more influence than might be expected. The references in the qualitative data suggest that this must be interpreted in relative terms (i.e., compared to its role in the past, the People's Assembly has grown in influence, although it is still far from exercising the kind of influence that a legislature in a liberal democratic state may have).

In addition, behind the scoring on this indicator is the question of how legislatures are organized. Some legislatures are new and have not yet developed a functioning committee system. These bodies lack resources that allow for in-house work on policies. Archives are poorly organized, if they exist at all. Elected representatives lack their own staff. Research capacity is most likely nonexistent. This limits the role that the legislature can play in shaping policy. This complaint is explicit in Mongolia. As long as committees remain confined to what is essentially a watchdog function, they are likely be in confrontation vis-à-vis government, not in collaboration. Oversight is an important part of legislating, but if that is the only role, then the executive is likely to treat legislatures as a nuisance, leading to an even more diminished oversight role. Again, legislatures that are well organized and have committee systems in place, with at least a minimum level of independent staff and research capacity, do well on the influence score. Chile, India, the Philippines, and Thailand are cases in point. We also notice that countries without effective committees (e.g., Jordan, Tanzania, and Russia) score much lower.

## Accountability

This indicator is meant to capture how well political society fosters public accountability. It is not only how legislators are elected that matters; also important for the legitimacy of political society is how they behave while in parliament. Most countries do not have a recall system, which allows the electorate to force a representative's resignation during the term of service. The common pattern is that voters must wait for the next election. Whatever system exists, it is meant to give voters a chance to punish legislators for unsatisfactory performance. The issue in many transitional societies, however, is that incumbents often have an advantage over challengers and can buy the support they need to get reelected. Our survey indicates that there are two issues at stake. The first is the extent to which an elected representative is seen as pursuing personal interests rather than those of constituents. The second is the extent to which the representative is seriously interested in policy as opposed to simply dishing out patronage.

The accountability score is lower than for the other political society indicators. There is a general lack of trust in elected representatives that cuts across national borders and types of political systems. Chile, India, and Peru, on the previous indicator, were high scorers. On accountability, they fall toward the lower end. In Chile, respondents made it clear that elected representatives have a poor image. They are seen as ignoring the public and working for themselves or their party. This view is echoed in other countries. We see it in comments from Indonesia and in the country coordinator's report for Argentina. Again, we find that skepticism toward representatives is exacerbated in systems of proportional representation. Because political parties approve lists, voters don't see how they can exercise control over representatives. The latter are seen as acting with little regard for the voters. Respondents maintain that in these systems the media play an especially important watchdog role, because voters' ability to do so is hampered by the electoral system. Because the link between voter and representative is not direct in systems of proportional representation, they tend to generate skepticism in transitional societies, where institutions are still in flux or in the process of consolidating.

Yet the plurality system, with its direct link between voters and elected representatives, is no guarantee of accountability. Because so much is at stake in single-member districts, candidates are more likely to spend considerable resources to win. Patronage tends to become especially important. It becomes especially significant during the campaigns, when it is crucial to get popular support. It is not uncommon for incumbents to rely on resources that are, from a legal perspective, public. For instance, ruling parties tend to take advantage of control over government resources and make them available to incumbents who seek reelection.

Although references to patronage are not common in our study, references to corruption are common. Some representatives bribe their way to power, an allegation made in Pakistan, the Philippines, and Tanzania. Again, it seems that plurality systems tend to cause this problem more so than proportional systems. The patronage issue is often more serious than it appears. Patronage is a way of rewarding people for past or future support. It is distributed on a personal basis regardless of the policy issue. In other words, it tends to take attention away from policy and instead institutionalizes informal rules that often run against the interest of constituents. This leads to a system of governance that is based on clientelism[24] rather than public issues that are of concern to constituents and country alike. Although clientelism may be a necessary feature of transitional societies and provide at least a tenuous link between elite and mass politics, its effects on governance are such that it doesn't help legitimacy.

## Implications for Research and Practice

Three implications are clear. The first concerns political society; the second relates to governance challenges inherent in political society; and the third is what our survey means for practitioners working to improve governance.

The World Governance Survey confirms that political society is the most difficult arena to govern. There are considerable differences across time, countries, and indicators. These differences stem from systemic or institutional variations, and they can be attributed to a discrepancy between prescribed rules and actual behavior. This discrepancy reflects a lack of experience and personal predispositions that are contrary to formal rules.

Many of the countries are newcomers to a system in which political society is meant to play an important part in the process. Institutions are only now being introduced or put into place. With regard to such key functions as adopting views from the public and transforming them into policy, our study confirms that individual actors and organizations are still learning. They make mistakes, and there is reason to consider whether the rules adopted thus far are the most suitable.

The governance challenges highlighted echo the literature on democratization. People do have expectations that representatives serve the interests of constituents, that the legislature is responsive to public opinion, and that it can exercise influence on policy. We do not conclude that there is one single path that leads all countries to good governance. Institutional differences exist (e.g., how party and electoral systems are constituted and how representatives are chosen). These cannot be altered without deference to the historical legacy and sociocultural context in which they developed.

Even if they sometimes function only suboptimally, their raison d'être should not be called into question. Countries in transition cannot necessarily be expected to function perfectly.

Many of the shortcomings of political society are directly attributable to the behavior of individual legislators. They do not necessarily live up to expectations associated with the rules, or they outright violate the rules. We see frequent reference to elected representatives having abandoned constituents or engaging in corrupt behavior. These breaches of expected norms have contributed to lowering the legitimacy of political society at large.

We also found that the perception of governance can vary over time in regard to key functions in political society. This is indicative of a lack of institutionalization. People do not trust institutions because their track records are too limited or uneven. They do experience an upswing, largely the result of other arenas performing poorly. For instance, there are windows of opportunities for political society to grow in significance and attain new legitimacy, as in Indonesia and Peru just before our survey.

Another important point is that high scores on governance of political society do not come from democratic countries alone. We differ from the international discourse on good governance, which has a very distinct bias in favor of liberal democracy. Our study confirms that high governance scores are obtainable in countries with other than a liberal political dispensation. China is the most obvious case. Its political society may not be as pluralist or open as in other countries, but it functions satisfactorily in producing results.

The concluding observations that we wish to make concern the implications for governance practitioners. With specific regard to political society, what does our study find that is important for people in the international community who advise on these issues? Despite all the money that has gone into strengthening legislatures and monitoring elections, remarkably little progress has been made. This should not be a source of despair but an invitation to accept the fact that any support of political society, whether the legislature or the electoral administration, is not merely a technical or capacity-building issue. Although greater capacity is surely needed in many countries, every gesture of support is political and will be perceived as such. There will be those who support, but also those who oppose. Governance work is not tantamount to some form of political engineering, an observation that may be especially true with reference to political society, because the arena is by definition so contested. Our study suggests that trust and social capital in the relationship between voters and representatives—civil society and political society—are as important as training, staff capacity, and archives.

## Notes

1. See, e.g., Gabriel A. Almond and James S. Coleman, *The Politics of Developing Areas* (Princeton, NJ: Princeton University Press, 1960); also Juan Linz and Alfred Stepan, *Problems of Democratic Transition and Consolidation: Southern Europe, South America, and Post-Communist Europe* (Baltimore: Johns Hopkins University Press, 1996).

2. Guiseppi DiPalma, *To Craft Democracies: An Essay on Democratic Transitions* (Berkeley: University of California Press, 1991); Samuel P. Huntington, *The Third Wave: Democratization in the Late Twentieth Century* (Norman: University of Oklahoma Press, 1991); Scott Mainwaring, G. O'Donnell, and J.S. Valenzuela, *Issues in Democratic Consolidation: The New South American Democracies in Comparative Perspective* (South Bend, IN: University of Notre Dame Press, 1992).

3. Arend Lijphart, *Democracy in Plural Societies: A Comparative Exploration* (New Haven, CT: Yale University Press, 1977).

4. Matthew S. Shugart and J. M. Carey, *Presidents and Assemblies: Constitutional Design and Electoral Dynamics* (Cambridge, UK: Cambridge University Press, 1992).

5. Larry Diamond, *Developing Democracy: Toward Consolidation* (Baltimore: Johns Hopkins University Press, 1999), pp. 96–98.

6. *Effectiveness* refers to the party fragmentation in the legislature. Although it is a continuous scale, an "effective" party is one that is significant enough to have a say in cabinet formation and in policymaking. See Marrku Laakso and Rein Taagepera, "'Effective' Number of Political Parties: A Measure with Application to Western Europe," *Comparative Political Studies* 12, no. 1 (April 1979): 3–27.

7. Linz and Stepan, *Problems of Democratic Transition and Consolidation,* pp. 181-182.

8. For a discussion of the African situation, see Shaheen Mozzafar, James R. Scarritt, and Glen Galaich, "Electoral Institutions, Ethnopolitical Cleavages and Party Systems in Africa's Emerging Democracies," *American Political Science Review* 97, no. 3 (August 2003): 379–391.

9. Michael Coppedge, *Strong Parties and Lame Ducks: Presidential Partyarchy and Factionalism in Venezuela* (Stanford, CA: Stanford University Press, 1994).

10. Scott Mainwaring and T. R. Scully, *Building Democratic Institutions: Party Systems in Latin America* (Stanford, CA: Stanford University Press, 1995).

11. Giovanni Sartori, "Political Development and Political Engineering," in J. D. Montgomery and A. O. Hirschman (eds.), *Public Policy* (Cambridge, UK: Cambridge University Press, 1968).

12. Maurice Duverger, *Political Parties: Their Organization and Activity in the Modern State* (New York: Wiley 1954).

13. Joel D. Barkan, "Elections in Agrarian Societies," *Journal of Democracy* 6 (1995): 106–116.

14. Andrew Reynolds, "The Case for Proportionality," *Journal of Democracy* 6 (1995): 117–124.

15. For a discussion of these issues, see Jorgen Elklit and Palle Svensson, "What Makes Elections Free and Fair?," *Journal of Democracy* 8 (1997): 32–46.

16. Shugart and Carey, *Presidents and Assemblies.*

17. Scott Mainwaring, "Presidentialism, Multipartyism, and Democracy: The Difficult Combination," *Comparative Political Studies* 26 (1993): 198–228.

18. Alfred Stepan and C. Skach, "Constitutional Frameworks and Democratic Consolidation: A Synthesis and Evaluation of Recent Theory and Research," review article, *World Politics* 46 (1993): 1–22.

19. Guillermo O'Donnell, "Delegative Democracy," *Journal of Democracy* 5, no. 1 (January 1994): 55–70.

20. Mick Moore, "Democracy and Development in Cross-National Perspective," *Democratization* 2, no. 2 (1995): 1–19.

21. It should be noted here that Zanzibar, though part of the United Republic of Tanzania, enjoys a high degree of autonomy. Our respondents were all from the mainland—originally called Tanganyika—and the scoring as well as comments by our Tanzanian respondents reflect this.

22. The military leader, General Pervez Musharaf, allowed competitive elections to the parliament to be held in October 2002. The strongest party represents a new coalition of interests in society.

23. Joel D. Barkan, "Protracted Transitions Among Africa's New Democracies," *Democratization* 7, no. 3 (2000): 227–243.

24. For an account of the role of clientelism in the context of national integration in Africa, see Rene Lemarchand, "Political Clientelism and Ethnicity in Tropical Africa: Competing Solidarities in Nation-Building," *American Political Science Review* 66, no. 1 (1972): 68–90.

# 5

# Government

The essence of governance is the way in which state-society relations are structured and managed. Managing a regime successfully has a lot to do with how citizens perceive the rules that guide their interaction with public officials. Much of this regime assessment takes place in the context of policy aggregation (see Chapter 4) and implementation (see Chapter 6). It equally occurs in the context of how well government deals with underlying issues that transcend policies. Is the regime so structured that citizens see that government cares about their welfare and security, whether individual or collective? This is the basic question guiding our assessment of governance in the government arena.

It may be helpful to spell out the key concepts. *State* refers here to all institutions that make up the public sector. It encompasses all public officers—elected or appointed—with a responsibility for implementing policy or, as in the case of police and judges, enforcing and adjudicating laws. It excludes elected officials with purely representative functions, such as lawmakers. *Government* is typically defined in reference to elected and appointed officials serving in core institutions at the national, provincial, county, city, and local levels. In this chapter, we refer to all appointed public servants as being part of the *bureaucracy* while confining the term *government* to those with responsibility for setting policy and making key appointments to public service. In many countries they would be *cabinet ministers*. They are responsible for the *executive dimension*, the term we introduced in Chapter 1. The rules that guide the behavior and actions of these officials concern us here.

More than anybody else, government officials are responsible for words and actions that influence the development of society. Their decisions are not merely a response to demands from groups in society. Government does not only revolve around the aggregation of interests, values, and preferences that come up via different channels to the executive level; it also implies transformative decisions that involve choices beyond interests and preferences. For instance, decisions go against particular interests but are viewed as necessary to protect the larger public or national interest. The readiness and ability to make hard choices is a product of how the polity is institutionalized. Governance in the government arena, therefore, is best understood as the nature of the state, what constitutes national interest, and the extent to which civilian government prevails.

The first section discusses the principal governance issues as they relate to the government arena, drawing on relevant literature. This discussion is meant to provide background. The second section analyzes the aggregate findings of our survey and discusses the differences between the high, medium, and low governance performers. The third section discusses each indicator in turn. The chapter concludes with a brief discussion of the implications of the findings.

## Governance Issues in the Government Arena

Western Europe was for a time a laboratory for social and political experimentation. Philosophers in France, Britain, and Germany pioneered ideas that guided new forms of political development. Baron de Montesquieu heralded the idea of separation of powers between the branches of government. Jean-Jacques Rousseau's principal message was sovereignty of the people. John Locke advocated the social contract between rulers and ruled. Georg Hegel and then Karl Marx pursued the notion that development is the product of opposing social forces. These ideas were both causes and consequences of political crises. They reflected the violent nature of European history over centuries. They were meant to provide hope for peace and development but often caused misery and violence. Europeans have not given up experimenting, as the European Union indicates. But since the end of World War II they turned attention to modifying interstate relations rather than transforming nation-states.

The frontier of political and social experimentation moved instead to the postcolonial world, or developing societies. We have witnessed experimentation with political systems aimed at finding ways to accelerate economic and social development. Bold but risky steps have been taken in Asia, Africa, and Latin America to catch up with the West, often transforming societies. Much of what guides discourse on governance and development today draws inspiration from such experiences. We review three sets of literature: the nature of the state, the search for a truly public interest, and relations between civil and military authorities. All three bear directly on the issue of governments providing security and development.

## Nature of the State

Here we look at what the state ought to be in relation to society. This is important because government ministers have a decisive influence on how the state should interact with society and realize such goals as peace and development.

This search for the reigning ideas about the nature of the state is relevant to governance. Much of the past is today dismissed as irrelevant. We believe that some issues important in the 1960s and 1970s are still valid. One of them is the extent to which the state enjoys autonomy vis-à-vis society.

This issue was at the forefront of the development discourse in earlier decades. Nationalist leaders in Africa and Asia, having gained independence by defeating colonial masters, came to power with a sense of making history. It is no coincidence that the literature on socialist revolution by Marx, Lenin, and Mao Zedong became important sources of inspiration for others in the developing world. All three provided arguments supporting the notion that the postcolonial era provided a unique political opportunity for reversing the trend toward capitalist hegemony.

Development, from this perspective, was not merely a matter of achieving incremental change. It was a grand project aimed at providing citizens with all they had been denied in the past. Little attention was paid to whether the means to realize this grand vision existed. Were the historical conditions present? Was the revolutionary consciousness or will of the elite developed? Were the masses ready to mobilize for a full transformation of not only society at large but also their own individual livelihoods? To so many nationalist leaders in the developing regions, the ends of the revolution were beyond question. Whichever ways these ends were sought could be justified.

Their view of the executive dimension—whether identified with a single ruling party's politburo or with a strong central government—was that it has a moral responsibility to take the lead for society. As in Africa, nationalist leaders expected deference to their vision of the national development project. Any opposition was treason. The role that ideology played in shaping the postcolonial world has been little studied because the assumption among academics was that objective structural conditions were more important.[1] What actually happened in most of these societies is best described as a disjuncture between the objective conditions and the subjective will of the political leadership. The latter acted as if there were no structural limitations, while history soon spun a tight web around them. Goran Hyden has described this contradiction by calling attention to the lack of control that the political leadership had over social forces[2] and to the problems of ignoring the historical conditions prevailing in African countries.[3]

This analysis draws attention to state power as a positive and negative factor in development. What difference can an ideologically ambitious political leadership make? The answers to this question have been sought along two lines. One has been that objective conditions set definite limits to what can be accomplished. Another has given more significance to human agency, assuming that it can make a positive difference.

The latter position was evident in the writings on political development in the 1960s that followed efforts to create a structural-functionalist framework for the analysis of politics.[4] This position has been present in the writings of Charles Tilly,[5] who sees significant political change as the result of purposive action by ideologically committed political leaders. For him—and others like Ted Gurr[6]—possibilities for changing governance arrangements occur as a result of underlying social changes, which the political leadership can exploit. For instance, in Gurr's case, such an opportunity arises because of growing social deprivation in key segments of the population.

Others have been more circumspect in attributing positive outcomes to human agency. Even if we ignore the economic determinism embraced by orthodox Marxists, there is a significant group of academic writers who stress the significance of objective conditions setting limits to what can be achieved. Foremost among them is Barrington Moore, who has devoted much of his professional career to explaining why people endure violence and repression. His most important book—*The Social Origins of Dictatorship and Democracy*[7]—sees class relations, notably those between lords and peasants, as key factors in the making of the modern world. In so doing, he acknowledges the role that repressive violence plays in sustaining or failing to sustain state power. In a subsequent book,[8] less heralded than the first but still important in this context, Moore points to the role that ideology and culture play in forming and reproducing cultures of compliance. His ideas have been influential in shaping the arguments of others, including Theda Skocpol, one of his students. In her work,[9] she questions the extent to which self-declared revolutionaries really achieve what they set out to do. She focuses her explanation on the structural crises that inevitably occur in society and produce the structurally determined opportunities for social and political change. Eric Hobsbawm echoes her argument when he maintains that what determines the possibilities for revolutionary action are idiosyncratic factors in a given situation.[10] In other words, a revolutionary political process cannot be easily modeled.

This review suggests that members of the political leadership—actors in the government arena—are far from free agents. Even if they wish to improve circumstances for people, the opportunities for doing so are few. More typical is the situation in which they have to settle for something less than transformation. This doesn't mean that political leaders fail in legitimizing their regime. It indicates that a political regime that gives too much autonomy to government may suffer a backlash. This set of issues has a bearing on how the summit of the political system is being governed.

## Defining the Public Interest

The second issue is defining the public interest. In theory, it is easy for a government to define it for citizens. It is more complicated if citizens are allowed input. Process complicates matters and raises a fundamental issue in political theory: How can the tension between substance and procedure best be resolved?

One of the real challenges to sustaining democracy is to give roughly equal dignity to every expression of preference in the public arena. Although every dollar carries equal value in the marketplace—whether spent by the most careless or the most careful consumer—in democracy political procedures impose a necessary arbitrariness of choice. As Kenneth Arrow pointed out long ago, even if all preferences are admitted to the democratic aggregation game, there is no single objective rule by which they could in fact be aggregated.[11] Whether we choose majoritarian or proportional rules for aggregating private preferences, we will fail to identify the one and only will of the people or its collective preference. Even if there were an objective or unobjectionable aggregation rule, it could not rule out the possibility that individuals, for example, would misrepresent their preferences for tactical reasons in order to ensure at least a suboptimal gain.[12]

Representative democracy is minimalist in the sense that it requires relatively little of those involved. It asks citizens only to cast a vote now and again. It requires of political leaders only an ability to bargain an acceptable outcome. In this respect, democracy produces at best suboptimal results. To some observers that is good enough. Democracy is about giving and taking. Bargain and compromise are at the bottom of a functioning democracy. Others, however, believe that this model of democracy is inadequate because it presupposes that each actor is an autonomous agent trying to maximize his or her own self-interest. This model fosters neither civic competence nor a valid notion of the common or public good.[13]

Deliberative democracy is different from representative democracy in that it presupposes a more demanding and complex system for arriving at what constitutes a public conception of a common good. Only those preferences that come out of special efforts such as self-examination, reflection, and deliberation deserve to be considered. The public good, in other words, is not merely the outcome of a mechanical aggregation of individual interests. What counts even more is how seriously a citizen or group have weighed a preferred option against those of others.[14] Even though this is a process that carries its own costs, careful and informed deliberations are believed to strengthen regime legitimacy.

Many politicians are inclined to avoid deliberation because it often undermines promises made to the public. The issue has taken on special significance in developing countries, where conservation versus development or sound public finance versus social welfare have become increasingly important long-term issues. For instance, Indonesia's president, Megawati Sukarnoputri, recently spoke of her determination to maintain cuts in fuel, electricity, and telephone subsidies despite public protests: "I chose an unpopular but constructive policy for the long run, rather than opting for a populist step that may trouble us further." Less than a week later she had changed her position and reinstated many of the subsidies.[15] The challenge that President Sukarnoputri and so many other leaders in developing societies face is how to reconcile public participation in expressing preferences with the need for a solution to a policy problem based on reasoning that transcends group interests and serves development in the long term. Perhaps no one has discussed constitutional and governance implications with greater sensitivity than the late Carlos Santiago Nino, an Argentine human rights lawyer and adviser who was a strong advocate of intersubjective means of establishing principles and policies guiding the public.[16] For governments around the world, defining the public interest in ways that balance substance with procedure continues to be a governance challenge with consequences for the public perception of the legitimacy of the regime.

### Civil-Military Relations

Governments in developing societies have often been described as powerful and overbearing in managing development. The paradox is that the problem is more often the opposite. Samuel Huntington emphasized this point years ago when he noted that the main distinction between states is not in the type of government but in the degree to which it really governs.[17] With specific reference to African countries, Aristide Zolberg argues along similar lines: "The major problem is not too much authority, but too little."[18]

Many authors have followed these statements. States have been variably described as soft[19] or weak.[20] It is in this institutional context that the role of the military in politics has acquired special interest. In the 1960s and 1970s, problems associated with lack of institutional capacity at the state level made the military look like the best-equipped institution to rule. It was viewed as a corporate entity with strong discipline and less inclination to engage in nepotistic and corrupt behavior. Retaining this image and behavior proved difficult once officers took the reins of civilian government. Their ranks were quickly politicized. Divisions sprang up, and their effectiveness in implementing policy did not meet popular expectations. The tendency for authoritarian rule, often relying on repressive methods, added to public disillusion.

This experience differs from one region to another. In Asia, the military has had an important role in the economy and politics without necessarily ruling alone. In South Korea, Taiwan, Thailand, the Philippines, and Indonesia, the military has played a positive role in building the economy (e.g., by exercising control over government-run public-sector firms). Yet the military in Asian countries has been reluctant to extend political rights to citizens and accept full accountability to a civilian government. In this respect, the militaries in Asia have differed from counterparts in Latin America. Although the military continues to be a key institution there, since the 1980s the militaries have returned to the barracks and transferred power to elected civilian leaders. The pattern in Africa is different in that military rule never led to greater political stability. One military regime succeeded another because of disagreements within the officers' ranks. Thus a succession of military coups occurred in a number of countries (e.g., Burkina Faso, Ghana, Nigeria, and Uganda).

The record of the military in power has not resulted in lasting legitimacy. Even in Asia, the military has been in political retreat. Many officers realize that the costs of running civilian affairs exceed the benefits. The general trend toward democratic governance has reinforced this orientation. Nowadays there is greater agreement between civilian and military authorities regarding a professional armed force with ultimate accountability to civilian government. This principle seems to apply regardless of whether the civilian form of governance is democratic or not. This does not necessarily mean that political development today is more institutionalized than before. Uncertainty continues to affect civil-military relations in some countries. Even where these were constitutionalized in a pact at the time the military handed over power to civilian rulers, these relations are more like a truce than a treaty.[21] The ongoing political tensions in Venezuela, as well as civil and political violence in neighboring Colombia, are cases in point. But now attempts by the military to intervene in civilian politics tend to have repercussions beyond boundaries. It causes uncertainty and anxiety in neighboring countries, enough to mobilize them to protect their own territory from incursions by soldiers or displaced persons. The notion that democratic countries do not fight one another may be accurate if confined to established democracies. It is yet to be established as a principle applied to countries still in the process of democratizing. These so-called diminished subtypes of democracy[22] suffer from a democratic deficit and lack some of the qualities that are requisites of democracies for which attacking a democratic neighbor would be taboo.

## The Government Arena: The Aggregate WGS Findings

The five indicators used in the World Governance Survey are drawn from the concerns expressed in the literature reviewed above. They have been constructed to indicate how well government in a particular political system is set to make large or transformative decisions on issues that affect citizens. This is a quality of the regime that can make a huge difference at critical junctures in development. The five specific indicators used here are as follows:

1. *Ensuring freedom from fear.* This indicator is meant to probe the extent to which governments promote rules that reduce the threat to personal security.
2. *Ensuring freedom from want.* This indicator aims at highlighting how far governments show interest in promoting social and economic rights.
3. *Readiness to make tough decisions.* This indicator is expected to assess how far rules enable governments to make decisions with the long-term interest of the country in mind as opposed to being driven by populist and short-term demands.
4. *Political-military relations.* This indicator is assessing the extent to which the military is subject to civilian control and largely confined to its professional role.
5. *Attitude toward peace.* This indicator is meant to measure how seriously government takes its task of reducing the risk of violence or war within its territorial boundaries as well as with neighboring countries.

These five indicators are important for sustainable development. The first focuses on the importance of *personal security,* a quality that citizens expect governments to be largely responsible for. The second relates to another key function that governments have typically been asked to oversee and develop: *social welfare.* The third refers to the role that government plays in defending and promoting the *national interest* as seen in a developmental perspective. The fourth speaks to the issue of *civilian control* of the military. The fifth refers to the ability of government to maintain *peace.* These issues cut across demands that individuals or groups make in society. They speak to a regime quality that in many respects is systemic yet conceived as stemming from how well government is doing its job. It is our belief that the best way to assess the governance quality of this arena is to focus on the big issues that affect not specific groups but everyone in society.

## Differences Among Countries

As we have done in the previous two chapters, we begin the analysis by looking at the aggregate arena score for each country. We also follow the same distinction between high, medium, and low performers (see Table 5.1). Some scores immediately catch the eye. One is the high score for civilian control of the military. Only Pakistan and Togo, where the military was—and still is—in power, have a low score on this indicator. With those exceptions, all countries' scores indicate that the military is generally ready to accept civilian control. Even countries that otherwise do not have a high score (e.g., the Philippines and Russia) come out favorably on this indicator.

Another notable point is the high score for the peace variable. Although governments are not necessarily seen as very good at providing for personal security, they do have a better record in keeping peace within territorial boundaries as well as with neighbors. Not surprisingly, given the conflicts between government and rebel forces on the island of Mindanao, the Philippines is the worst performer.

**Table 5.1    Aggregate Government Arena Scores by Country, 2000**

| Country | Personal Security | Social Welfare | National Interest | Civilian Control | Peace | Average |
|---------|-------------------|----------------|-------------------|------------------|-------|---------|
| **High-scoring countries** | | | | | | |
| Chile | 3.70 | 3.63 | 2.87 | 3.20 | 4.20 | 3.52 |
| India | 3.00 | 2.81 | 2.35 | 4.67 | 3.69 | 3.30 |
| Jordan | 3.93 | 3.13 | 3.13 | 3.98 | 4.13 | 3.66 |
| Mongolia | 2.77 | 2.82 | 2.67 | 3.04 | 3.54 | 2.97 |
| Tanzania | 3.15 | 2.95 | 3.05 | 3.97 | 3.24 | 3.27 |
| Thailand | 3.10 | 3.29 | 2.99 | 3.66 | 3.66 | 3.34 |
| **Medium-scoring countries** | | | | | | |
| Argentina | 2.69 | 2.66 | 2.40 | 4.23 | 3.89 | 3.17 |
| Bulgaria | 2.12 | 1.95 | 2.90 | 3.44 | 3.46 | 2.77 |
| China | 2.79 | 2.85 | 2.88 | 3.36 | 2.97 | 2.97 |
| Indonesia | 1.94 | 2.17 | 2.31 | 3.09 | 2.74 | 2.45 |
| Peru | 3.03 | 2.64 | 2.51 | 2.97 | 3.38 | 2.91 |
| **Low-scoring countries** | | | | | | |
| Kyrgyzstan | 2.49 | 2.44 | 2.85 | 3.31 | 3.85 | 2.99 |
| Pakistan | 2.27 | 2.09 | 2.24 | 1.33 | 2.48 | 2.08 |
| Philippines | 2.37 | 2.00 | 2.00 | 3.34 | 1.97 | 2.34 |
| Russia | 2.18 | 2.16 | 3.24 | 3.63 | 2.74 | 2.79 |
| Togo | 2.43 | 1.79 | 2.07 | 1.75 | 2.71 | 2.15 |
| Average, all countries | 2.75 | 2.59 | 2.65 | 3.31 | 3.29 | 2.92 |

Generally speaking, governments do better maintaining law and order than development. To be sure, there is variation with respect to personal security. For instance, the government in Indonesia in 2000 was not viewed as capable of providing personal security, not very surprising given the uncertainty and increased violence surrounding the transition from the Suharto regime. It is worth noting that former communist countries, notably Bulgaria and Russia, also scored low. There is no evidence that the form of government plays a major role in regard to the ability to guarantee personal security. The views of the respondents coincide regardless of regime type. It is high in democratic countries like Chile, India, and Peru but noticeably high also in Jordan, a Muslim country where the monarchy is generally more influential than the parliament. Other high-scoring countries include Tanzania and Thailand, whose governments are democratically elected but not foreign to autocratic rule.

The lowest score is recorded for social welfare. It reflects problems governments have in meeting popular expectations in health care and education. These services used to be free, but in the 1980s and 1990s they were available at some cost to households. The high-scoring countries do well on this indicator, but outside that group it is only one country—China—where the opinion of government performance with regard to this variable is at the same level. Countries that have undergone structural adjustment programs are foremost among those with low scores.

Government's ability to make long-term decisions in the national interest is also called into question in many countries. Although it is not clear that countries with democratic forms of governance necessarily fare worse than others, it is interesting that countries like Argentina, Chile, India, and Peru on this particular indicator score lower than countries with forms of government that are less democratic like China, Kyrgyzstan, Russia, and Tanzania.

One country stands out more than any other: Jordan. Its high governance score must be viewed in the context of the tensions that exist in the Middle East. There is a general sense that the Hashemite monarchy has successfully guarded the Jordanians from many of the calamities that have afflicted other peoples in the region, notably Palestinians. The widespread and great appreciation of governance in the government arena in Jordan should not come as a big surprise.

If we compare the aggregate scores for each category of country, they are considerably higher for this arena than they were for political society. It applies especially to the high and low scoring categories (see Table 5.2).

It may be a surprise that the scores for this arena are so much higher given that governments in developing countries have been forced to contract their involvement in the development process. These scores, however, conceal the fact that there is variation on the five indicators. A closer examination of each indicator will tell us more about the specific governance features of the government arena. Before proceeding, some comments on the changes over time are warranted.

## Changes over Time

Compared to both the civil and political society arenas, the changes over time here are modest. There is much greater continuity or stability in the government arena. To the extent that there is a difference, it is in the form of a slight improvement, although the single biggest change is negative—in the Philippines. The specifics for each country are contained in Figure 5.1.

Improvements and declines are also more scattered in this arena than in

**Table 5.2    Mean Scores on Government Arena Indicators by Groups of Countries**

| Category of Countries | Mean Score |
| --- | --- |
| High scoring | 3.34 |
| Medium scoring | 2.85 |
| Low scoring | 2.53 |

**Figure 5.1    Changes over Time in the Government Arena, 1995–2000**

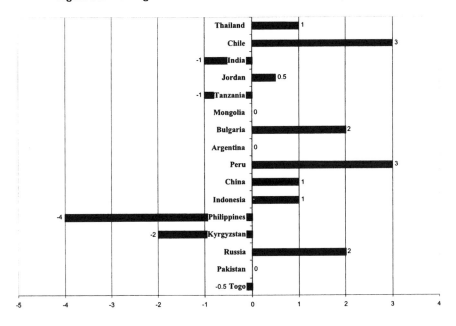

the others. Although all countries in the medium-scoring category, with the exception of one, have recorded improvement, there is variation in the other two groups. The declines in Kyrgyzstan and the Philippines can be explained by the growing inability of governments to provide personal security and peace. The recorded declines in India and Tanzania are in part for the same reason, but more influenced by the perceived sense that government is unable to secure freedom from want.

The improvement recorded for Chile is related to the ability of civilian rulers to increase control over the military, and in Russia it is related to the role that President Vladimir Putin is playing in enhancing security. Although his record is not impeccable, compared to that of his predecessor Boris Yeltsin he looks better in the eyes of Russian respondents. The change to the better in Peru is explained by the ability of the Fujimori government to eliminate the threat of the Shining Path movement, and the removal of the man in charge of the security services of the country, Valdomiro Montesinos.

A final comment is that the government arena was not a key place for change in countries like Indonesia and Mongolia, which have undergone significant political reforms, but where the changes over time are more noticeable in other arenas.

## Analysis of Individual Indicators

Each indicator refers to how the regime is structured to deal with issues that are cross-cutting and fundamental to the security and welfare of the citizenry and thus citizens' sense of how well their government is able to protect and promote their common interests. The discussion of each indicator below draws on the statistical data already provided, as well as qualitative comments provided by respondents.

### Personal Security

This indicator is included because it refers to a fundamental aspect of how governance relates to development. Freedom from fear is a basic human right that is referred to in Articles 3-5 of the UDHR. It is also stated in no uncertain terms as a right in the Convention Against Torture. Governments' ability to provide personal security, however, is not easy, especially in societies undergoing rapid social change or suffering economic crisis.

This is confirmed by our study. A few cases deserve special attention. The first is Jordan, which scores higher than any other country (3.93) on this indicator. It reflects a widespread belief among respondents that the government pays attention to public safety and security in accordance with the principles of Islam. There has been no real change, suggesting that religious principles underpinning government action are firmly in place. Comments by individual respondents indicate that government policy on this issue is in tune with the majority's principles.

Mongolia stands in contrast to Jordan. Both are among the high performers, but Mongolia's score on this indicator (2.77) is considerably below that of the others. A major reason is the extent to which Mongolian respondents focused on the prevalence of domestic violence. It is not necessarily more common than anywhere else, but it has acquired special attention in Mongolia because of widespread reporting of women being raped and beaten by men, especially husbands. This behavior contradicts the culture of gender equality that was developed under communism. The facts that many Mongolians are nomads and that the country is large may be exacerbating factors.

It is generally true that countries with some tradition of democratic governance tend to score higher. For instance, Chile, India, Peru, and Thailand fall into this category. There are exceptions. Argentina and the Philippines—countries with a tradition of democratic governance—score low. Respondents recognize that there has been a decline in the ability of government to provide personal security as a result of corruption and other manifestations of a soft state. Respondents in the Philippines suggested that it was possible in 2000 to get away with murder as long as one had the right political connections. This, they argued, was a marked deterioration from the situation five years earlier. Similar sentiments were expressed by respondents in Russia who noted the presence of a local mafia as a growing threat to personal security. They suggested that government was still in need of showing that it could contain these threats to citizens around the country.

Doubts about governments' ability to protect citizens from fear were expressed in countries like Indonesia and Bulgaria and may be less surprising given the political transitions there and the uncertainty they generated. It is important to note that the respondents were members of the elite, but they empathized with the situation of the poorer populations and the threats to which they are exposed. Although in most countries there has been no significant deterioration in regard to how respondents perceive personal security, the qualitative comments that we received indicate an ongoing and genuine concern about the ability of governments to enhance freedom from fear.

### Social Welfare

This indicator refers to the ability of governments to ensure freedom from want. As such, it comments on the extent to which citizens are able to benefit from the promotion of social and economic rights, as reflected in Articles 23-25 of the UDHR as well as the International Covenant on Economic, Social, and Cultural Rights. Governments vary in their commitment and capacity to satisfy citizen demands for a better life. People also differ in terms of expectations as to what governments should be doing on their behalf. Our findings suggest that citizens do expect governments to care about their social and economic needs, but not to the extent that an earlier generation did. For instance, the revolution of rising expectations that Samuel Huntington saw as a threat to political development and stability in the latter part of the 1960s seems to have faded.[23] Some respondents believe government should not be concerned with securing social and economic rights; rather it should stay out of development and be concerned only with securing order and justice.

And to the extent that development is being approached from a rights rather than a needs perspective, popular expectations and demands on government to secure acceptable livelihoods for all stay alive. The scores on this indicator across countries should be viewed against this background. We want to make the following specific comments.

The government's role in securing adequate livelihoods for people is most widely appreciated in developed countries, notably Chile and Thailand. To be sure, there are those in Chile who accept that government has been more responsible for growth than redistribution of the benefits of economic development, but in both countries there is a sense that government is improving its role in securing freedom from want. Given budgetary limitations in light of structural adjustments of the economy in a neoliberal direction, government may not be involved directly to the same extent as in the past, but new partnerships with private and voluntary agencies are seen as important initiatives to improve the living conditions for poorer segments.

Countries scoring low on this indicator tended to have strong government involvement in the development sector in the past. This applies especially to former communist and socialist regimes. Thus it is not a coincidence that the sense of disappointment—bordering on cynicism—is noticeable in Bulgaria and Russia, where the transition from communism to capitalism has created widespread opportunities for abuse of power. This sentiment is present in Kyrgyzstan and Tanzania—two other countries with a socialist legacy—but is less pronounced. Pakistan and the Philippines also have low scores, but the reason is different. Respondents make it clear that corruption has undermined citizens' belief in the government's interest in caring about their welfare.

Another item that cuts across countries is the gap between government rhetoric and practice. Several Indonesian respondents made the point that during the Suharto regime there was political repression but also progress on the economic and social fronts. Following his resignation and the arrival of a new regime with high aspirations, the political language in 2000 was correct, but there was very little evidence that the promises that politicians were making could be realized.

Respondents in some countries stressed that the government's role in securing freedom from want for all citizens requires institutional reform. Mongolians were making references to the need for strengthening local government, a point that was echoed in comments from Russia and Tanzania. A strong centralized government, especially in large countries, lacks the outreach that makes it sensitive to local concerns. It tends to act in more general terms with little understanding of the variations that exist in living conditions for different groups. Even though it may have good intentions, it fails because it acts according to a blueprint rather than in response to real-life circumstances.[24]

### National Interest

Government often has to make tough decisions that are unpopular or go against majority opinion. This is true in countries that are resource-scarce or that undergo crisis. In an era of structural adjustment, this has become a real political issue. How well equipped is the regime to handle hard prioritizing that sets short-term gains in opposition to longer-term necessities? Government is ultimately the only agency capable of resolving this dilemma.

Our respondents recognize the significance of this indicator. With growing interest in making development more sustainable, persons concerned with the way their country is governed are more aware of how government policy makes a difference in the long run. "Development has become more demanding and difficult" is how one respondent in Argentina expressed it. The various conditions that are being placed on what development option is selected, and what the potential implications might be of such a choice, have raised the ante for government.

No government is rated as doing particularly well. There is some evidence to suggest that governments in countries with democratic forms of governance may be less well situated to make tough decisions. Countries like India, Argentina, Peru, and the Philippines have a lower score than countries like China, Jordan, Kyrgyzstan, and Russia. Even Chile, which has a high average score for the arena as a whole, comes out considerably lower than the average on this indicator. This indicates that democratically elected governments are sensitive to public opinion and inclined to take the demands for immediate action in response to interests as an important impetus for political action. Taking into consideration the long-term interest of the nation as a whole is typically much more difficult.

Opportunities to do so tend to occur at particular conjunctures. Windows of opportunity may open as a result of an economic or political crisis. This helps explain why the higher scorers are not necessarily the same as with the other measures. Russia is the top scorer, followed by Jordan and Tanzania. Our respondents provide valuable insights into why these three countries come out generally well. President Putin's ability to lead Russia from chaos is associated with his ability to rise above the partisan crowds that tended to take advantage of an increasingly infirm Yeltsin. He is described as having brought Russians together. By standing above partisan interests, he is also said to have acted in the country's national interest. For some others, he is viewed as having brought pride back to Russia.

We have already commented on the situation in Jordan, where respondents point to the ability of the king to act in the interest of all Jordanians in a volatile region. Although King Abdullah had been in power only a short time at the time of our survey, he enjoyed the same reputation as his father—King Hussein—as someone who acts wisely with the long-term interest of the country in mind. The Tanzanian case is a bit different but still indicative of the same capacity. By the time President Benjamin Mkapa took over in 1995, Tanzania's economy was not in very good shape. By 2000 the new president had turned things around. Through prudent policies, public finance was under control. The International Monetary Fund, the World Bank, and bilateral donors were all impressed by the turn of events and gave the government high marks for its commitment to cleaning up public finance without losing sight of the need for poverty reduction. Although the latter—as could be expected in a resource-poor country—has proved to be complicated and is an issue that needs longer time to produce results, our respondents give the president and his government credit for having been able to do things that they see as necessary for the country's ability to develop in the long run.

In the same way that good policy has spilled over into appreciation of governance, bad policy has undermined the legitimacy of some regimes. This is true in the Philippines, where the Estrada administration was seen as having lost sight of the national interest; and in Togo President Eyadema in 2000 was viewed as acting in partisan ways at the expense of the national interest.

### Civilian Control

Civilian control has become a major governance issue because of the past failure of democratically elected governments in developing societies to demonstrate discipline and commitment to modernization, a broad expectation of governments in the 1960s. In those days, the military was regarded as a legitimate substitute for civilian governments that failed to meet popular expectations.[25] Civilian governments that were seen to stray ideologically from this objective, or displayed signs of being corrupt or bogged down in disagreements, were overthrown by military juntas, which believed that they were better equipped to rule the country.[26] Although the situation varied, in several countries the military was received as saviors by large segments of the population. Members of the democratically elected elite had lost their support among the public, including the oppressed classes.

Military rule was prevalent in the 1970s and into the 1980s in Africa, Asia, and Latin America. Efforts were made to civilianize rule by bringing expertise into government. Such efforts notwithstanding, the regimes were controlled by the military. Officers were in charge and unaccountable to elected civilian leaders.

The professionalism and discipline that the military displayed prior to running governments, however, dissipated once the officers had taken on the task. Their style of running affairs of government generated opposition, especially if it involved the denial of political and civil rights. Violation of human rights became an albatross for the military. In Latin America, civilian populations began to organize and protest military rule. These protests grew strong enough to force the military to reconsider its involvement in politics. In Argentina, Brazil, and Chile, where the militaries had kept a strong hold on the reins of power, this retreat took place during the 1980s and resulted in a return to democracy.[27] With a few recent exceptions—notably Pakistan—the military has retreated and stayed out of power in other developing regions (e.g., Indonesia in Asia and Nigeria in Africa).

Our survey suggests that civilian control of the military is a broadly accepted principle in practice. The overall score is among the highest we received across the board. To be sure, there are two notable exceptions—Pakistan and Togo, where the military remains in control—but elsewhere respondents generally agree that the military is ready to accept accountability to civilian government. Some countries are behind on this issue. Rights and political prerogatives reserved for the military in the new democratic constitution in Chile remained a question of how far the military really was willing to accept civilian control. The political uncertainty surrounding the regime in Indonesia and Peru in 2000 contributed to respondents' doubts when asked to rate their country on this indicator.

By and large, when it comes to the military accepting its role as a professional corps working on the defense of the nation—or in nation-building capacity under a civilian government—there has been a dramatic change. The incentive for the military to get back into government is not there, which explains why it has remained in the barracks even in countries like Argentina, where the economy completely collapsed in 2001 due in part to shortcomings in the way the elected government was handling economic policy.

## Peace

This indicator was included to give a sense of how respondents assessed government attitudes toward resolving conflict. Our assumption was that even though war may be justified in certain circumstances, such as defending the homeland, it is more costly than trying to resolve a conflict by peaceful means. This premise is in line with a prevailing opinion among member-states of the United Nations. Willingness to consider peaceful means of resolving conflict is seen as preferable.

This applies to conflict resolution both among and within states. Government may decide on using repressive means to resolve a conflict between different groups within a country, as Iraq did in the 1980s when it killed large numbers of Kurds and Shiites, or as the government of Sudan has repeatedly done vis-à-vis the southern provinces. Governments may also be problematic neighbors, either because they are outright provocative or because they are ready to take economic or political advantage of a weak neighbor.

The prospect of conflict or war brings uncertainty and tends to negatively affect development. For instance, investors—whether local or foreign—are likely to be reluctant to contribute to development if they see hostilities on the horizon. Being able to avoid violence is an important indicator of prospects for economic and social development.

Our respondents are ready to give governments high marks for readiness and the ability to seek peaceful resolution of conflicts. There seem to be two reasons for this rating. One is that governments in highly volatile regions are rated favorably because of their ability to avoid conflicts that would negatively affect citizens. Cases in point are Jordan, Kyrgyzstan, and India. The other reason is the government contribution to the legacy of peace. This applies to Chile in Latin America and Tanzania in Africa. Since the war with Bolivia more than 100 years ago, Chile has been a good neighbor. Although there has been civil conflict on the islands of Zanzibar, Tanzanian respondents tend to assess their government foremost in relation to other countries in the region, many of which suffered civil war or war with neighbors. When the Tanzanian government fought a war with Uganda in the late 1970s it was to defend its sovereign territory (although it ended up with the Tanzanian armed forces invading Uganda to get rid of its erratic and autocratic ruler at the time, Idi Amin).

Argentina and Peru are interesting cases, as both were involved in military conflicts—Argentina with Britain over the Falkland Islands, Peru with Ecuador over a contested border. Respondents' ratings reflect the readiness of governments to avoid the costs of nurturing such conflicts. In other words, respondents believe that government is no longer seeking a confrontational solution to conflicts with other countries.

It may be no surprise that on this indicator the government of the Philippines gets the lowest mark of all. It has been unable to resolve its conflict with the Muslim minority population on the island of Mindanao. Indonesians were somewhat more favorable in assessing their government, pointing to its readiness to transfer sovereignty to East Timor in spite of human rights violations committed by Indonesian soldiers in previous years.

## Implications for Research and Practice

We would like to conclude this chapter with three observations. The first is relevant to research but also has practical implications: the need to make a distinction between *government* and *regime*. There is often a tendency to conflate the two, associating regime with government (or with the head of state). Our survey shows that by disaggregating governance into six arenas, it is possible to get a more detailed appreciation of how government relates to regime. If government is treated as just one of six governance arenas, the concept of regime is much broader because it refers to the rules applying to the other arenas. What we found is that high scores for the government arena are not necessarily associated with a particular type of political regime. The monarchic regime of Jordan scores as high as the democratic regimes of Chile and India. Even the communist government of China is viewed as doing well with regard to the various key functions. Although respondents identify shortcomings with regimes in other arenas, their rating of government is generally higher than average.

The second point is that governments generally score lower on the ability to ensure adequate standards of living for citizens than on the ability to provide security. In regard to promoting social and economic rights, as well as making tough decisions based on long-term national interests, governments are seen as performing less well than in regard to enhancing personal security and taking a peaceful approach to resolving conflict. Our respondents indicate in qualitative comments that the political rhetoric of governments is correct, but practice differs for two reasons: lack of commitment and/or insufficient resources. Some adjustment downward seems to have taken place with regard to popular expectations about the role of governments in development, but even so expectations remain higher.

The third and final observation concerns the role of the military. There is a general sense that the military is ready to accept civilian control. This does not mean, however, that everything has returned to normal. It is important that the international community, through its various agencies, continues to pay attention to how the militaries in developing countries can be further professionalized. The U.S. government, through its armed forces, is already doing this. The incentives that this kind of professional development gives to officers are important for regime stability as well as national development. Other governments, especially those in the European Union, could assist in improving the conditions of governance in the government arena by paying more attention to how civil-military relations can be institutionalized through incentives for professional development of the military.

## Notes

1. An exception is Crawford Young's book, *Ideology and Development in Africa* (New Haven, CT: Yale University Press, 1982).
2. Goran Hyden, *Beyond Ujamaa in Tanzania: Underdevelopment and an Uncaptured Peasantry* (London: Heinemann Educational Books, 1980; and Berkeley: University of California Press, 1980).
3. Goran Hyden, *No Shortcuts to Progress: African Development Management in Perspective* (London: Heinemann Educational Books, 1983; and Berkeley: University of California Press, 1983).
4. The landmark contribution was the book edited by Gabriel A. Almond and James S. Coleman, *The Politics of Developing Areas* (Princeton, NJ: Princeton University Press, 1960). It was followed in the 1960s by a series of edited volumes devoted to a particular set of variables meant to correlate and explain political development.
5. See, e.g., Charles Tilly (ed.), *The Formation of National States in Western Europe* (Princeton, NJ: Princeton University Press, 1975).
6. Ted Gurr, *Why Men Rebel* (Princeton, NJ: Princeton University Press, 1970).
7. Barrington Moore Jr., *The Social Origins of Dictatorship and Democracy* (Boston: Beacon Press, 1966).
8. Barrington Moore Jr., *Injustice: The Social Bases of Obedience and Revolt* (White Plains, NY: M. E. Sharpe, 1978).
9. See, notably, Theda Skocpol, *States and Revolutions: A Comparative Analysis of France, Russia and China* (Cambridge, UK: Cambridge University Press, 1979).
10. Eric J.Hobsbawm, "Revolution," paper presented at the Fourteenth International Congress of Historical Sciences, San Francisco, August 1975, cited by John Dunn, *Rethinking Modern Political Theory* (Cambridge, UK: Cambridge University Press, 1985), p. 76.
11. Kenneth J. Arrow, *Social Choice and Individual Values* (New York: Wiley, 1963).
12. For a discussion of this set of issues as they affect modern democracy, see Claus Offe, "Micro-Aspects of Democratic Theory: What Makes for Deliberative Competence of Citizens?" in Axel Hadenius (ed.), *Democracy's Victory and Crisis* (Cambridge, UK: Cambridge University Press, 1997), pp. 81–104.

13. See, e.g., Jon Elster, *Deliberative Democracy* (Cambridge, UK: Cambridge University Press, 1998).

14. See, e.g., John Dryzek, *Discursive Democracy* (Cambridge, UK: Cambridge University Press, 1990); also Jules L. Coleman and John Ferejohn, "Democracy and Social Choice," *Ethics,* no. 97 (1998): 6–25.

15. "All the Spine of a Jellyfish," *The Economist* 366, no. 8308 (January 25–31, 2003): 42.

16. See Carlos Santiago Nino, *The Constitution of Deliberative Democracy* (New Haven, CT: Yale University Press, 1996).

17. Samuel P. Huntington, *Political Order in Changing Societies* (New Haven, CT: Yale University Press, 1968).

18. Aristide Zolberg, *One-Party Government in the Ivory Coast* (Princeton, NJ: Princeton University Press, 1969), p. x.

19. With reference to Asian countries, see Gunnar Myrdal, *Asian Drama: An Inquiry into the Poverty of Nations* (New York: Pantheon, 1968).

20. See, e.g., Joel Migdal, *Weak States and Strong Societies* (Princeton, NJ: Princeton University Press, 1988); with specific reference to Africa, see Robert H. Jackson and Carl Rosberg, *Personal Rule in Black Africa* (Berkeley: University of California Press, 1982).

21. For a discussion of pacting between outgoing and incoming rulers, see, e.g., Adam Przeworski, *Democracy and the Market* (New York: Cambridge University Press, 1991).

22. The notion of diminished subtypes of democracy comes from an article by David Collier and Steven Levitsky, "Democracy with Adjectives: Conceptual Innovation in Comparative Research," *World Politics* 49, no. 3 (April 1997): 430–451.

23. Huntington, *Political Order in Changing Societies.*

24. For a review of how governments with good intentions may end up undermining development efforts, see James C. Scott, *Seeing Like a State* (New Haven, CT: Yale University Press, 1999).

25. For a discussion of the role of the military in development, see. e.g., J. J. Johnson (ed.), *The Role of the Military in Underdeveloped Countries* (Princeton, NJ: Princeton University Press, 1962).

26. The various ways by which democratic regimes were overthrown are analyzed in a volume edited by Juan Linz and Alfred Stepan, *The Breakdown of Democratic Regimes* (Baltimore: Johns Hopkins University Press, 1978).

27. The return to democracy in Latin America during the 1980s is analyzed in great detail in a four-volume publication edited by Guillermo O'Donnell, Philippe C. Schmitter, and Laurence Whitehead, *Transitions from Authoritarian Rule* (Baltimore: Johns Hopkins University Press, 1986).

# 6

# The Bureaucracy

The bureaucratic arena includes all state organizations engaged in formulating and implementing policy as well as in regulating and delivering services. Although issues of bureaucratic governance are not constitutive of development per se, they are seen as crucial determinants of social and economic progress. These issues have been of concern since the advent of centralized administration, but they have taken on particular significance to academics and practitioners alike since the work of Max Weber[1] many years ago. There has been increasing evidence, from case studies and cross-country empirical analysis, that bureaucratic performance is important for development performance.[2] The literature on the role of the bureaucracy during the period of rapid growth in East Asia supports the view that the bureaucracy was a key ingredient of the miracle.[3] At the same time, a substantial literature argues that the weakness of bureaucracy in Africa helps explain the poor development performance of many countries on the continent.[4] Again, our emphasis is on the rules that govern bureaucratic processes; these rules have an impact on performance as a result of how they are constituted and managed.

Governance issues in the bureaucratic arena become important given the pressures on public agencies to become leaner, more efficient, and accessible to people. In many developing countries—often as part of structural adjustment programs—there have been pressures to reduce the role of the state in relation to the market and to cut civil service (numbers of employees and wages).[5] Lack of economic and social progress there has also led to calls for improving the managerial efficiency of bureaucracies.

The bureaucracy should be studied not only in the context of policy implementation but also that of governance. The rules that determine procedures in the bureaucracy, formal and informal, are especially important for public perceptions of how the state operates. As we know, many contacts that citizens have with government are with first-level bureaucrats responsible for processing requests for services and assistance. The *Voices of the Poor* study commissioned by the World Bank provides a demonstration of the importance of this set of issues—the poor highlighting that their experiences with bureaucrats are often unpleasant, unfair, and corrupt.[6] The implication is that the way countries organize relations within the bureaucracy—and between the bureaucracy and other arenas in the public realm—may make a substantial difference when it comes to policy outcomes as well as the legitimacy of the regime.

But which rules matter? Following Weber, the view that bureaucratic rules must be legal-rational has dominated. Others have perceived bureaucracies in negative terms, highlighting the problems of combining formal rules and procedures with positive substantive outcomes.[7] Much of the evidence has been limited to case studies and exploratory survey work. The lack of systematic data—over time within countries and between countries around the world—means we are uncertain as to what kind of bureaucratic structures and processes—in different contexts—lead to better bureaucratic performance (and thus development performance). What rules matter most for efficiency *and* legitimacy? Are there tradeoffs? Are certain issues more important at different levels of development?

A single study cannot provide all the answers, but we can offer insights into the importance of the rules that guide policy implementation. We begin by reviewing literature around the key issues of bureaucracy and development. It focuses on links between bureaucratic rules and performance in the context of development performance. Following the analysis of the aggregate findings, we discuss findings in relation to each indicator. The concluding section discusses implications for research and practice.

## Main Themes in the Literature

There is a growing literature in the field of public administration on governance. Much of it is focused on the specifics of interagency cooperation given that problem issues are perceived as cutting across administrative jurisdictions (see Chapter 1). Although that section of the literature is important, we focus on writings that bear directly on issues facing developing countries—notably how bureaucratic performance can be improved and how such performance relates to development outcomes. We begin with the latter.

### Bureaucratic Rules, Performance,s and Outcomes

The relationship between bureaucratic performance and economic growth and development outcomes has been a subject of interest to the international development community as well as scholars. In the 1960s, it centered on the role of *development administration*, an approach to public administration meant to differ from the more conventional bureaucratic approach.[8] Since the 1990s, the same assumption has reappeared with the additional insight that the quality of bureaucratic rules is essential for understanding how bureaucratic performance relates to developmental outcomes. The current assumptions may be summarized, as follows:

Bureaucratic rules > Bureaucratic performance > Socioeconomic development

For instance, the current focus on governance in institutions like the World Bank and the Organization for Economic Cooperation and Development (OECD) is almost exclusively on finding links between improved government performance and development outcomes. Using the tool of regression analysis and a conception of governance primarily associated with qualities of state institutions, World Bank analysts[9] have created six scores for six dimensions of governance, of which Government Effectiveness is particularly relevant here. That dimension includes ratings on such issues as the quality of bureaucracy, the quality of service provision, and the competence of civil servants. They find that government effectiveness is positively associated with per capita incomes and adult literacy and negatively associated with infant mortality. The evidence suggests that the level of economic development does not necessarily lead to better governance and that the causality runs from good governance to better growth and development performance.[10]

The team at the World Bank is not alone. A growing number of other actors have begun to rate the degree of bureaucratic performance in different ways (as part of broader assessments of country risk). For example, the Economist Intelligence Unit (EIU) provides ratings on various aspects of regulatory quality, the rule of law, and corruption (among other issues) from a global network of national information gatherers reviewed by regional panels. The International Country Risk Guide (ICRG), produced by Political Risk Services in New York, provides a direct measure of bureaucratic quality using a variety of indicators. Transparency International (TI) issues its annual Perception of Corruption Index. In sum, these agencies provide subjective assessments on key issues of bureaucratic performance—including government efficacy, red tape, and corruption among public officials.

Several important studies used these data sets in empirical work investigating the importance of different aspects of bureaucratic quality for development outcomes. For example, using EIU data, it was found that the efficiency of the bureaucracy was associated with better rates of investment and growth, whereas corruption was negatively related.[11] Relying on ICRG data, others found that bureaucratic quality, being used as part of a broader governance index, was positively associated with improved investment and growth rates.[12] And others have reported a similar positive relationship between institutional quality and economic growth, although they also conclude that the reverse is true—economic growth leads to better institutional quality.[13]

After going through the contemporary literature on the role of government in development, we concluded that there is a lack of good primary source data. Most of it is based on an attempt to correlate various objective measures of performance; to the extent that it is subjective, measures are aggregate in nature. For instance, differences with regard to such key functions as collecting revenues, providing public services, and regulating the economy cannot be measured only in statistical terms, especially if the objective is to identify ways of improving performance.[14] The answers to such questions lie in the more qualitative sphere of data. As one research team put it, "While the cross-country statistical evidence reinforces the idea that differential governmental performance may have an impact on economic growth, it tells us little about what kind of institutional characteristics are associated with lower levels of corruption or red tape".[15] That is why in our own study we have not only collected fresh data, but we have made a deliberate decision to complement statistical information with qualitative comments by our respondents.

### What Rules Matter for Bureaucratic Performance

There are several ways in which bureaucratic incentives and structures are thought to affect bureaucratic performance—again with much of the theoretical support from the classic work of Weber.[16] The main argument is that "replacing patronage systems for state officials by a professional bureaucracy is a necessary (though not sufficient) condition for a state to be 'developmental.'"[17]

Public servants should act in the public interest. Weber argued that a key aspect was the distinction between "public moneys and equipment" and "the private property of the official".[18] Evidence from the miracle era in East Asia highlights meritocratic recruitment and deep bureaucratic traditions as crucial to development success.[19] In contrast, it has been a standard theme in the literature on African states that public officials serve their own interest rather than that of the public.[20] Much of the literature on how bureaucracies perform centers on this fundamental issue. More specifically it deals with themes such as merit in recruitment and promotion, adequate incentives, rule orientation, and accountability.

The need to have objective entry requirements or an independent body deciding on public-service employment and promotion issues is a key concern. Competence, and thus better performance, is seen as stemming from competition based on merit rather than personal contacts or illicit payments. Governments have been accused of being more preoccupied with securing public employment than promoting the quality of the civil service. Even in the face of fiscal pressure, public employment has often been maintained and even expanded at lower skill levels. The World Bank has put it starkly: "[African] governments have become employers of last resort and dispensers of political patronage, offering jobs to family, friends and supporters".[21] This is not necessarily only an African problem, so we decided to focus on this issue in our study.

Paying reasonable wages should encourage talented people to enter and remain in the civil service. In East Asia, adequate compensation of civil servants has been used as one means of attracting and retaining competent staff. It is not clear, however, how far higher pay makes a difference when it comes to better performance and less corruption. For instance, most studies conclude that there is no positive link between higher salaries and lower levels of corruption, with one exception.[22]

Another important issue is the extent to which officials follow rules. Clear rules relating to how decisions are made and how civil servants conduct themselves are important for performance.[23] Although the existence of clear rules is often related to how the public views the bureaucracy, it is also linked to how efficient it is. Clear decisionmaking rules are typically seen as enhancing efficiency. The risk of misuse of public office and poor decisions is seen as higher, the less clear rules are.[24] Probing how our respondents experience the decisionmaking rules in the bureaucracy, therefore, is another indicator in our survey.

Rules are also important for holding officials accountable. Rules internal to the bureaucracy may not be enforced unless there are control mechanisms and watchdog organizations. Audits, ombudsman institutions, anticorruption commissions, public censure, and courts are mechanisms that have been used to hold civil servants accountable. Given the significance attached to the accountability issue, it is also included as an indicator in the survey.

Policy issues in society are typically complex and multidimensional, requiring the insights of civil servants with professional and specialized competence. Structuring the policy formulation and implementation process such that government operations can benefit from the advice of professionals is seen to be an important issue affecting bureaucratic performance. The extent to which authority is given to specialized agencies to formulate policy indicates a strong role for bureaucrats. The existence of deep layers of political appointments in the bureaucracy would indicate a lesser role. The finding that the depth of political appointments was low in

East Asia has been cited as one important reason for that region's economic success.[25] We have opted to include the issue of professional influence in public policymaking as yet another indicator in this arena.

Although there are varied opinions about the extent to which participatory approaches can be accommodated with bureaucratic decisionmaking,[26] bureaucracies need a definite measure of autonomy from both politicians and the public. It cannot afford to be responsive to every demand placed upon it. A degree of autonomy, therefore, seems to be helpful when it comes to formulating and implementing development strategies. Yet links to certain groups in society are common and sometimes institutionalized, as in Japan and Korea,[27] where relations between bureaucrats and businesspeople have for a long time been close. On a Weber-type scale,[28] these two countries would not score high on the autonomy measure, but they do have other qualities that would place them high on such a scale. Research comparing thirty-five countries largely from Asia and Latin America concluded that Weberian characteristics of the bureaucracy are positively correlated with economic growth—even when controlling for level of development and human capital. A study of twenty countries in Africa was carried out to compare the original data set.[29] The original results were confirmed: better bureaucratic performance is associated with greater power and autonomy of agencies to formulate policies, good career opportunities in the public sector, and good pay for public servants. Countries with a merit-based bureaucracy perform better, have lower corruption and higher efficiency in their service delivery, and provide a better framework for the private sector.

A final issue for discussion concerns public access to the bureaucracy. Although autonomy may be important for its functions, it must be tempered by accessibility. Without the latter, the legitimacy of the guiding rules is in question. This is particularly the case since some groups in society are more powerful than others. In our survey, we were interested to know to what extent efforts were made by state officials to ensure equal access to public services.

## WGS Data on the Bureaucracy: Aggregate Findings

The framework for implementing policy is important. Day-to-day management of government operations affects the impression citizens have of individual departments and often the regime as a whole. In other words, how policy implementation is structured constitutes an important aspect of governance. The specific questions we used were

1. To what extent are higher civil servants a part of the policymaking process? (the "influence" indicator)

2. To what extent is there a merit-based system for recruitment into the civil service? (the "meritocracy" indicator)
3. To what extent are civil servants accountable for their actions? (the "accountability" indicator)
4. To what extent are there clear decisionmaking processes in the civil service? (the "transparency" indicator)
5. To what extent is there equal access to public services? (the "access" indicator)

## Aggregate Findings

As reported in Chapter 2, there is much discontent about the bureaucracy in many countries. The aggregate scores are among the lowest of all the arenas, even among the higher-scoring countries. The bureaucracy also records relatively modest improvement over time. There are plenty of references in the commentaries that nepotism and various forms of corruption continue to affect the civil services in many countries. This section looks at two issues: the aggregate scores for the countries and the changes over time and some of the reasons behind these changes. Also interesting is the diversity of the top-scoring group of countries. It includes, for 2000, long-democratic India, Southeast Asian tiger Thailand, very poor Tanzania, Islamic Jordan, and middle-income Chile. It suggests that bureaucratic performance is not necessarily dependent on level of gross domestic product (GDP), type of regime, or a particular culture. The five countries that score low on this dimension—Togo, Kyrgyzstan, Indonesia, Philippines, and Argentina—are perceived to suffer from prevalent political patronage and a lack of transparency and accountability. It is worth looking at some of these high- and low-scoring countries in more detail (see Table 6.1).

The reputation of the higher echelons of the Indian civil service as being the backbone of the government is generally confirmed. Indian respondents recognize the bureaucracy's input into policy and its recruitment on the basis of merit criteria (though the overall rating fell marginally between 1995 and 2000). Both in international comparison and compared to the ratings for other arenas within India, the bureaucracy scores well.

In Mongolia respondents indicate that the power given to specialized agencies to formulate policy is limited. The excessive role of political parties in bureaucratic appointments at all levels of public administration contradicts the principles of a merit-based system of recruitment and equal access to public service. Since the structure of accountability at all institutional levels is underdeveloped, the transparency and responsiveness of the public administration are low.

Bulgaria provides an interesting case in reforming the bureaucratic arena after its shift to a market economy. Commentators noted that this was

**Table 6.1  Aggregate Bureaucracy Arena Scores by Country, 2000**

| Country | Influence | Meritocracy | Accountability | Transparency | Access | Average |
|---|---|---|---|---|---|---|
| **High-scoring countries** | | | | | | |
| Chile | 3.00 | 2.47 | 2.83 | 2.93 | 3.37 | 2.92 |
| India | 4.00 | 4.06 | 2.92 | 2.94 | 2.83 | 3.35 |
| Jordan | 3.03 | 2.50 | 2.95 | 3.03 | 3.48 | 3.00 |
| Mongolia | 3.38 | 2.67 | 2.41 | 2.82 | 2.67 | 2.79 |
| Tanzania | 3.42 | 3.18 | 3.03 | 3.15 | 2.61 | 3.08 |
| Thailand | 3.59 | 2.98 | 3.07 | 3.10 | 3.20 | 3.19 |
| **Medium-scoring countries** | | | | | | |
| Argentina | 2.94 | 1.70 | 2.11 | 1.86 | 2.77 | 2.28 |
| Bulgaria | 3.61 | 2.17 | 2.05 | 2.34 | 2.54 | 2.54 |
| China | 2.58 | 2.73 | 2.39 | 2.09 | 2.45 | 2.45 |
| Indonesia | 2.57 | 2.17 | 1.97 | 2.03 | 2.46 | 2.24 |
| Peru | 3.00 | 2.16 | 2.54 | 2.14 | 2.65 | 2.50 |
| **Low-scoring countries** | | | | | | |
| Kyrgyzstan | 2.85 | 2.03 | 2.08 | 2.05 | 2.10 | 2.22 |
| Pakistan | 3.85 | 2.94 | 2.48 | 2.39 | 1.94 | 2.72 |
| Philippines | 2.57 | 2.37 | 2.14 | 2.37 | 2.03 | 2.30 |
| Russia | 3.68 | 2.39 | 2.16 | 2.11 | 2.58 | 2.58 |
| Togo | 2.79 | 1.98 | 1.95 | 2.02 | 2.29 | 2.20 |
| Average, all countries | 3.18 | 2.53 | 2.44 | 2.46 | 2.62 | 2.65 |

the most difficult arena to reform in the years of transition, and the low average scores reflect that. The small improvement is attributed to the Law on Public Officials, elaborated and enacted by the government in 2000. This new legislation reduced the number of political appointees and defined the rights and obligations of civil servants. Some parts of the old communist order are still present. Corruption is seen as widespread, accountability almost absent.

Given that the survey was conducted before the financial crisis in Argentina, it is a little surprising that its scores are so low. The country has been undergoing public-sector reform for some time with support from international financial institutions. Our respondents indicate that there is little evidence of improvement in spite of hefty investments. They are critical of the rules relating to good governance within the bureaucracy (i.e., with regard to hiring, transparency, and accountability).

Another surprise is Pakistan, but for the opposite reason. Although governance in Pakistan is generally rated low, respondents are more appreciative of the rules applying to the bureaucratic arena. This seems to reflect the decline in other arenas. Party politics in the late 1990s was both chaotic and corrupt, eventually causing the military to step in and take over. In this situation, the civil service has looked like a backbone capable of getting the things done where other institutions failed.

Although the civil service has appeared in increasingly favorable light in Pakistan, the opposite applies to Togo. President Eyadema's long-standing rule—himself a military officer—has politicized public policymaking to a point where professional expertise is no longer valued as much. As one of our respondents put it, "Policies are implemented in compliance with the interests of the ruling group in power." Since civil servants are seen as essentially incompetent and corrupt, the low score is no surprise.

The reasons for the low scores in Indonesia seem to vary from 1995 and 2000. In 1995, the main concern was the hold that President Suharto and his immediate associates had over the public service. Corruption was seen as widespread; even if it functioned, it did so in an arbitrary fashion that left large segments of the public dissatisfied. In 2000 it was the uncertainty associated with the transition from the Suharto era that explains the low score. Our respondents indicated that the situation after Suharto's resignation was characterized by confusion. Old rules continued to exist, but many of them had lost their credibility. New ones had yet to be agreed upon. Management of public affairs had suffered in quality.

### Changes over Time

Our findings regarding change over time are summarized in Figure 6.1. Two countries are rated considerably higher in 2000 than in 1995: Peru and Tanzania. The reasons behind these perceived improvements differ. In Peru, there seems to be spillover effects of the regime change that took place as President Alberto Fujimori was forced out of power. In Tanzania, however, the increased ratings seem to reflect a genuine satisfaction with improved public-sector performance.

For those who have studied Tanzania, the scores in this arena may at first be a surprise. It has not been known for an effective or efficient public sector. The noticeable improvement in scoring is a genuine reflection of the appreciation that respondents have of the implementation of public-sector reforms since President Mkapa took over as head of state in 1995. This progress is now broadly acknowledged in the international community. Tanzania has often been held up as a success story in public finances and operations. Among the range of governance reforms are five major components: organization and efficiency reform, personnel control and management reform, capacity-building, local government and regional administration reform, and rationalization of government employment reform. The successful implementation of these reforms is evident in our data: although still short of target, accountability and transparency are on the increase in Tanzania; greater equality of access is noted; appointments are increasingly

**Figure 6.1    Changes in Aggregate Bureaucracy Arena Scores, 1995–2000**

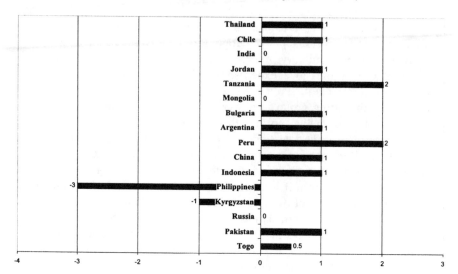

based on merit; and expertise is now more appreciated. That pressures from the international community have played their part in this process should not overshadow the appreciation that the Tanzanian respondents have with the progress that their country has made in this arena.

Like Tanzania, China has long suffered from a bureaucracy with little autonomy of its own. During the heyday of Maoist rule in the 1960s and 1970s, party leaders made all decisions of importance with little regard for the costs and benefits and feasibility. Professional expertise was scorned. This has changed subsequently, but to this day the Communist Party has remained the principal policymaking organ. Nonetheless, with economic reform since 1978 has come an incremental change in the way civil servants contribute to development. Several public organs—not just enterprises—have received greater autonomy. Our respondents acknowledge that China has a long way to go with regard to opening up its bureaucracy to greater public scrutiny, but they also note that reforms keep occurring. In their view, changes in this arena are going in the right direction.

Thailand also shows an increase in this arena, not a surprise. The bureaucracy has generally been viewed as a key contributor to its economic growth and tiger status. It has also been an institution unto itself (i.e., it has enjoyed autonomy and power vis-à-vis other institutions in society). This has begun to change. Thanks to a variety of reforms in the late 1990s, there has been a conscious effort to reach a better relation between the legislative, administrative, and judicial sectors. Although these reforms do not explain everything behind the high scores in Thailand, they are an integral part of the sense among our respondents that governance in this arena has improved considerably.

We cannot rule out the possibility that the marked improvement in Peru is a reflection of the euphoria that the end of the Fujimori regime brought to large segments of the population. Our respondents note that the bureaucracy had little, if any, input into policymaking during the Fujimori days. Moreover, civil servants were hired, fired, and promoted with little respect for the rules that guide public employment. Even though things remained somewhat uncertain in 2000, respondents reported significant improvements in public-sector institutions and regulatory agencies. Especially appreciated is the rising level of professionalism. Another important improvement is the increased bureaucratic accountability. Holding the public service accountable in the Fujimori days was a matter for government and therefore highly politicized. It now lies with an independent judicial authority.

Among countries registering a decline between 1995 and 2000, the Philippines exhibited the biggest fall. Respondents attributed this primarily to the corrupt and clientelistic rule of former president Estrada. His patronage system diluted the accountability of civil servants and transparency of bureaucratic processes. As one respondent put it, "One good indicator of the strength of accountability mechanisms is the number of top public servants who have been sent to jail. There has been none in the Philippines." All these issues negatively affected the effectiveness of the system.

In Kyrgyzstan, the bureaucracy received the lowest average score of all arenas—and there was a noticeable overall decrease of the aggregate scores since 1995. This decline was present in all indicators, although it was especially noticeable with regard to meritocratic recruitment and equality of access to public services. One reason for this may be that administrative authority is so highly decentralized that civil servants easily end up under the control of local political patrons. Reform of the civil service system is being attempted, aimed at increasing central direction and control, while also strengthening its transparency and the professional competence of individual government employees. But continuous conflicts within the government about how the reform should be implemented have prevented much progress.

## Analysis of Individual Indicators

As suggested above, each indicator included reflects a major focus in the vast literature on bureaucracy, but also a contemporary concern with how public services should perform. It is possible that additional relevant indicators could have been included, but we believe that we have captured the most significant determinants of bureaucratic performance: *influence, meritocracy, accountability, transparency,* and *access.* We examine each below.

### Influence

We were interested here in the extent to which higher civil servants were part of the policymaking process. Three main issues deserve attention. The first is the broad agreement among respondents across countries that higher-level civil servants have influence on policy, albeit not just as experts. Pakistan and India stand out in this regard. In both countries, respondents point out that civil servants are an important part of the policymaking process. The same is true for some other countries, including Russia, but respondents there mention that only some top bureaucrats—notably in the president's office—are really influential. Higher civil servants in sectoral ministries are much less influential.

The second observation is that many respondents see politicization of top positions in the bureaucracy as inevitable and not necessarily harmful. The point that respondents are making (e.g., in Chile and Thailand) is that reliance on public servants who are first and foremost technocrats may make the bureaucracy less sensitive to public interests and, by extension, less concerned about accountability and transparency. There is also the question of where to draw the line of responsibility between elected and appointed officials. In countries with relatively stable bureaucratic structures, such as Chile, there is a tendency among respondents to argue for more input by elected political officials. Respondents in the Philippines, however, harbor the opposite view. As one of them noted, "The more personalized and populist the leadership, the more diminished the role of technocrats and professional civil servants."

Indonesia provides an interesting case of change and complexity. By the end of the Suharto regime, the policymaking process was highly centralized. Some higher civil servants had a significant influence on policy, but only those advisers who formed the inner circle of his government. On other issues such as public finance, technology, and public health, Suharto was more dependent on his ministers. Thus the ability of higher civil servants to influence policymaking was not universal or guaranteed. It depended on personal loyalty to the president. It is interesting that, according to our respondents, Suharto's departure has not increased the influence of civil servants. On the contrary, because of the introduction of a more genuine multiparty democracy than in the past, elected politicians demand to have more influence than the experts in the public service.

The third issue is that respondents across countries believed that bureaucrats were more influential in the implementation rather than the formulation of policy. Interestingly, this issue came out most repeatedly and strongly among Chinese respondents. They noted that the influence varies from one sector to another. For instance, local bureaucrats often have enough discretion to twist central government policy in directions other than those originally intended. Comments by respondents in other countries tend to confirm the point that policy implementation in the end boils down to what street-level bureaucrats decide to do.[30] The conclusion to be drawn is that top bureaucrats do not always have as much influence in the end as is often implied.

## Meritocracy

The rules guiding recruitment have long been regarded as a key issue for successful policy implementation, regulation, and provision of services. We refer not only to formal issues—such as the existence of an exam—but also to the ways that they operate in practice. Our survey, and comments by our respondents accompanying it, makes clear that very few countries have a merit-based system of recruitment. India stands out as the main exception. Merit recruitment prevails there, although respondents indicate that scheduled castes and tribes are not able to compete with other groups in society. None of the other countries scored above 3 points on this indicator except for Tanzania, which reflects its improvements. For most countries, commentators seem to agree that recruitment is done arbitrarily, with little or no reference to merit.

Qualifications are not taken into account in an objective way in choosing bureaucrats. Many commentators point to the lack of a proper exam or that exams are seen as a sham. In Togo, there used to be an exam, but it has now been stopped. In Jordan one commentator lamented that the main problem is that government agencies are overstaffed and that employment rules in the public sector need improvement, giving priority to qualifications.

The most commonly used reference is to political interference in civil service appointments. Having the right personal connections is important, as the respondents in the Philippines suggested. Nepotism is an issue in countries like Indonesia and Togo. The situation in Latin American countries seems problematic. In Argentina, most experts noted that there is no merit-based system for recruitment into the civil service. This means that family members and friends are recruited into government. Suggestions for reform included the introduction of a more competitive recruitment system to increase professionals in civil service. Even in Chile, which is generally scoring high, the ratings for the bureaucratic arena are lower than the country average. Our respondents complain about the immobility of the civil service and the need for new statutes to reduce politicization of appointments and to attract more professionals.

In Russia, recruitment of bureaucrats is a major problem. One respondent after another noted that there is little use of merit criteria. Recruitment depends on personal ties. The result is that people without training or experience fill high posts.

Although merit-based recruitment to the bureaucracy is only one of five indicators, our survey suggests that the lack of it in most countries is a serious shortcoming. Not only does it affect performance; it also calls into question the role that government plays in development. The sense of unfairness and discontent that it breeds adversely affects the whole regime on which governance rests.

### Accountability

Civil servants often have some discretion in their work, and how they implement rules and provide services can have significant impact on citizens. Therefore systems of accountability are considered important to reduce corruption and other misuse of public office. We asked respondents to consider the degree to which civil servants were accountable for their actions. As can be seen, the accountability scores are generally low, indicating that this is another problem area. The main issue seems to be that institutional mechanisms, although they exist, don't really work. The main exceptions are Thailand and, interestingly, Pakistan under military rule.

Administrative reform in Thailand has been far-reaching and includes the establishment of institutions aimed at holding bureaucrats publicly accountable. These include an Anti-Corruption Commission, the special Administrative Court, and an ombudsman for lodging complaints against administrative decisions. Implementation of these reforms has been facilitated by the fact that all government officials—including those elected—must declare their interests and show private assets and liabilities. These steps are bold and have changed the overall perception among the public of the civil service in a positive direction.

Accountability of civil servants in Pakistan has improved since the military took over. This is the message from our respondents. In fact, they argue that even though they don't know for how long this will last, accountability of public service has become a major priority of the military government. Several civil servants have been dismissed, and some have been prosecuted for abuse of public office. These steps have been in response to the soft nature of the state apparatus during the previous democratically elected government. Laws and institutional mechanisms for holding public officers accountable existed but were not systematically enforced, leaving the public with the impression that the system was corrupt. Civil servants took advantage of the corruption at ministerial levels, allowing it to become institutionalized from the top down.

It is clear that behavior in the civil service is very much dependent on how the political leadership behaves. If elected politicians are not corrupt, they tend to set an example emulated in the bureaucracy. If they are corrupt, this tends to spread to the civil service. The cases of the Philippines and Russia highlight this. Cronyism and political patronage set the stage for undermining both merit-based recruitment and efforts at holding civil servants accountable. The latter often use their offices to get rich and promote their own interests at the expense of the public.

The conclusion that we like to draw from this study is that holding civil servants accountable is a complicated issue. Establishing institutional mechanisms, such as the ombudsman, auditor-general's office, and onetime commissions aimed at curbing corruption, is only an important first step. The real challenge is to make these bodies have and use teeth. Our respondents in most countries indicate that these specific institutions have been largely ineffective. Instead, accountability has come from demands made by the media or, as in Indonesia, public pressure. Although the media cannot really be described as the fourth estate in the countries included in our study, we believe that when it comes to holding officials accountable, they are at least as effective in many countries as other mechanisms in place.

*Transparency*

Although transparency is a controversial issue in some governments, there is an increasingly widespread view that clear rules and openness reduce the risk of misuse of public office. Similarly, if the public is not adequately informed about how decisions are made, this adversely affects the image of the bureaucracy. Our survey investigated the extent to which there are clear decisionmaking processes in the civil service in the sixteen countries.

The overall results are worrying. The scores for this indicator are generally low for each country and are among the lowest obtained in the whole survey. Clearly, many respondents believe that the operations of the civil service lack real transparency. There is some variation, with Tanzania, Thailand, and Jordan scoring a bit better (only around 3), and Argentina, Kyrgyzstan, Indonesia, and Togo scoring more poorly (around 2). That Argentina was the lowest-rated country will raise eyebrows, but the respondents were extremely critical of the situation.[31] Generally, it is interesting that many respondents comment that they perceive a public demand for greater transparency.

Not surprisingly, the scores for transparency tend to be close to those for accountability. One tends to go hand in hand with the other, the only exception being Pakistan. Although accountability improved notably with military rule, transparency deteriorated marginally. Commentators note that decisionmaking rules became more obscure and consultation with the public less frequent.

It is worth mentioning that transparency is an issue that cuts across regime type. We find this being a source of disaffection in Argentina and Peru—countries with a democratic legacy—as well as in China with its long legacy of communist rule. This is not to imply that the issue of transparency is the same everywhere. We find that some countries try to introduce it, while others do not even try. The country coordinator for Bulgaria may have stated the problem better than anyone else when he commented that this is definitely an issue that takes time to address. It involves an attitudinal change not only among bureaucrats but also among politicians and the public at large. The important thing is that any measures taken enhance the degree of legitimacy of the regime, even if incrementally. Although progress is slowly being made, not the least thanks to organizations like Transparency International, judging from our study much more needs to be done to enhance the legitimacy of bureaucracy and regime.

### Access

The final indicator in this arena concerns equal access to public services. This is seen as an important issue for the legitimacy of the civil service as well as for development outcomes. Given what has been said about the bureaucracy already, it is no surprise that access to services is perceived to be unequal in many of the WGS countries. The scores for most countries are low, with the exception of Thailand, Jordan, and Chile. They are particularly low in Pakistan and Kyrgyzstan. The reasons for the scores seem to vary along four different lines.

The first is the recognition that a country's size complicates access. This comes across in comments made by respondents both in China and Indonesia. The vast expanses of western China are handicapped compared to the eastern coastal belt. In Indonesia, respondents point to the outlying islands as having more difficulty taking advantage of public services than the main island of Java. Smaller countries like Jordan and Togo score comparatively better on this indicator than on others, confirming the thesis that geography matters. In Jordan, for instance, the Civil Service Bylaw of 1998 goes far toward local district control of government services and human resource development.

The second point is that urban residents are favored over rural residents. This is no surprise given the cost of extending infrastructure to the countryside. Respondents in the Philippines note that residents of the metropolitan areas, especially Manila, are much better served . By and large, these people have easier access than those in the villages, especially the outlying islands. Respondents in Chile, India, and Russia make the same point. The rural population is seen at a disadvantage in access to government services.

The third point regards differential access and social stratification. There are relatively few references to unequal access being the result of social or economic inequalities in society. This does not necessarily mean that respondents ignore this aspect. It certainly matters, especially in the comments provided by Indian and Pakistani respondents. Access to public services among the poor in these countries is low. Thus even if the bureaucracy is meritocratic and civil servants have an influence on policy, this seems to make little difference on the ground for the poorer population. Respondents also suggest that the better-off in society often have privileged access to services as a result of being able to pay bribes. In sum, the inclusion of the access variable has convinced us that changes in the governance of the bureaucratic arena are difficult to achieve from within and may be more easily facilitated by thinking about how its relations to other arenas— notably government and civil society—are constituted.

The fourth point concerns the fact that even if there is officially equal access, the quality of services differs from one area to another. Wherever demand is high, as in the urban areas, quality tends to be better. This difference may stem from political favoritism. The quality of public services in areas where government ministers come from is often better.

The issue of access to public services is important. Unequal access is the result of more than one factor. Often geography, demography, and social stratification coincide to make greater equality in access to public services a complicated and costly issue. Mustering the political will to achieve a transformation is not easy. One can expect that overcoming deficiencies associated with this indicator may be more difficult than those identified in relation to the other four indicators.

## Implications for Research and Practice

Four observations of our findings stand out as especially important. The first is that bureaucracy is one of the more problematic arenas of governance. Respondents in most of the WGS countries were not impressed with governance in this arena. Hiring is rarely on merit, bureaucrats are seldom seen to be accountable, and the operations of the civil service often lack real transparency. Respondents rated these issues lower than most other indicators in the survey and commented extensively on their frustrations. It is clear that issues of bureaucratic governance tend to adversely affect the legitimacy of the public realm—and that this is the case for *all* the indicators we focused on.

The second point is that the relationship between rules and structures versus performance is difficult to establish. It is not that the link is unimportant. Even when disaggregated, it is hard to know what rule has what kind of effect. More research on this set of issues is warranted.

Our third observation is that reforming the bureaucratic arena is difficult. One of our country coordinators summarized it well: "This arena has proved hardest to reform in the years of transition and the average scores are just another evidence of these difficulties." It is clear that reforms take time to implement and even longer to have an impact on development outcomes. Above all, it must be recognized that it is not merely a technical issue. The bureaucratic arena cannot be treated in isolation from other governance arenas, although public-sector reform efforts have tended to do so. Our findings indicate that a pure public administration perspective may be too narrow and technical in many cases and fails to focus on the real problem.

The fourth observation is that reforming the bureaucracy requires sensitivity to regime-specific issues. Context matters, but it is encouraging that the level of development, according to our study, is not a critical issue. It is possible for poor countries to improve bureaucratic governance. Socioeconomic conditions are not necessarily impeding reforms in this arena. Tanzania and Thailand are two very different countries where reforms have been undertaken and progress has been registered.

Given the importance of the work done by the World Bank team, led by Daniel Kaufmann, it may be especially appropriate that we discuss the implications for research in conjunction with that work. We are hesitant to make a direct comparison between our study and theirs, given differences in conceptualization and operationalization of the concept, but by choosing our access indicator and comparing it with the World Bank's Government Effectiveness measure, we find a high correlation coefficient of 0.658.[32] When examining the relationship between the other four indicators and bureaucratic performance, we found that the findings are more ambiguous, as the relationships vary considerably. Meritocracy seems to be the least significant. Although qualitative comments by our respondents indicate that merit criteria in appointment and promotion are important for the credibility of the civil service, there is no clear link between this indicator and performance.

Participation by higher civil servants in policymaking is another enigmatic indicator. We found little evidence to suggest that participation of higher civil servants in policymaking is necessarily a good thing in and of itself. Our respondents make comments to the effect that a certain degree of politicization is not only inevitable but sometimes a good thing. This indicator, therefore, is highly regime-dependent: the strength of expert advice works well in some regimes but may be less valued in comparison to other criteria, such as political loyalty, in others. This is where we recognize that the purely quantitative analysis of governance shows its limitations. Additional case studies may be needed in order to throw more light on the issues where there is a deviation from the ideal model advocated by agencies in the international development community.[33]

In our study, transparency and accountability proved to be the indicators where there is some evidence of a correlation with performance. Comparing our average scores on this indicator with the World Bank's Government Effectiveness scores for 2000 and 2001, we found correlation coefficients at 0.48 and 0.49, respectively. Even if we allow for problems with comparability, our study indicates that these two variables seem to be especially important for improving bureaucratic performance. Given this finding, we also carried out a simple additional piece of analysis by comparing the two indicators with the access indicator. What we found is that: (1) if both transparency and accountability are low, service performance is rated low; (2) if either transparency or accountability are low and the other is rated high, service performance is likely to be in the medium-low range; and (3) if both transparency and accountability are medium, service performance is also rated medium. This gives us an additional indication that transparency and accountability do have a potential influence on performance.

This is an interesting and important finding for those in the business of improving public administration and public-sector performance. Our study suggests that these issues should be given primary attention. This study also provides encouragement for organizations like Transparency International that are in the forefront of combating corruption by working practically on issues such as accountability and transparency.

## Notes

1. M. Weber, *The Theory of Social and Economic Organizations* (New York: Free Press, 1947).

2. See D. Kaufmann, A. Kraay, and P. Zoido-Lobaton, "Governance Matters," *Policy Research Working Paper No. 2195* (Washington, DC: World Bank, October 1999); Peter Evans and J. E. Rauch, "Bureaucracy and Growth: A Cross-National Analysis of the Effects of 'Weberian' State Structures on Economic Growth," *American Sociological Review* 64, no. 5 (October 1999): 748–765; and Peter Evans and J. E. Rauch, "Bureaucratic Structure and Bureaucratic Performance in Less Developed Countries," *Journal of Public Economics* 75 (January 2000): 49–71.

3. Peter Evans, *Embedded Autonomy: States and Industrial Transformation* (Princeton, NJ: Princeton University Press, 1995); and World Bank, *The East Asian*

*Miracle: Economic Growth and Public Policy* (New York: Oxford University Press, 1993).

4. See, e.g., P. Blunt, *Organization Theory and Behaviour: An African Perspective* (London: Longman, 1983); and Goran Hyden, *No Shortcuts to Progress: African Development Management in Perspective* (Berkeley: University of California Press, 1983; and London: Heinemann Educational Books, 1983).

5. Given the focus of our study, this chapter does not directly address issues of the size of the bureaucracy. Various studies have found that there is no relation between larger bureaucracies and weaker development performance—indeed the opposite may be true. See A. Goldsmith, "Africa's Overgrown State Reconsidered: Bureaucracy and Economic Growth," *World Politics* 51 (July 1999): 520–546.

6. D. Narayan, R. Patel, K. Schafft, A. Rademacher, and S. Koch-Schulte, *Voices of the Poor: Can Anyone Hear Us?* (Washington, DC: World Bank, 2000).

7. Michel Crozier, *The Bureaucratic Phenomenon* (Chicago: University of Chicago Press, 1964).

8. An interesting account of the early efforts to launch development administration, see Bernard Schaffer, "The Deadlock in Development Administration," in Colin Leys, ed., *Political Change in Developing Countries* (London: Cambridge University Press, 1969).

9. Daniel Kaufmann, Aart Kraay, and Massimo Mastruzzi, "Governance Matters III: Governance Indicators for 1996–2002" *Policy Research Working Paper* (Washington, DC: World Bank, May 2003).

10. Ibid.

11. Paolo Mauro, "Corruption and Growth," *Quarterly Journal of Economics*, no. 110 (1995): 681–712.

12. Stephen Knack and Philip Keefer, "Institutions and Economic Performance: Cross-Country Tests Using Alternative Institutional Measures," *Economics and Politics* 7 (1995): 207–227.

13. Alberto Chong and Cesar Calderon, "Causality and Feedback Between Institutional Measures and Economic Growth," *Economics and Politics* 12, no. 1 (2000): 69–81.

14. For example, a number of scholars have argued that raising income tax revenue requires an organization possessing Weberian features. See, e.g., Margaret Levy, *Of Rule and Revenue* (Berkeley: University of California Press, 1988); Mick Moore, "Death Without Taxes: Democracy, State Capacity, and Aid Dependence in the Fourth World," in G. White and M. Robinson, eds., *Towards a Democratic Developmental State* (Oxford, UK: Oxford University Press, 1997); and Charles Tilly, *Coercion, Capital, and European States, AD 990–1992* (Oxford, UK: Blackwell, 1990).

15. Evans and Rauch, "Bureaucracy and Growth."

16. Stemming from the original work of Weber, Evans, and Evans and Rauch developed a set of hypotheses that can be found in Evans, *Embedded Autonomy*, and Evans and Rauch, "Bureaucratic Structure."

17. Evans and Rauch, "Bureaucracy and Growth"; see also Evans and Rauch, "Bureaucratic Structure."

18. Weber, *The Theory of Social and Economic Organizations*.

19. World Bank, *The East Asian Miracle*.

20. Hyden, *No Shortcuts to Progress*; also Richard Joseph, *Prebendalism and Democracy in Nigeria* (New York: Cambridge University Press, 1987).

21. World Bank, "The State in a Changing World," in *World Development Report 1997* (New York: Oxford University Press, 1997), p. 95.

22. Caroline Van Rijckeghem and Beatrice Weder, "Corruption and the Rate of Temptation: Do Low Wages in the Civil Service Cause Corruption?" *IMF Working Paper No. 97/73* (Washington, DC: International Monetary Fund, 1997).

23. Weber, *The Theory of Social and Economic Organizations.*

24. Robert Klitgaard, *Controlling Corruption* (Berkeley and Los Angeles: University of California Press, 1988).

25. World Bank, *The East Asian Miracle.*

26. See Bernard Schaffer, "The Deadlock in Development Administration," in Colin T. Leys, ed., *Political Change in Developing Countries* (London: Cambridge University Press, 1969).

27. E.g., Sylvia Chan, *Liberalism, Democracy and Development* (Cambridge, UK: Cambridge University Press, 2002); also Evans 1995, *Embedded Autonomy.*

28. Evans and Rauch, "Bureaucracy and Growth."

29. J. Court, P. Kristen, and B. Weder, "Bureaucratic Structure and Performance: New Evidence from Africa," *United Nations University Working Paper* (Tokyo: United Nations University Press, 1999).

30. M. Lipsky, *Street-Level Bureaucracy: Dilemmas of the Individual in Public Services* (New York: Russell Sage Foundation, 1980).

31. To us this reinforces the point that the impression from rating agencies and the international media do not always accurately reflect the situation on the ground and highlights the value of governance assessment approaches that seek local views.

32. See Kaufmann et al., "Governance Matters II."

33. Work along these lines is being done by a group of scholars in East and Southeast Asia. The project, Governance in Asia Revisited, is led by professor Yasutami Shimomura, Hosei University.

# 7

# Economic Society

$E$ *conomic society* means state-market relations.[1] It is an arena all its own because of the significance that such relations play in society, especially in the era of neoliberal economics. The arena is constituted by the rules that apply to state-market relations. It is different from civil society in that economic society is made up of actors engaged in the pursuit of monetary gain. Thus a private corporation or a single-owner small business are both included in this arena. Any organization that speaks on behalf of businesspersons (e.g., a chamber of commerce) carries out activities in civil society. Like civil society, economic society has gained prominence in academic and policy-oriented circles. Two recent Nobel laureates in economics—Douglass North and Joseph Stiglitz—devoted much of their professional career to examining the nature of economic society. The World Bank, the most visible and influential actor in this field, has devoted two of its recent reports on the state of the world economy to the significance of state-market relations.[2]

Although there has been a convergence in economic thinking toward accepting the value of free markets, no country follows a pure laissez-faire approach to economic management. No less an advocate of the invisible hand of the market than Adam Smith acknowledged that the state is necessary to perform certain economic functions. These include formulating economic policy, regulating the economy, providing economic infrastructure and services, providing public goods, and dealing with market failures. Governments fulfill these tasks in different ways to different degrees.

The rules that apply to economic society are often referred to as the economic regime of a country. That regime is shaped by several factors; at least three deserve mention. The first is the extent to which economic and financial markets have been liberalized. Much economic reform has focused on reshaping public finance through monetary, budgetary, and trade policies that reduce state control. The second is political democratization. Some countries have carried out extensive political reforms simultaneously with economic liberalization; others have been more cautious. Argentina is an example of the first approach, China an example of the second. The third factor is globalization. With fewer regulations at the state level, international economic factors are bound to play a greater role in shaping national economies. Countries with developed economies dependent on modern technology start from a stronger position than those that are economically less developed and in a more peripheral position in the global economy. How much the latter will benefit from globalization is an important factor in shaping the rules of this arena.

It is against this background that our survey was conducted. We are concerned with the perception of the rules of the arena, not the outcome per se. The legitimacy of the rules is an important determinant of policy outcome. Governance interventions to shape or reshape rules tend to be noted not only by the business community but also by many other people. Thus it is clear that how rules are actually handled matters to national development.

This chapter is organized in similar fashion. We review the literature on the subject matter, then analyze the aggregate findings of the World Governance Survey with a comparison both among countries and over time. After examining more closely responses related to each individual indicator, we conclude with a discussion of the implications for research and practice.

## Governance Issues in Economic Society

State-market relations have come to occupy an increasingly important position in the literature on development. The first part of this section discusses this literature in more general terms, focusing on some of the more important contributions. The second part concentrates on which specific issues are of interest in the governance context of this arena.

### Economic Society and Development

Several theorists have contributed to our understanding of the role that rules and institutions play in economic development. On the academic side, at least three authors stand out as especially influential: Douglass North,[3] Ronald Coase,[4] and Oliver Williamson.[5] North demonstrated that institutions, the formal and informal rules of the game, create a powerful incentive system for a society, thus affecting decisionmaking by public and private actors. North also argued that the rules—at least formally—are often created to serve the interests of those with the bargaining power. The result is that benefits and other outcomes are not distributed evenly. As one can see in many countries—developed and developing—what is good for the group in power is not necessarily good for the country. Private interests are pursued at the expense of a common or public interest. Similarly, the interests of those living and benefiting now are often favored over those of coming generations. These are issues that countries around the world increasingly face because of the way state-market relations have been structured.

Because so much of a person's welfare or a country's development rests on the rules of this arena, it is no coincidence that such principles as transparency, accountability, efficiency, and fairness have become of special significance here. A growing number of studies commissioned by the World Bank and other international bodies like Transparency International confirm this observation. Based on an extensive survey of firms, the *World Development Report 1997* demonstrated the importance of policy stability, the nature of regulations, and the effects of corruption on business performance.[6] Others highlight the importance of institutions that protect property rights for investment and growth.[7] And still others show that corruption is negatively associated with economic growth.[8] In its 2003 global corruption report, TI discusses the relationship between access to information, corruption, governance, and development.[9]

Some of the clearest evidence about the importance of state-market relations for growth and development comes from the work of Daniel Kaufmann and his colleagues.[10] Based on aggregating much of existing data, they created indices for Corruption and Regulatory Quality (the latter including policy issues such as price controls as well as perceptions on issues such as excessive regulation) and ran regression to see whether governance mattered.[11] Their findings are clear: better regulatory quality and lower corruption are positively associated with per capita incomes and adult literacy and negatively associated with infant mortality. Another recent contribution by this group of analysts was prepared for the World Economic Forum.[12] It shows convincingly that the business climate in a given country is very much shaped directly by governance issues. In short, how transparent rules are, how reliable they are, and what results they encourage make a lot of difference to investment as well as other related indicators of economic development.

## Which Rules Matter?

Governance issues in economic society have an important bearing on the overall quality of governance as well as economic development. But are some rules more important than others? In designing this project, we were faced with prioritizing those that both literature and development practice indicated are the most important.

Although we were unable to rely on it in 2000 when this study was designed, the *World Development Report 2002* provides a useful framework for our discussion here since it synthesizes the latest research and practice regarding why and how institutions affect growth and poverty reduction. When the World Bank refers to *institutions* it implies rules that guide specific phenomena in the economy (e.g., ownership of property, conduct of business, or resolution of conflict between contending parties). More specifically, it argues that institutions support the functioning of markets with regard to access to information, protection of property rights, and regulation of competition. Our approach is similar and covers much the same ground. Thus we include here four specific issues that are of relevance: *information sharing*; *property rights*; *competition, regulation, and corruption*; and *global influences*. We cover each in turn.

Institutions support markets by channeling information about markets' products, participants, and conditions. It is easy to see that this has a critical impact on the efficiency of markets. Buyers and sellers need to know about prices in order to make informed decisions about purchases and investment. Some scholars are known for studies on information and its impact on economic efficiency.[13] Actors in the marketplace are not equally well placed to take advantage of information. Some are even excluded from it by virtue of their location. This is especially true in developing countries, where markets are still emerging and functioning in less efficient ways. A sense of being at the mercy of the invisible hand of the market is a common reason for aversion to its operations. For instance, smallholder farmers and microentrepreneurs in Africa and Asia are often reluctant to use the market, because they suspect that others who are better informed and more powerful exploit them.[14]

Information sharing goes beyond the issue of how it affects business in the short term. Information sharing is a key indicator of trust; information flows more easily and effectively in some channels or circles than in others.[15] It typically begins with relatively closed circles (e.g., a family or clan). Once it reaches efficiency at that level, the challenge becomes sharing information over longer distances and with strangers. This is an issue that businesses face in most developing countries but is rarely covered in the literature because it deals with corporate entities that already are operating across national and cultural boundaries. These consolidated giants have their own culture, and sharing information within them for purpose of effective corporate governance is much less of an issue.

Information sharing within or among businesses, however, is not the sole issue here. The extent to which businesspeople have access to information stemming from government and may actually be part of a policy consultation process is also important. Do rules allow for such consultation and information sharing? This is an important question in many countries where transparency is not institutionalized and government officials make decisions at their own discretion. We know from business leaders that consultation and information sharing is not only good for business but also for the government, because it tends to enhance the legitimacy of the rules that guide economic society.

Issues of relevance include, among others, whether firms are consulted about potential changes in economic policy, whether forums for interaction exist (e.g. consultation committees), whether information is provided in an exclusive manner, and whether private-sector groups are seen as legitimate and representative.[16] Much of the literature on this set of issues comes from Asia.[17] For example, Japan is seen to have deep and multiple mechanisms for interaction between state and private sector actors, both formal and informal.[18] In Thailand, business-government collaboration is institutionalized in many industries but coexists with endemic corruption.[19]

As for property rights, security of property has been a universal concern for a long time. It was a sufficiently strong issue when the United Nations was formed, and nations came together to draft and adopt the Universal Declaration of Human Rights in 1948. This document states in Article 17 that "everyone has the right to own property alone as well as in association with others" and "no one shall be arbitrarily deprived of his property." This universal principle has been turned into a global policy prescription: private property provides the best incentive for material progress.

The theory of property rights comes out of economics. Some scholars accept that the structure of property is a more powerful predictor of organizational behavior than any other variable.[20] Property rights specify the social and economic relations that people must observe in their use of scarce resources, including not only the benefits that owners are allowed to enjoy but also the harms that they are allowed to cause.[21]

Some authors have taken the issue of property rights to a different level,[22] suggesting that in a historical perspective there is a relationship between private property rights and national economic development. What works at the micro or intermediate level also works at the macro level. Herman de Soto makes a similar point with reference to Peru. He argues that, among many benefits, having clear title to land allows owners to use property as collateral for loans that assist home development.[23] The *World Development Report 2002* brings much of the recent evidence together and points to evidence that property rights are highly correlated with variables at the micro and macro levels.[24]

The problem that many developing countries encounter because property rights are not fully institutionalized is that there is lack of respect not only for private but also public property. Because the line between the two is not respected, private property may be confiscated on flimsy grounds and public property is being used to feather private nests. One of the first to draw attention to this issue was Colin Leys in an account of President Jomo Kenyatta's Kenya in the 1970s.[25] He provides a rich sample of ways in which public property was being used by well-connected managers to build personal capital. The point here is that this form of abuse of public office is harmful not only to the individual enterprise but also to the reputation of the regime at large. In other words, without governance interventions to enforce the rules, the legitimacy of a key aspect of the arena is in doubt.

As for competition, regulation, and corruption, the *World Development Report 2002* provides a wealth of evidence that the level and nature of competition in markets affect innovation and growth.[26] Although one of the hallmarks of a market economy is competition, it rarely functions without some form of regulation. The market alone does not produce all the goods on which a society's development depends. For instance, regulations are often needed to protect the public interest against private profit motives. The challenge in economic society is that businesspeople and the public at large view regulations differently. What looks like a blessing to the ordinary citizen is a curse to the businessperson. Because of such differences, one of two problems tends to arise. The first is that regulations are unevenly applied. Those with the right political connections can escape them without being penalized. Others who are not so lucky are being sought out with a view to making them pay. This is one of the softer spots in the governance realm in many countries. Rules are not sufficiently transparent and often applied in discretionary ways. This leaves the business community in uncertainty about what rules prevail. This issue tends to become especially pronounced in countries with a privileged minority dominating the economy. Examples are the Chinese minority in Indonesia and several other Southeast Asian countries, the Lebanese in West Africa, and the Indians in East Africa.[27]

There have been massive efforts placed on studying corruption and the practice of combating it.[28] A favorite concern has been to examine the process associated with obtaining a business license. Governments typically have a formal licensing procedure for establishing a business. How long it takes to get such a license and the additional payments involved are often viewed as indicative of the business climate in a country. In some countries, investors—foreign and local—are unable to obtain licenses without first paying a bribe to some public official. Such situations increase transaction costs and make the process less efficient in the long run. However, corrupt payments also substantially affect the trust that key actors have in the system. The legitimacy of the regime is being called into question.

As for globalization, changes in economic society have been very much influenced by global factors. With economic liberalization has come a greater scope for exchanges across national—and cultural—boundaries. This is particularly true in trade, finance, and technology.[29] Governments often fall behind on these challenges. Conflicts arise between government and business. The task of managing conflicting relations is exacerbated by the fact that economic liberalization and political democratization are not always mutually supportive. Several scholars have devoted their attention to this issue and called into question the extent to which these two processes are complementary.[30] Economic liberalization gives the wealthy a greater chance to win, while pressures from the losing majority tend to challenge the extent to which democracy can be consolidated. Events in Argentina remind us of this reality.

In sum, the literature indicates that governance in the economic society arena is full of challenges. We are unable to deal with all of them, but after careful scrutiny of the literature and consultation with practitioners, we chose five indicators that reflect the prevailing concerns among those who have given thought to governance issues in this arena.

### Economic Society: Aggregate WGS Findings

Before presenting the aggregate findings for economic society, we like to briefly introduce the indicators that we chose.

1. *Respect for property rights.* To what extent do persons in public office promote respect for property rights? This is our decency indicator for this arena. It speaks to how far public officials really respect a set of rights that are important not only to individual persons but also to a society's development at large.

2. *Equal application of regulations.* To what extent are economic regulations applied equally to firms in the economy? This indicates the extent to which fairness applies in the application of rules in this arena. It has important implications for the business climate and how people, especially investors, view the legitimacy of the regime.

3. *Corrupt transactions.* To what extent is obtaining a business license associated with corrupt transactions? This indicator tries to measure the level of transparency. It is a generally accepted measure of transparency that we include here together with our other measures.

4. *State and private-sector consultation.* To what extent is there consultation on policy between public and private sector actors? This indicator has been chosen to measure the level of trust and cooperation that exists between private sector actors, on the one hand, and government officials, on the other. In an era when private sector enterprises have been given greater recognition as important contributors to development, their relationship and interaction with the state has taken on special significance.

5. *New global economic rules.* To what extent does the government

take the new rules of global trade, finance, and technology flows into account when formulating policy? Globalization brings new challenges to economic and political actors alike. How they respond to and manage the new international rules for trade and business transactions with adequate attention to the welfare and security of their respective countries cannot be ignored. This indicator is meant to measure the level of adjustment that these actors are able to make in the light of the challenges of new global rules.

### Differences Among Countries

By disaggregating economic society in this way, we expect to get a sense of what the more critical and controversial dimensions of economic society are. The discussion below of the aggregate scores draws on country ratings and contextual comments by the experts. For consistency, we divide the countries into the same groups—high, medium, and low—based on their overall 2000 WGS scores.

The average scores for economic society are not as high as those for civil society or the government arenas but slightly better than bureaucracy and political society. Compared to other arenas, there is less variation in the ratings among individual indicators. We remind our readers that respondents are a cross section of well-informed persons, some in business and civil society, others in government and judicial offices. Although there are obvious variations by country, no issue emerges as a particular challenge across countries. Regulatory issues are more problematic; somewhat surprising, adjustment to global economic rules is the issue that respondents regard as least challenging. The most salient, though not surprising, difference among countries is that those with a longer tradition of a functioning market economy score higher than those who lack such a legacy. Thus countries that have embarked on economic liberalization (e.g., Bulgaria, China, Mongolia, and Russia) tend to have a lower score for this arena (see Table 7.1).

Several countries deserve attention here. Jordan is the biggest surprise. It is the second-highest-rated country in this arena. This score reflects the relative success of liberal economic reforms undertaken in the 1990s. As a result of these reforms, Jordan joined the World Trade Organization (WTO) and established free-trade areas with Arab countries, the European Union, and the United States. Its laws and regulations for this transition are in place and working satisfactorily, according to our respondents.

It is also worth noting that Asian countries tend to score on the low side. This reflects the disappointments that respondents in many countries felt as a result of the Asian financial crisis in the late 1990s. Although the average score for Thailand is well above 3, respondents highlight prob-

**Table 7.1    Aggregate Economic Society Scores by Country, 2000**

| Country | Decency | Fairness | Transparency | Cooperation | Adjustment | Average |
|---------|---------|----------|--------------|-------------|------------|---------|
| **High-scoring countries** | | | | | | |
| Chile | 3.87 | 3.83 | 3.80 | 3.50 | 4.18 | 3.84 |
| India | 3.21 | 3.18 | 2.43 | 3.22 | 3.89 | 3.19 |
| Jordan | 4.03 | 3.50 | 3.25 | 3.00 | 4.18 | 3.59 |
| Mongolia | 2.92 | 2.72 | 2.44 | 2.67 | 3.13 | 2.78 |
| Tanzania | 3.12 | 2.97 | 3.33 | 3.27 | 3.35 | 3.21 |
| Thailand | 3.41 | 3.12 | 2.78 | 3.41 | 3.59 | 3.26 |
| **Medium-scoring countries** | | | | | | |
| Argentina | 2.74 | 2.36 | 1.91 | 3.16 | 3.54 | 2.74 |
| Bulgaria | 2.76 | 2.27 | 3.83 | 2.76 | 2.85 | 2.89 |
| China | 2.94 | 2.94 | 2.12 | 2.32 | 3.30 | 2.72 |
| Indonesia | 2.26 | 2.40 | 2.06 | 2.66 | 3.09 | 2.49 |
| Peru | 2.70 | 2.78 | 2.88 | 2.41 | 3.16 | 2.79 |
| **Low-scoring countries** | | | | | | |
| Kyrgyzstan | 2.38 | 2.41 | 3.77 | 2.69 | 2.85 | 2.82 |
| Pakistan | 2.58 | 2.67 | 2.82 | 2.39 | 2.94 | 2.68 |
| Philippines | 2.77 | 1.60 | 2.37 | 2.34 | 3.54 | 2.52 |
| Russia | 2.29 | 2.32 | 2.34 | 2.87 | 2.84 | 2.53 |
| Togo | 2.67 | 2.76 | 2.90 | 2.02 | 2.57 | 2.59 |
| Average, all countries | 2.92 | 2.74 | 2.81 | 2.79 | 3.31 | 2.91 |

lems associated with corruption and the enforcement of government regulations.

The situation in China is of special interest. Corruption is an issue that most respondents identified as problematic. Much of it stems from the legacy of overregulation that characterized its socialist economy before liberalization. Also highly problematic in China is the relationship between the public and private sectors. Genuine privatization is slow in coming, and there is little, if any, consultation between actors in the two sectors. Many respondents see unfair competition as another issue that adversely affects the perception of this arena. These comments confirm points highlighted in the literature on China's economic transition.[31] Although governance of economic society in China has weaknesses, there is much praise for its adjustment to the global economy. It scores high on the question of how well it has taken on its entrance into the world economy, including membership in the WTO. There is, however, a simultaneous realization that as China enters the world economy more head-on, new issues are arising, notably growing social stratification and the tensions between rich and poor.

Russia has liberalized to a greater degree than China and provides another interesting case of a troubled economic transition. Respondents highlight privatization of former state-owned property and mention that private property generally remains vulnerable and poorly protected. The enforcement of regulations is inadequate and/or unfair. The most common comment was about cronyism—special treatment given mostly to friends and relatives. Licenses are a main source of official bribery; other forms of corruption are widespread. There is no systematic consultation between private and public organizations. Our respondents noted that those in power consult only with oligarchs of their own choice. The only real bright spot in Russia is the same as in China: a more active role in the world economy, including negotiations to join the WTO, ongoing in 2000.

We also like to add a few comments about Argentina. Our survey was undertaken in 2000 (i.e., before the economic situation turned into a crisis in Argentina). Ratings as well as comments by our respondents suggest an awareness of the problems underlying the country's economy and the causes of its crisis since 2001. They specifically refer to the prevalence of corruption, poor or unfair enforcement of economic regulations, and discrimination against small and medium-sized enterprises. The ratings stand in marked contrast to the perceptions prevailing elsewhere in the world at the time—not the least in the United States—of Argentina as a country taking advantage of best practices in economic development.

Finally, the mean scores for each category of countries suggest that the high scorers do particularly well in this arena. They are well above the other two groups, even though one country—Mongolia—is an outlier scoring much lower than the average. Governance of the economic society arena in Mongolia is problematic because the transition to a market economy continues to be associated with the same kind of problems present in the transitions in Russia and China (see Table 7.2).

The relatively low average scores for the other two categories suggest that governance in the economic society arena is going to be problematic as long as the rule of law is not institutionalized. This raises the question of whether the quality of the judicial arena is a determinant of what happens in some of the other arenas, such as economic society.

**Table 7.2   Mean Scores of Economic Society Indicators by Groups of Countries**

| Category of Countries | Mean Score |
| --- | --- |
| High scoring | 3.31 |
| Medium scoring | 2.73 |
| Low scoring | 2.63 |

*Changes over Time*

In spite of the shortcomings associated with the economic society in 2000, there was modest improvement from 1995. The median rating for the mid-1990s was 2.76, compared to 2.92 for 2000, slightly more than 3 percent. Only one country—the Philippines—showed marked deterioration. Improvement is associated especially with adjustment to the world economy, but there is also some shift to the better in respect for property rights and consultation between government and the private sector. In short, market reforms have continued, although each step forward creates its own problems that tend to overshadow some of the progress made (see Figure 7.1).

It is worth noting that although former socialist countries scored lower than those with a market economy legacy, many of the countries that show great improvement are in the former category. For instance, both China and Bulgaria record a considerable improvement, as do Tanzania and Russia, albeit to a lesser extent. Such improvement does not apply to all former socialist countries. Mongolia saw no improvement in this arena, as progress toward a market economy ran into problems in the late 1990s.

Improvement in countries with a market economy in place has been less dramatic but steady. India, Indonesia, Pakistan, and Thailand do slight-

**Figure 7.1    Changes over Time in Economic Society, 1995–2000**

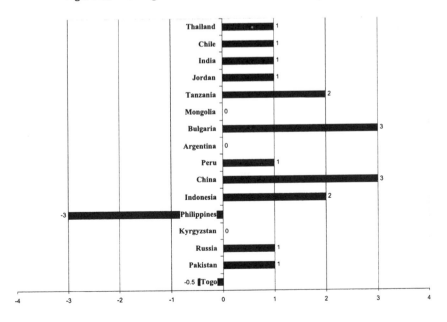

ly better than our sample from Latin America. Chile and Peru showed modest gains over the five-year period and Argentina was flat, although all three were very much the target of economic liberalization. In Africa, there is a big difference between Tanzania and Togo. Although the former is seen as having made good progress with regard to financial stabilization and structural adjustment, Togo has gone slightly backward. Widespread corruption, accentuated favoritism, and dishonest transactions by the government are cited as main reasons for the decline there.

In sum, like in the other arenas, improvement exceeds decline, but there is variation among individual indicators.

## Analysis of Individual Indicators

It has been impossible to cover everything that possibly might fall under the rubric of economic society. Our set of indicators, however, represents a cross section of important variables. They were all treated as being of equal importance in our survey. We shall begin our discussion on that basis.

### Decency

There are three important observations that we want to make in regard to this indicator. The first is that decency—respect for property rights—varies and is not necessarily linked to level of development. The best scores on this indicator belong to a range of different countries: Islamic Jordan, middle-income Chile, technologically advanced India, rapidly growing Thailand, and rural and agricultural Tanzania. This suggests to us that property rights can flourish in different settings.

The second observation is that countries where private property has been enshrined in law—Argentina, India, Peru, Philippines, and Thailand—may have an advantage, but they face problems with enforcement. The situation in the Philippines has been alarming. Respondents told us that violation of property rights in order to enhance private interests increased during the Estrada regime in the late 1990s. Favoritism and other forms of corruption are mentioned as common in several of these countries. These problems also feature prominently in countries with autocratic governments (e.g., Indonesia, Pakistan, and Togo).

Although enforcement is a serious issue everywhere in our sample, the countries that have made the transition from a socialist economy face special problems. Weaknesses in those countries often stem from lack of clarity in the laws and from a lack of public understanding of the new laws. As respondents told us in Kyrgyzstan, there was no such thing as private property, let alone laws protecting it. How this affects the relationship with others in society is something that people are still learning. Thus in Kyrgyzstan, as well as Russia, respondents indicated that there is widespread anger with the way private property is allocated—or seized—as a result of inadequacies in legal systems. The respondents in Russia talked about the destruction of state property by those responsible for privatization, because it was allocated to a small group of well-placed individuals with connections in government.

Although the issue in most former socialist countries is lack of control in privatizing state property, the issue in China is different. It has undertaken far-reaching economic reform but has been more cautious with political reform. Appreciation of these reforms is recorded in our survey, but there is also awareness that economic reforms need to be complemented by changes in governance. Uncertainty about the future stems from the fact that China lacks a road map for political development. People are not sure how things will develop, and that adds to worries about the sustainability of economic reforms.

In Tanzania property rights were very much ignored in the past. During the socialist 1970s, violations of these rights were frequent. The situation since then has changed and is now stabilized. Private property rights are respected. To the extent that people feel threatened, it has more to do with personal security. It is in this light that the relatively high score for Tanzania should be seen.

Our concluding observation is that many countries included in this study do face problems with regard to respect for property rights. Although progress may have been made, most countries are far from living up to the obligations in the Universal Declaration of Human Rights.

*Fairness*

How fairly regulations are applied matters. To some extent, the problems associated with this indicator are similar to those identified in relation to decency. This is especially true for former socialist countries, where legal apparatuses are outdated, causing problems for emerging market economies. We want to comment on two other issues that came out strongly in our study.

The first is the extent to which personal connections play an important but often detrimental role in economic society. Everyone knows that business deals are dependent on trust and direct personal contacts. These contacts, however, sometimes become too close and operate at the expense of regulations. This phenomenon, which many respondents call cronyism, is prevalent to varying degrees in virtually all countries. It is mentioned frequently by respondents in Bulgaria, Indonesia, Pakistan, Russia, and Togo—countries that scored low on this indicator. In these places, comments by our respondents suggest that relatives and friends of powerful politicians often enjoy privileges that others are denied.

The second point is that our respondents indicate that problems of fairness exist even where cronyism is not such a big issue. They suggest that government officials are more prone to listen to representatives of big business than to those who operate smaller enterprises. This sentiment was articulated in Argentina as well as the Philippines. In the latter, respondents believed that some sectors are favored over others. In countries like Tanzania, there is a common belief that foreign enterprises are favored over local ones. It is no coincidence that our Tanzanian respondents had the lowest score of all.

Our findings confirm that this is a problematic part of economic society. The market is not supposed to discriminate, but in practice unfairness is common. Our respondents had few suggestions about what to do, although increased transparency and accountability should produce results.

## Transparency

Transparency is a challenge to many governments because they often have so much to hide from the public. Misappropriation of funds and corruption are among the main reasons why transparency tends to be low. As our respondents tell us, corruption is rife in many countries included in this study. It is associated with obtaining licenses and other aspects of conducting business. This suggests that focusing only on the issue of obtaining a license may underreport the extent to which corruption is a problem in a given country.

The main complaint is that authorities are ineffective or slow in dealing with corruption. This is especially true in countries that are undergoing economic liberalization. Respondents from Mongolia and Russia lament the fact that corruption and political patronage remain despite a decade-plus of economic reforms. The case of Indonesia provides some insights into why progress has been limited. Although certain forms of corruption—collusion and nepotism—that were associated with the Suharto government have become less prevalent, new forms—notably bribes—have emerged as serious threats to the legality of business deals. The lesson learned is that opening up the economy is much easier than getting it to function in a credible and reliable fashion.

Surprising were the very low ratings for Argentina and India. These ratings are considerably below their average for this arena or the country average. This indicates a problem that our respondents also highlighted. Bribery in business was viewed by some Indian respondents as an everyday practice, but many also point to it as a detrimental feature. The sentiments in Argentina, which has a much lower score than Chile, and even Peru are very similar to what their Indian counterparts told us.

The problem is that most countries lack effective institutional mechanisms for controlling corruption. Even where they exist, they don't have much effect, as the cases of India, Pakistan, Tanzania, Togo, and China imply. In terms of what is possible, Peru and Thailand offer some constructive lessons. In Peru the Fujimori government was seen as so corrupt that it caused public outcry. The incoming president could not afford to let officials engage in corrupt practices. Relying on public opinion—and the media—as the sole mechanism of control is not likely to be enough. That is why the Thai case is of interest. The government there has set up an independent agency—the National Counter-Corruption Commission—to monitor its performance. It is instructive that in a 2002 poll it was found to be Thailand's most trusted government institution.[32]

## Cooperation

Consultations between government and the private sector are generally considered important for effective development. Information sharing creates trust and facilitates negotiations on policy. Rules for such activities and what they are expected to achieve are important for understanding governance of economic society.

Our study suggests that consultations on economic policy issues do not happen often, but the fact that the high-scoring group of countries does better on this indicator confirms the value of information sharing between the government and the private sector. On the one extreme are countries where respondents tell us that government never consults business. It prefers to spring surprises on the latter. This happens in Russia, and it seems that the former socialist countries have fewer mechanisms for consultations, if any at all, that work. These countries generally score lower on this indicator. In Argentina and Bulgaria some consultation takes place, but the issues raised are never acted upon. In other places, consultation is with individual enterprises rather than corporate bodies representing the business community at large.

Although many countries have bodies like chambers of commerce, confederations of industries, and manufacturers' associations, their involvement in policymaking is often marginal and ad hoc. There is nothing resembling a corporatist arrangement whereby the state creates a special chamber or council for consultation on economic policy. Governments prefer to decide policy on their own and tend to see regular consultation with the private sector as a complicating factor. There are two exceptions to this point. One is Chile, which scores high on this indicator; the other is Thailand.

Both countries have established patterns of policy consultations, and this type of collaboration between the private sector and public institutions is seen as an important factor contributing to economic success. China has succeeded economically without any such consultative practices, yet our study indicates that professional and businesslike consultations between government and the private sector are helpful for national economic development. The challenge is to make them more effective and representative of the business community at large.

## Adjustment

Governments face new challenges as the result of global economic liberalization. New rules and practices regarding trade, finance, and technology flows have become a factor in shaping conditions for economic and social policy. The degree to which governments can adjust by incorporating considerations of international opportunities and risks in policymaking is an important governance indicator. The governance challenge is how to manage these rules to enhance the benefits and mitigate the negative effects to people and the country. We asked respondents to consider the extent to which government takes international economic rules into account in formulating economic policy.[33]

This indicator received the highest average rating in the economic society arena—3.31 in 2000. Many respondents believe that government is capable of taking new global economic issues into account in formulating policy. They do cope with adjustments in the rules well. It is also evident that the high-scoring group tends to do best on this indicator. The former socialist countries generally have lower scores, but they are also among those that have made the greatest strides forward. As one respondent put it, "Five years ago Bulgaria was isolated from the rest of the world. Now our country is mostly open and we are part of the global processes."

Based on the ratings and comments by respondents, countries can roughly be divided into three groups with regard to government response to the new economic rules. The first group is somewhat agnostic—they see globalization as inevitable and government needs to take rules regarding trade, finance, and technology into account. But they grudge about it. Countries in this group include Bulgaria, Indonesia, Philippines, Russia, India, Togo, and Tanzania.

India provides an interesting case study. Substantive comments by respondents support approval for the economic liberalization policies implemented since 1991. There is certainly a better relationship between the state and private sector, which had been antagonistic. The increased consideration of international economic issues is seen as necessary. But this does not mean that respondents are blind to the potential adverse effects of globalization. Several make references to the challenges that these new policies pose to the poorer segments of society.

A second group of countries is more positive. Although accepting the challenges and risks, this group tends to see an outward-oriented strategy as good. It includes Chile, Thailand, China, Jordan, and Kyrgyzstan, countries with an ambition to join the World Trade Organization, if they haven't already done so.

The third group has a negative view of new global rules and views changes coming as a result of pressure from outside. This is present in countries where economic problems have required external intervention: Argentina, Mongolia, and Pakistan. Respondents are critical of specific international institutions like the IMF and suggest that members of the public as well as the media view globalization as favoring developed countries and discriminating against the third world.

Despite these variations, there are concerns that cut across the groups. The first—and most common—is that not enough is done to protect people against the negative effects of social changes due to new global rules. A second concern is that the pace of change does not enable countries to react. Globalization is simply too fast. The third is that governments have not yet found solutions to the economic risks and challenges the new global rules will bring. Many of them are still fumbling in the dark.

## Implications for Research and Practice

Governance in the economic society arena can make a difference regardless of existing level of economic development and cultural orientation. The top scorers in this arena have different backgrounds. Former socialist countries seem to encounter greater difficulties in this arena. Their transition to a market economy is recent and will require more time. Yet most countries have made progress, including those with problems. Economic reform is paying off, even if it is slower than consultants and advisers would like. Even if globalization and liberalization have positive impacts, most continue to battle with issues that affect the business climate and governance of the regime.

Regarding implications for research, property rights has received growing attention in the literature. Our study concludes that more work is needed to understand how property rights affect development. Because private property rights have been seen as the most effective, there has been less interest in other types of rights—common and public—that may be the most appropriate in certain circumstances.[34] This is true in many countries where communal property legacies are still present and affect the way people think about ownership and inheritance. It is also necessary to take a critical look at the results of implementing private property rights in developing countries. What does the record tell us? Furthermore, given that so many rights are informal (i.e., not contained in a written contract), it is necessary to study how informal rights serve formalization and the development of a legalized property rights system.

There is a prevalence of informal relations, and how they affect the enforcement of rights and contracts is important. Our study has shown that a good number of respondents believe that regulations are not applied evenly. Patronage and favoritism, rather than formal rules, often determine the outcome. This issue is receiving growing attention in the literature as researchers realize that formal institutions are not always as important as they appear on paper.

What is going on in economic society should be considered in the context of what happens elsewhere in the governance realm. Countries which do well in our governance survey do well in this arena. So there may be reason to look at the effects of a strong civil society on economic society. What effects does media freedom have on development?[35] As for the judicial arena, how does it bear on what happens in economic society? A focus on economic society alone may be too narrow and technical in many instances. Real underlying problems are not adequately understood through such an approach.[36] For instance, a closer examination of the corporatist models that were popular in the past, especially in Western Europe, may be one way of bringing a new perspective to these issues.

We make four points regarding implications for practice. The first concerns the scope of issues that is important for understanding economic society and how it operates. There is a tendency to regard it primarily in terms of efficiency: how can transaction costs be lowered? Although that is a legitimate concern, our study highlights the importance of including other objectives, among which the legitimacy of the rules and regulations that apply is of special salience.

Second, the market is often promoted as the only hope. There is no question that the move toward a market economy has been beneficial for development in many countries, but unleashing the private sector largely unregulated also carries risks. Argentina and Russia illustrate how easy it is for a radical restructuring of economic society to go awry. Our study suggests that a more comprehensive strategy of improving both state and market institutions as well as linkages between them may be more sustainable.

Third, although the majority of countries are seen to make progress in economic society, much remains to be done, especially in former socialist countries. One issue is how private-sector voices can be incorporated into the policymaking process. There is little, if any, effort to listen to private-sector representatives and their concerns. Policy is made above the heads of the latter. Organizing the economic society regime to allow for more consultation on a regular and formal basis would be an important way to improve governance in this arena. In so doing, it is important to pay attention to context, especially the extent to which there is a legacy of state-market relations involving private-sector representatives.

Fourth, globalization has costs and benefits for individual countries. Our study shows that globalization is associated with gains and risks, especially for vulnerable groups in society. More attention needs to be paid to the social implications of the new economic rules that globalization is bringing to each national economy. Thus although the existing liberal orthodoxy continues to be the driving force behind much of the improved governance in this arena, it needs to be tempered so that its gains are not reversed by a backlash.

## Notes

1. Juan Linz and Alfred Stepan, *Problems of Democratic Transition and Consolidation: Southern Europe, South America, and Post-Communist Europe* (Baltimore: Johns Hopkins University Press, 1996).

2. World Bank, *World Development Report 1997: The State in a Changing World* (New York: Oxford University Press, 1997); and World Bank, *World Development Report 2002: Building Institutions for Markets* (New York: Oxford University Press, 2002).

3. Douglass North, *Institutions, Institutional Change, and Economic Performance* (Cambridge, UK: Cambridge University Press, 1990).

4. Ronald H. Coase, "The Institutional Structure of Production," *American Economic Review* 28, no. 4 (1992): 713–720.

5. Oliver Williamson, "The Institutions and Governance of Economic Development and Reform," in *Proceedings of the World Bank Annual Conference on Development Economics 1994* (Washington, DC: World Bank, 1995).

6. World Bank, *World Development Report 1997*.

7. Stephen Knack and Philip Keefer, "Institutions and Economic Performance: Cross-Country Tests Using Alternative Institutional Measures," *Economics and Politics* 7 (1994): 207–227.

8. Paolo Mauro, "Corruption and Growth," *Quarterly Journal of Economics,* no. 110 (1995): 681–712.

9. Transparency International, *Global Corruption Report 2003* (London: Profile Books, 2003).

10. D. Kaufmann, A. Kraay, and P. Zoido-Lobaton, "Governance Matters," *Research Policy Working Paper No. 2196* (Washington, DC: World Bank, 1999); D. Kaufmann, A. Kraay, and P. Zoido-Lobaton, "Governance Matters II: Updated Indicators for 2000/01," *World Bank Policy Research Working Paper No. 2772* (Washington, DC: World Bank, 2002); and D. Kaufmann and A. Kraay, "Governance and Growth: Causality Which Way?" *World Bank Research Working Paper* (Washington, DC: World Bank, February 2003).

11. Kaufmann, Kraay, and Zoido-Lobaton, "Governance Matters."

12. D. Kaufmann, "Rethinking Governance: Empirical Lessons Challenge Orthodoxy," *World Bank Research Working Paper* (Washington, DC: World Bank, March 2003).

13. For example, see Joseph E. Stiglitz, "Information and Economic Analysis: A Perspective," *Economic Journal* 95 (supplement: conference papers) (1985): 21–41.

14. James C. Scott, *Weapons of the Weak* (New Haven, CT, and London: Yale University Press, 1985).

15. Francis F. Fukuyama, *Trust: The Social Virtues and the Creation of Prosperity* (New York: Free Press, 1995).

16. I. Marsh, "Economic Governance and Economic Performance," in Ian Marsh, Jean Blondel, and Takashi Inoguchi, eds., *Democracy, Governance, and Economic Performance: East and Southeast Asia* (Tokyo: United Nations University Press, 1999).

17. World Bank, *The East Asian Miracle: Economic Growth and Public Policy* (New York: Oxford University Press, 1993); and Peter Evans, *Embedded Autonomy: States and Industrial Transformation* (Princeton, NJ: Princeton University Press, 1995).

18. D. Okimoto, *Between MITI and the Market* (Stanford, CA: Stanford University Press, 1989).

19. Anek Laothamata, *Business Associations and the New Political Economy of Thailand: From Bureaucratic Polity to Liberal Corporatism* (Boulder, CO: Westview Press, 1992).

20. H. Demsetz, "Toward a Theory of Property Rights," *American Economic Review* 57 (1967): 347–359; L. De Alessi, "The Economics of Property Rights: A Review of the Evidence," *Research in Law and Economics* 2 (1980): 1–47.

21. P. Starr, "The Meaning of Privatization," in S. B. Kamerman and A. J. Kahn, eds., *Privatization and the Welfare State* (Princeton, NJ: Princeton University Press, 1989).

22. North, *Institutions, Institutional Change, and Economic Performance.*

23. H. de Soto, *The Mystery of Capital: Why Capitalism Triumphs in the West and Fails Everywhere Else* (New York: Random House, 2002).

24. World Bank, *World Development Report 2002.*

25. Colin Leys, *Underdevelopment in Kenya* (London: Heinemann Educational Books, 1975; and Berkeley: University of California Press, 1975).

26. World Bank, *World Development Report 2002.*

27. Amy Chua, *World on Fire* (New York: Doubleday, 2003).

28. See Mauro, "Corruption and Growth"; also Robert Klitgaard, *Controlling Corruption* (Berkeley and Los Angeles: University of California Press, 1998); and Transparency International, *The 2003 Anti-Corruption Report* (London: Profile, 2003).

29. See, e.g., Linda Weiss, *The Myth of the Powerless State: Governing the Economy in a Global Era* (Cambridge, UK: Polity, 1998; and Ithaca, NY: Cornell University Press, 1998).

30. Adam Przeworski, *Democracy and the Market* (New York: Cambridge University Press, 1991); John Dryzek, *Democracy in Capitalist Times: Ideals, Limits, and Struggles* (Oxford, UK: Oxford University Press, 1996).

31. J. Howell, *China Opens its Doors: The Politics of Economic Transition* (Boulder, CO: Lynne Rienner Publishers, 1993); see also T. Saich, *Governance and Politics of China* (London: Palgrave, 2001).

32. "Thailand: Beware of the Watchdog," *The Economist*, August 17, 2002, p. 35.

33. Some respondents commented to us that this question was phrased too broadly; *global economic rules* could simply include too many things. For instance, some argued that it was not enough to consider just what governments had done in formulating policy but also how serious they have been in implementing it.

34. Elinor Ostrom, *Governing the Commons: The Evolution of Institutions for Collective Action* (New York: Cambridge University Press, 1990).

35. The *World Development Report 2002*, for instance, presents evidence to show that the quality of regulation declines with less competition in the media.

36. This is a conclusion that Kaufmann also reaches; see Kaufmann, "Rethinking Governance."

# 8

# The Judiciary

The judicial arena is an integral part of the political-process approach to governance, but it is also different from the others we analyze and discuss in earlier chapters. Its raison d'être is derived from the social or political dynamics in the other arenas. As individuals live their lives, they inevitably get into conflict with others. Some conflicts may be of a purely private or civil nature (e.g., a dispute over inheritance rights). Others may be public (i.e., stemming from a person's interaction with government agencies). Many of the latter involve a group or an organization. Each society, whether developing or developed, requires bodies to resolve disputes between contending parties. We are interested in the extent to which rules constituting the judicial arena are viewed by the respondents as effective in administering justice.

Administration of justice may take different forms. In the historical perspective, resolving conflicts in premodern societies typically rested with the sovereign—the king or chief. In such places, many of the functions that we consider separate today—legislation, implementation, and adjudication—were controlled by the sovereign authority. As societies became more complex and spanned larger territories, the need for differentiation and decentralization of authority increased. Thus while each society had an authority dispensing justice in one form or another, the evolution of a legal system with special courts was a product of growing social differentiation and expansion of economic and political scale.[1] Part of the inspiration for this development can be found in religion, part in the secular realm. Few have paid more attention to this process than Max Weber. He examined it with a view to differentiating between the premodern and modern systems of law, the latter being a product of the capitalist system. Weber was also sensitive to tensions that arose in the Western legal tradition as a result of its dual religious and secular origins. Thus he argued that law was based on either substantive rationality or formal rationality.

The latter signifies the formulation and application of abstract rules by a process of logical generalization and interpretation. Its emphasis is on collecting and rationalizing by logical means all the valid rules and forming them into an internally consistent set of propositions. As capitalism expanded across wider reaches of the world, this type of reasoning became necessary to sustain that economic system. Substantive rationality, by contrast, accords prominence not to logical consistency but to ethical considerations, utility, and expediency. It reflects the belief that all human beings act with certain values in mind, whether or not they are utilitarian, and regardless of their origin.[2]

This outline of the Western legal tradition leads to important observations on the issues analyzed in this chapter. The first is that legal tradition in the West is not uniform but has given rise to a variety of legal systems, one being the difference between civil (associated with the French legal tradition) and common law (associated with that of Anglo-Saxon countries). The second is that rules for administering justice were originally part of an oral tradition. The extent to which they were formalized, and when it happened, vary from one society to another. For example, in the West the formalization of a legal system and the creation of professional courts began in earnest in the eleventh and twelfth centuries.[3] As this transition continued, old rules were recast. Nature became property; economic relations became contract; and conscience became will and intent. The third point is that as the West extended its influence around the world during the era of imperialism in the nineteenth and twentieth centuries, its agents encountered the persistence of old rules. A major issue was what to do: Eliminate them because they were seen as archaic or barbaric? Or leave them alone and superimpose Western laws on top? The legacy left behind in most developing countries is mixed. There are both modern and customary courts, both formal and informal bodies dispensing justice. And regardless of the differences, the role of law means subjecting human conduct to the governance of rules.[4] The emphasis is not only on rules but also on how rules are applied in society. For this reason, the judicial arena, from a governance perspective, is important for socializing and enforcing rules. The legal culture that develops in society as a result of how arbitration is carried out is important for how people perceive the judiciary and the political system. And the way in which judicial institutions operate may also have an impact on economic and development performance.

We examine some of the major issues in the field of law and justice before analyzing the findings of the WGS. We present the aggregate findings and then discuss what is interesting about each individual indicator. The final section deals with the implications for research and practice.

## Governance Issues in the Judicial Arena

Two sets of issues have been dominant in the literature on governance in the judicial arena. The first relates to the role that law plays in development. The second concerns whose rules and which ones matter. We discuss each in turn.

### Law and Development

Although transplantation of law has been a permanent feature of world history,[5] the idea that the rule of law is important for a country's development became a special concern in the 1960s when development was perceived largely as a matter of imitating the success of Western societies. Driven by the intellectual energy of U.S.-based scholars like James C. N. Paul, Clarence Diaz, and Robert Seidman, reshaping the legal education syllabus and the role of lawyers in society became priorities. Achieving a transformation of legal systems in newly independent and developing countries proved more elusive than its protagonists had expected. Soon this approach lost its appeal. Two other members of this law and development school—David Trubek and Marc Galanter—subsequently admitted that the demise of their effort was very much due to the misguided notion that the U.S. model, which they called liberal legalism, could be exported to and take root in developing countries.[6]

The notion that the rule of law matters disappeared when development was seen more in political economy terms, first as redistribution of resources to the poor, later as providing incentives for greater participation in the market. This does not mean that issues of justice disappeared. Police acted brutally and were more often associated with corruption than with protection. Access to justice was difficult, delivery of judicial services weak. Evidence was mounting that lawlessness and weak legal institutions were having a negative impact on economic and social progress.

It was not until the 1990s, with a renewed emphasis on democracy and good governance, that issues related to the role of law in development were revived. As Thomas Carothers noted, "One cannot get through a foreign policy debate these days without someone proposing the rule of law as the solution to the world's troubles."[7] The two concepts of governance and rule of law are clearly interrelated: without a fair and effective judiciary based on the rule of law, one can hardly imagine good governance.

The literature that has developed as a result of the renewed interest in law and development has given rise to two different approaches. One argues that the judicial arena is an integral part of development; development is defined by the presence of rule of law. Another argues that the judicial arena contributes to development; it affects economic performance and people's welfare. We differentiate between the two by labeling the first the *constitutive approach,* the second the *instrumentalist approach.*

The works of John Rawls and Amartya Sen are relevant to the constitutive approach. Rawls's discussion of the rule of law forms part of his overall view of "justice as fairness."[8] Margaret Radin interprets "Rawls as making the stronger claim that the rule of law is *required* for liberty."[9] In a somewhat similar vein, Sen argues that "legal reform advances freedom—a crucial and constitutive quality of comprehensive development. Legal reform is thus important on its own."[10] Development depends on people being able to enjoy basic legal rights. A recent study of the poor conducted under the auspices of the World Bank confirms that these people view safety, security, and access to justice as high priorities.[11]

The instrumentalist approach focuses on the questions of whether and how legal institutions affect development performance. Economic theory suggests that the judiciary might affect economic outcomes. Adam Smith argued that "a tolerable administration of justice" along with peace and low taxes were all that was necessary to "carry a state to the highest degree of opulence."[12] Ever since, scholars have argued about the ways in which administration of justice can make a difference to development. What is more important, upholding property rights, enforcing contracts between economic actors, checking abuses of government power, or ensuring the rule of law? The *World Development Report 2002* brings much of the recent evidence together and concludes that income and the rule of law—encompassing the collective importance of property rights, respect for legal institution, and the judiciary—are highly correlated.[13] The same report also shows that the absence of formal contract enforcement mechanisms limited the growth of firms and the development of financial institutions, citing evidence of a direct relation between independent courts and the expansion of trade.[14] Another study finds a strong correlation between legal protections to creditors and investment.[15] These studies notwithstanding, causality remains uncertain. And other studies indicate that widespread legal reform is not necessary to attract foreign investment and that legal reforms are inherently slow.[16] Thus while the evidence points to the positive impact of solid legal frameworks on economic performance, the evidence is not yet sufficient to draw definite conclusions.

Even if legal reform may not influence foreign investment, it may make a difference to the welfare of ordinary citizens. For instance, work in Asia indicates that legal empowerment can improve the circumstances of the poor—and that a vibrant civil society, and laws that protect it, are important for legal empowerment strategies.[17] Michael Anderson suggests that the ways that the poor may be adversely affected by the performance of the justice system include the failure of the justice system to protect people from "theft, violence and official abuse"; the failure of the justice system to "enforce legitimate entitlements and legal rights (e.g. to wages or inheritance)"; "the prevalence of police extortion, unjust imprisonment and courtroom bribery"; and lawlessness forcing poor households to use "scarce disposable income for self-protection (e.g. bribes and weapons)" in order to protect themselves.[18]

These overviews of recent research are helpful, but they leave us with the conclusion that empirical research on the impact of the judiciary on human development remains thin; more work is required.

### Whose Rules and Which Matter?

Legal systems are embedded in culture and customs. Finding the common denominators of a universal legal regime is difficult, although since the adoption of the Universal Declaration of Human Rights in 1948 this has been the ambition of the international community. To start, they have had to cope with differences inherent in the four predominant contemporary legal systems of the world: common law, civil law, socialist law, and religious law. Common law systems are found in Anglo-Saxon countries and those colonized by Britain. It emphasizes the rights of the individual vis-à-vis the state, checks and balances between the branches of government, and the courts' use of precedents and individual cases in adjudication. Its strength lies in flexibility to adjust to changing social, economic, and political circumstances.

Civil law is most closely associated with France and francophone countries, although it is present elsewhere on the European continent. It was introduced as the Code Napoleon. Although it does pay attention to how individual rights can be protected from state interference, its basic premise is that the government executive and the legislature exist to regulate individual behavior. In this system, the individual is not autonomous but is wedded to the state through a series of obligations. Adjudication in courts is based on a rational interpretation of the law. Legislation is more important than precedent in settling disputes.

Socialist law is a category in decline since the demise of the Soviet Union. To the extent that it still exists in countries like China, Cuba, North Korea, and Vietnam, it is characterized by the premise that the state is a dominant actor and the absence of concrete power-sharing mechanisms. Even more than in civil law countries, rights of the state take precedence over those of the individual. In fact, individual rights are subordinated to the ideological goal of the state.

Religious law resembles socialist law in that both presuppose the full subordination of individuals to a supreme authority, religious or secular. The development of law is not a prerogative of elected legislators but constrained by texts of a religious nature. The Islamic sharia is a good case in point.

Most legal systems, especially in developing countries, are mixed. For instance, in many African countries the legal system is a mix of common or civil law traditions together with customary law. In countries with Islamic law, there is an influence from other sources, be they Western or customary. In former communist countries elements of socialist law may contend with new influences from civil or common law traditions, as in Central Europe and Eastern Europe.

So does it make a difference to development what kind of legal system a society has? Some have examined this question and concluded that countries with common or civil law are more democratic than others and that pure legal systems—common, civil, religious—perform best in terms of economic development. Countries with mixed legal systems perform as much as twice as poorly in terms of GDP per capita than those with pure systems.[19]

This inevitably leads us to ask whether there are common denominators for judging what constitutes universally applicable principles and rules for the judicial arena? We believe that there is a growing consensus around at least a reasonable set. For instance, drawing together findings of studies devoted to the rule of law, Lawrence Solum[20] has identified seven requirements that need to be present before one can talk of "good" governance: arbitrary decisions by government officials must not serve as the basis for legal verdicts; government officials must not perceive themselves as being above the law; the law must be known to the public through clear methods of promulgation; legal rules must be stated in general terms and not aimed at particular individuals or groups; similar cases must be treated in an equivalent manner; procedures for determining must be fair and orderly; and actions required and forbidden by the rule of law must be easy for citizens to identify.

Other scholars[21] come to similar conclusions in trying to identify what constitutes key values associated with the rule of law. In sum, there is a reasonable consensus about the more important principles and indicators of governance in this arena.

## The Judicial Arena: Aggregate WGS Findings

Before proceeding to the analysis of our findings, it is necessary to present the indicators at some length. The existing consensus has been important in determining the indicators that we chose for this arena.

1. *Fairness.* To what extent is there equal access to justice for citizens? Equal protection under the law is a human right that is universally acknowledged, as Article 7 of the UDHR shows. In practice, however, access to justice varies. The extent to which rules of the judicial arena address this issue is an important governance concern.

2. *Transparency.* To what extent are there clear decisionmaking processes in the judicial system? Procedural clarity is another principle that is acknowledged in the UDHR, more specifically in Articles 9 and 11. This principle applies not only to what happens in the courtroom but also to all other aspects associated with a legal case, including the way evidence is collected. Rules must be clear and easy to understand. The more transparent the rules are and the more systematically they are adhered to, the greater the likelihood that the legal system is being viewed as authoritative and respected.

3. *Accountability.* To what extent are judicial officials accountable for their actions? Judges need a definite measure of autonomy in order to be able to carry out their job. The discretion that follows with this autonomy could, willfully or not, be misused. For this reason there must be mechanisms in place for holding judicial officials accountable. Appeal, judicial review, and special inquiries are examples. The importance of these mechanisms was acknowledged in a World Bank report, which argued that greater accountability of judges to the users of the judicial system has been more important in increasing efficiency than simple increases in financial and human resources.[22] Finally, the media, NGOs, and parliamentary committees are examples of mechanisms that fall outside the judiciary but that can have an impact on the actions of judicial officers.

4. *Decency.* To what extent are international legal norms in the human rights field being incorporated into the national rights regime? An interesting development has been the emergence of an international jurisprudence that draws inspiration from human rights and other legal conventions. Because principles articulated in international jurisprudence tend to be daring, they pose a challenge for the development of universal norms. Although every country in the world has ratified at least one of six principal human rights treaties, and more than half have ratified all six treaties, there is a lag when it comes to translating principles into practice at the national level.

5. *Flexibility.* To what extent are nonjudicial processes in place for fair resolution of conflicts? Because so many legal systems are mixed, it is no surprise that many mechanisms for settling disputes are informal. In many rural areas of the world, community representatives may administer justice. For instance, one study notes that 80–90 percent of all local disputes in southwestern Nigeria are taken to traditional rulers.[23] These informal instances are often preferred because access is easier and costs are lower.

They do also have downsides (e.g., a tendency to discriminate against women and the absence of mechanisms for appeal). Nonetheless, because of their prevalence in developing countries, they form an integral part of governing the judicial arena.

These five indicators capture dimensions of dispute resolution that are vital to any society. They relate to some key principles of governance (see Chapter 1). Access to justice refers to fairness, due process to transparency, judicial autonomy to accountability, international human rights to decency, and nonformal mechanisms to the flexibility of the system. By disaggregating the judicial arena in this way, we hope to identify some of the most important and contested issues. First, we discuss the aggregate scores for each country for the judicial dimension and changes over time.

### Differences Among Countries

Our findings confirm that the judicial arena is problematic in most countries. The average score for this arena is generally on the low side, and only a few countries score anywhere near their average for other arenas. By looking at the individual country scores for 2000 in Table 8.1, we intend to provide a better sense of what is at stake. We begin with a few comments about those that scored highest.

Somewhat to our surprise, Jordan and Thailand emerge as the top scorers. Respondents give a higher rating than, for instance, their Indian counterparts or those in Latin American countries, which all have been exposed to the Western tradition for longer periods. Jordan and Thailand are both reform-minded monarchies. They have a uniform legal tradition that draws not on colonial but on indigenous values. They are not known for separation of powers, but institutions have stood the test of political turmoil stemming from domestic and international challenges. The judiciary is no exception. For instance, in Jordan respondents were of the view that the judiciary is independent and protects human rights. At the time of our survey, a royal commission was looking into how the judicial system could be reformed and improved. Respondents mentioned the need to upgrade judges and improve conditions as a special challenge. These two cases raise an interesting governance issue: whether countries should keep reforming existing institutions on the assumption that they can enhance regime legitimacy or need to introduce new institutions.

Chile's relatively low score may look like a surprise. The score is attributed to the many inefficiencies in the judicial system. The main complaint was that the administration of justice tends to be slow and expensive—and influenced by the government in office. In this regard, our findings reflect those of other surveys, which suggest that while other

**Table 8.1    Aggregate Judiciary Scores by Country, 2000**

| Country | Fairness | Transparency | Accountability | Decency | Flexibility | Average |
|---|---|---|---|---|---|---|
| | | **High-scoring countries** | | | | |
| Chile | 2.67 | 3.00 | 3.03 | 3.70 | 2.67 | 3.01 |
| India | 2.86 | 3.31 | 2.92 | 3.47 | 3.00 | 3.11 |
| Jordan | 3.78 | 3.53 | 3.15 | 3.48 | 3.33 | 3.45 |
| Mongolia | 2.28 | 2.54 | 2.49 | 3.46 | 2.49 | 2.65 |
| Tanzania | 2.73 | 3.12 | 2.88 | 3.09 | 2.85 | 2.93 |
| Thailand | 3.37 | 3.46 | 3.51 | 3.52 | 3.01 | 3.38 |
| | | **Medium-scoring countries** | | | | |
| Argentina | 2.43 | 2.16 | 2.21 | 3.80 | 2.91 | 2.70 |
| Bulgaria | 2.44 | 2.34 | 2.27 | 3.54 | 2.15 | 2.55 |
| China | 2.58 | 2.30 | 2.48 | 2.67 | 2.94 | 2.59 |
| Indonesia | 2.43 | 2.11 | 2.00 | 3.26 | 2.97 | 2.55 |
| Peru | 1.92 | 1.78 | 2.05 | 3.68 | 2.68 | 2.42 |
| | | **Low-scoring countries** | | | | |
| Kyrgyzstan | 2.21 | 2.08 | 2.09 | 2.71 | 2.72 | 2.36 |
| Pakistan | 1.82 | 2.15 | 2.03 | 2.36 | 2.42 | 2.16 |
| Philippines | 1.97 | 2.63 | 2.46 | 2.94 | 2.97 | 2.59 |
| Russia | 1.79 | 2.13 | 2.03 | 2.89 | 2.71 | 2.31 |
| Togo | 2.19 | 2.17 | 2.12 | 3.04 | 2.75 | 2.45 |
| Average, all countries | 2.47 | 2.55 | 2.48 | 3.23 | 2.79 | 2.70 |

institutions have contributed to democratization in the country, the judiciary is still lagging. The ratings and comments we received indicate that the Pinochet legacy was still present in the judicial arena. It has taken time for citizens to respect the judiciary after the dictatorship. There have been significant improvements, with the reopening of cases and changes in the judicial doctrine to deal with human rights violations. A good number of respondents expressed a belief that recently launched reforms will have a positive impact on the judiciary in Chile.

Tanzania is typical of what may happen once a country has embarked on political reform. The commitment to reform in government circles is wavering, and lack of financial resources places limits on what government can accomplish. Thus while the government has signed most human rights–related conventions, and human rights have been included in the constitution, implementation has been slow. Respondents indicate that financial constraints are one of the main issues hampering equality. Similarly, corruption is seen to inhibit implementation of justice, although the arrest of some magistrates on charges of corruption indicates that there is progress. Respondents also point out that the low capacity of courts to clear cases—there are too many undecided cases—is another problem.

Tanzanians often face the situation that justice delayed is justice denied. This is the case especially if a party is unable to bribe court officials to take up the case quickly. Although generally critical in their comments on our questions, Tanzanian respondents also had positive things to say. They highlighted the importance of traditional and community institutions. They are seen as capable of offering fair resolution to conflicts, especially in rural areas. They also mentioned the ongoing judicial reform program as well as the existence of several nonjudicial institutions, such as the Media Council of Tanzania, the Tanzania Business Council, and several other tribunals, playing an important role in mediating between key actors in society.

Chinese respondents were open in their comments on the judicial arena. Although China's score is only slightly lower than the average, respondents highlight challenges facing the judicial system in China. The first concerns the lack of independence of judicial institutions and the importance of the Communist Party in guiding judicial procedures. As one respondent put it, "The ruling party and its organizations enjoy the biggest power in Chinese political life." Respondents noted that the ability of the judicial system to resolve conflicts remains limited as long as there is no significant change in the political system. A second but related problem is that the party organization at all levels is often above the law. The judiciary in China will never be fair as long as officials are allowed to ignore the law of the land. A third issue relates to corruption, with respondents highlighting the need for greater supervision. Again, it was noted that this was prevalent at the local level. The fourth issue concerns the importance of having connections. People can get away with crimes because they know someone in a powerful position. The comments suggested that people are not equal before the law.

Scores for the judicial arena in Argentina were just about average for this particular arena and for the country average, reflecting a mixed impression. There are positive aspects, but there are also shortcomings. On the positive side, respondents made it clear that rules affecting the business sector were clearer and more efficient than those shaping the government sector. In other words, the judicial arena dealt with complaints by the private sector more effectively than it did with complaints involving government institutions. Because of the frustrations many people have encountered in dealing with courts, respondents suggested that nonjudicial mechanisms for resolving conflicts have gained popularity because they are cheaper and easier to access. Two criticisms were reiterated by more than one of our respondents. The first is that access to justice depends on finance—"access is inversely proportional to the amount of money citizens have." The second is the lack of internal accountability in the judicial system. Courts enjoy a definite measure of autonomy, but there are no institutional mechanisms in the system for holding judges accountable. External monitoring by the media through investigative journalism emerged as the most effective check.

Although the Philippines is in the low-scoring group overall, the judicial arena was rated surprisingly well by respondents. They noted that judicial reform programs were in place and that efforts were progressing despite the adverse wider governance context of the Estrada administration at the time. Because of the credibility of the chief justice, the supreme court enjoyed an especially high level of legitimacy. This appreciation was tempered by the perception that at lower levels in the judicial system things were not so good. Ordinary citizens had little trust in lower courts. Like in so many other survey countries, the issue of unequal access was raised, as was the absence of accountability. Because of these problems, alternative dispute resolution mechanisms were seen as useful. For example, respondents pointed to tribal mediation processes and *barangay* (village) mediation systems as working because of the ineffectiveness of mainstream judicial procedures, and they highlighted the increasing role of NGOs in conflict resolution.

Pakistanis rated their judicial arena low. In fact, Pakistan was the lowest scoring country. The judicial system has structural problems. Respondents insisted that the judiciary is "corrupt to the core" and that "there is no such thing as justice" in Pakistan. In addition to corruption, respondents identified the cost of going to court and the time involved as key issues reducing access to justice. Women suffered due to their social and financial situations. Although accountability mechanisms exist on paper (such as appeal, judicial review, etc.), they are ineffective. The only silver lining in the judicial arena in Pakistan, respondents suggested, was that much conflict resolution takes place through informal systems (village elders or *jirga* processes through feudal lords). These informal processes have grown in importance because of the failure of the formal mechanisms. One respondent estimated that 50 percent of conflict resolution in villages is done by local elders. Although alternative mechanisms are seen as fairer than formal systems, this varies considerably. Others point out that they totally exclude women and marginalized groups and serve, in some cases, to perpetuate human rights abuses (e.g., honor killings) (see Table 8.2).

Before we conclude, we highlight the differences in average score by category of countries. The high-scoring group does considerably better, although its average compared to that of other arenas is on the low side. The difference between the other two categories is less marked, indicating that the medium group is scoring considerably lower in this arena than in the others.

## Changes over Time

The changes over time are summarized in Figure 8.1. The most striking thing is that twelve of the sixteen countries improved their ratings. In fact, this arena experienced the highest percentage growth of all. Mongolia and Kyrgyzstan held steady, while the Philippines and Togo decreased by 1 point. The improvement was noticeable in Indonesia and Peru but considerable also in India and Chile.

The massive improvements in Peru and Indonesia are a reflection of the euphoria felt when corrupt regimes were coming to an end. In Peru, the coordinator noted that an important factor influencing public opinion was the release of videos made by Valdimiro Montesinos, the presidential intelligence adviser, which exposed the corrupt nature of the judicial system during Fujimori's watch. Although the situation improved in Peru in every one of the governance arenas, respondents indicated that dealing with

**Table 8.2　Mean Scores on Judiciary Indicators by Groups of Countries**

| Category of Countries | Mean Score, 2000 |
| --- | --- |
| High-scoring | 3.09 |
| Medium-scoring | 2.56 |
| Low-scoring | 2.37 |

**Figure 8.1　Changes in Aggregate Judiciary Scores, 1995–2000**

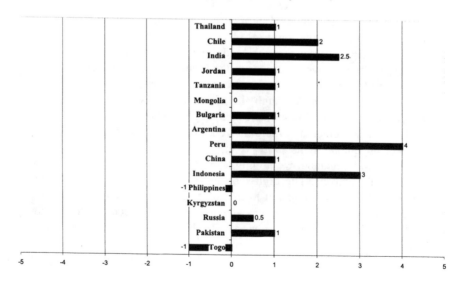

weaknesses in the judicial arena was the highest priority. The respondents in Indonesia were of the opinion that things had definitely changed for the better after the fall of Suharto, but there was lingering suspicion that reform was difficult, especially with regard to basic principles such as access to justice, transparency, and accountability.

Although improvements in most other countries are less marked and almost expected, as in the cases of Argentina and Chile, the changes in Thailand are especially interesting. They have taken place since the country went through a constitutional reform that included not only a more distinct separation of power between the various branches of government but also a greater emphasis on human rights. Thus, for instance, the powers of the monarch to resolve disputes were reduced while a variety of human rights protections were enacted. Although the implementation of these 1997 constitutional and legal reforms was still new when we conducted our survey, the majority of respondents indicated that the situation was improving. Special mention was made of the appointment of outside persons to review the judiciary and the ensuing improvements they noted in accountability and transparency.

## Analysis of Individual Indicators

The five indicators refer to issues that are important in developing countries as they deal with governance. By looking specifically at each one, we gain a better understanding of what is at stake. In addition to commenting on the ratings, we include qualitative comments provided by respondents.

### Fairness

This indictor, which measures access to justice, has one of the lowest overall ratings in the whole survey, not just the judicial arena. Four countries—Peru, Pakistan, the Philippines, and Russia—are given ratings below the 2-point level. Only Thailand and Jordan scored above the 3-point level. There are several reasons for the low scoring; judging from the comments, some are purely geographical, others administrative. For instance, the capacity to administer justice efficiently is not present in every country, as suggested by respondents in Argentina, Chile, the Philippines, and Tanzania. Delay is common and tantamount to denial of justice. The most common reasons go beyond geography and lack of capacity. Four are worth highlighting.

The most common is that money buys justice. In one country after another, respondents noted that the rich have easier access to legal recourse and can affect the outcome of trials. In practice, many citizens are denied their rights because they do not have enough money. One Indian respondent summed it up this way: "People can hardly afford the legal expenses, delays make justice almost unavailable, and legal aid to poor is a farce in reality." The second reason is political connections and patronage. This issue was highlighted in Bulgaria and China but was also articulated in Mongolia, where patronage is seen to reduce honest and fair resolution of disputes. In Kyrgyzstan one expert said that personal connections determine everything. A third reason is direct political interference. Political leaders want to avoid embarrassment and thus attempt to affect the outcome by threat or intimidation directed at judges. This seems to be common in countries with an autocratic legacy. In our sample, this was mentioned in China but was also highlighted in Bulgaria, Russia, and Togo. A fourth reason is the relative ignorance among the public of both the law and opportunities that exist for redressing injustices. This is not surprising in countries where poverty is widespread and illiteracy extensive, yet it is clear that it is common everywhere.

India provides a fascinating example of the opportunities and constraints that exist in access to justice. Although higher courts are progressive in their judgments, and the highest court has initiated the use of public interest litigation (i.e., the court itself taking the initiative to redress an injustice), the lower echelons of the system are far less progressive, often inefficient, and corrupt. The additions of Lok Adalats (People's Courts) and various informal conflict resolution mechanisms have provided outlets for some, but even so the situation in India is far from satisfactory. Thus the high score for India is due to the appreciation respondents have of institutions outside the formal judicial system.

*Transparency*

Transparency and predictability of the legal system in most countries are low. Laws on paper are different from law as practiced. Neither laws nor legal procedures are adequately understood. This issue seems especially pronounced where the transformation of the legal system has been rapid and far-reaching. We provide helpful illustrations from different countries.

It is no coincidence that Mongolia, one of the top scorers in our sample, comes out low on this indicator. Mongolia, despite being in the top group, is a case of an incomplete legal transition. Procedural rules are outdated, and even though they were being revised at the time of our survey, judges are left with discretion in how justice is administered and in determining the outcome of cases. It is no surprise that transparency is seen as the weakest element of the governance realm in that country.

In Russia, another low-scoring country on this indicator, the laws that are necessary for a functioning market economy are taking shape. Our respondents make the point that judges often relapse to the laws of the old bureaucratic system. The response in Bulgaria is similar, with frequent references to the relative clumsiness of the new legal system. Too many changes in laws and procedures represent a problem in Indonesia, although legal reforms have not been as extensive as in the former communist countries. Much of the dissatisfaction there is also related to the ease with which judges can be corrupted and totally ignore due process. This is referred to as *mafia peradilan* (court mafia) in Indonesia.

The complaints about the lack of transparency also extend to law enforcement. For instance, as one respondent in Pakistan put it. "Evidence is doctored, there is no scientific procedure for recording evidence, and witness protection is not guaranteed." The ineffectiveness of the police, often exacerbated by corruption, leaves citizens without a sense of security. Although this complaint is specific to the judicial arena, its ramifications are wider. As suggested in Chapter 5, it tends to backfire on the perceived ability of the executive to guarantee the security of citizens.

In sum, the scores for this indicator are higher, but there are problems of transparency and people do not have a high level of trust in court systems. The top scores are those where the rule of law has been in place for some time, like India and Chile, but it includes a few surprises. In Jordan Islamic law is widely known and the courts are open. Thailand has been able to modernize its governance system and has achieved a set of credible institutions. Tanzania is also among the top. It would be fair to assume that procedures are less institutionalized and transparent there, but our respondents are generally appreciative of the steps forward.[24]

### Accountability

Autonomy in the judicial arena is important if courts are to play an effective role in society. The discretion that follows from autonomy must be tempered by mechanisms ensuring accountability, the latter being a key principle of good governance. Such mechanisms tend to be weak, if not absent, in the countries included in this survey.

This time, only Chile, Jordan, and Thailand are rated above the 3-point level. Thailand is the only country where respondents strongly express the view that accountability mechanisms are in place and work. They point to the separation between the executive and the judicial branches. In their view, courts operate free of political interference and corruption. They also make reference to constitutional provisions for public organizations to carry out inspections of the judiciary, although many admitted that accountability processes are slow.

The lack of public scrutiny, and the implications for accountability, became a common theme in China and Russia, where there is little public scrutiny. "Accountability of judges to the public is insignificant" was a frequent comment by Russian respondents. In China, one respondent noted, "It is almost commonly accepted that 'without money, don't go to the court.'" In India and Tanzania public scrutiny may exist in theory but does not have an impact on the accountability of judicial officers.

Although there is criticism of how judges use discretion, there is also praise. Individual judges can serve as role models and make a difference by reversing lower-court decisions. This was highlighted in the Philippines, where the chief justice at the time of our survey was seen as a man of substantial credibility. Many respondents admitted that their inclination to give a high score on this indicator was related to his role in the administration of justice.

Corruption was cited as a serious problem undermining the autonomy of the judiciary. A respondent from Kyrgyzstan captured the feeling of many of his fellow countrymen when he said that "the problem is that authorities do not want courts to really be independent." A similar view was expressed in Togo: "There is no real independence of the judicial system because of corrupt magistrates and frequent political pressure."

Although the ombudsman deals primarily with administrative law, wherever such an institution has been introduced it faces the same accusations of being inefficient and corrupt. It is clear that the problem of accountability affects not only the executive and legislative branches but also the judicial branch.

It should be added that with the exception of Thailand the scores differ less dramatically. Given that the average score is low, accountability of judicial officers is a widespread problem.

## Decency

A growing number of international treaties and conventions have created a growing interest in international jurisprudence. Behind this lies the idea that the international community can agree on a set of legal norms. The nature of international legal norms varies. Some that stem from the Universal Declaration of Human Rights are fundamental and easier to present as mandatory hard law. A large number of other treaties belong to soft law (i.e., norms that have less immediacy and are not deemed obligatory for national legal systems to adopt). A variety of intergovernmental organizations and international NGOs have spearheaded the dissemination of international norms. The 1993 World Conference on Human Rights in Vienna is one example. Regardless of the nature of the norms, they raise the issue of establishing standards of decency across national and cultural boundaries.

We were interested in the extent to which legal norms from the outside have been considered by governments and the legal profession. We asked respondents specifically to comment on the extent to which norms from international conventions have been adopted.[25]

As shown in Table 8.1, the average score for this indicator is high in relation to others in this arena and to the averages for each arena. This may reflect the fact that respondents were asked to comment on something that is in most countries not controversial. To be sure, there are countries where attempts to incorporate international legal norms created a political storm, but our study indicates such is not the case in any country included here. Even Togo scores high, reflecting the fact that the public has learned more about human rights as political opposition and organizations in civil society battled the autocratic administration. Thus one explanation for the high score here as in other countries is that respondents see the internalization of international legal norms as being confined not only to governments but also to other groups in society, whether activist or professional.

Our respondents are critical of governments. One Indian respondent noted that the government is quick to sign conventions but slow to ratify them and even slower to implement them. Similar comments were made by respondents in Argentina, China, Indonesia, Kyrgyzstan, Peru, and Togo.

Another observation of interest is that respondents were aware that Western governments and international NGOs pressure governments to sign and ratify human rights agreements. Some approve; others see it as a form of neocolonialism. There seems to be broad agreement that foreign governments and NGOs can merely support changes; actual changes must come from within. The encouraging thing is how much respondents acknowledge the progress made by organizations in this field outside government.

### Flexibility

Formal judicial institutions are not the only mechanisms for resolving conflict. Nonjudicial institutions and processes that participate in the administration of justice are also important. The ability to accommodate such institutions is a measure of institutional flexibility that often matters in governance. They have their own rules and are important in the wider national context. It is no surprise that respondents indicated that these institutions and processes are important. Ratings were generally high. Nonjudicial and nonformal mechanisms are typically found at the local level and usually involve civil rather than criminal cases. Examples of such institutions are courts of elders in Kyrgyzstan, tribal mediation processes in the Philippines and Tanzania, traditional chiefs in Togo, and religious groups in Thailand. In other countries, reference was made to the existence of village mediation systems. We were also informed that NGOs sometimes performed the role of resolving local conflicts. Thus there is a variety of institutions and processes in place. It may be important to point out that such institutions have developed in former communist countries.

This is another indicator where the scoring is flat (i.e., the difference between top and bottom is not large). The average is on the high side, although not markedly. The figures we have for the indicator tend to underline what has been stated above: nonjudicial mechanisms are important in every country included in the study. The reasons vary, but they are often preferred because they are less costly and because local parties to the conflict are familiar with the procedures. Another reason is the corrupt nature of the judicial system. People avoid formal courts because they do not trust them. It is clear from comments we received in China and Russia that nonformal mechanisms are not always a blessing. They tend to be biased against women, and there is room for corruption and violence. For instance, honor killings of women were mentioned as problematic in Jordan and Pakistan.

Nonformal mechanisms seem to exist because they fill a void left by formal courts. There is no evidence that they are in decline. In fact, in India, the country coordinator notes that these institutions are necessary and thus promoted by organizations working with rural and urban poor. Any effort to assess the state of governance in a country has good reason to include nonformal mechanisms for resolving conflict.

## Implications for Research and Practice

The judicial arena is problematic in virtually all countries included in our survey. Access to justice remains low and interest in improving national legal systems by incorporating norms from outside is similarly faint. And the reasons for the weakness of the judicial system are worrisome. Administration of justice is slow and often corrupt. People lack trust in the court system. Moreover, the problems may be pronounced in former communist countries, including China, because of the pace and extent of economic and political reforms. Laws are often outdated and create problems for the transformation of these regimes.

Turning to implications for research, there is still a need for more and better data. This applies to nonformal institutions and processes and to the performance of formal courts and other institutions. Compared to data availability in other arenas, the situation in the judicial arena is problematic.

Issues of justice are important to people. Much of what is going on in the judicial arena has an intrinsic value to people. Thus it is not enough to look at the legal system merely in instrumental terms (e.g., how it contributes to socioeconomic development). Our survey has made it clear that a fair way to administer justice is not just a means but also an end in itself.

We still know very little about how different legal systems work. Although many of the problems that the WGS identified seem to cut across systems, there may be reason to follow up the work of Ole Norgaard and Karin Hilmer Pedersen[26] on how legal systems relate to democracy and development. Does the legacy of a civil or common law system make a difference? Do mixed systems pose more problems than those that are pure? Our survey suggests that further research would be important and rewarding.

Then there is the relationship of the judicial arena to other governance arenas. Our survey shows that the executive branch often interferes in the affairs of the judiciary. Especially intriguing is the relationship to civil society and the prevalence of nonformal, often community-based institutions that play an important role in resolving conflicts at the local level. This is a complementary function, although it may also be conflicting, as local justice administration by nonformal institutions is not always sufficient or satisfactory.

Finally, the judicial arena is important, but the way it functions is not very satisfactory. Although some of these problems may be addressed through capacity-building, it is clear that they are more political than technical in nature. Our survey points to many cases of political interference, lack of accountability, and widespread corruption. Respondents have repeatedly drawn attention to the fact that connections matter and money buys justice.

We do not suggest that the international donor community should stop funding work in the judicial arena, but we do agree that aid to this arena has not been very effective to date: "After more than ten years and hundreds of millions of dollars in aid, many judicial systems in Latin America still function poorly . . . Russia is probably the single largest recipient of such aid, but is not even clearly moving in the right direction."[27] Our study confirms that judicial reform typically takes longer than donors allow for their project support. A revision of the time horizon for supporting reform may be the first step.

Finally, there is virtue in flexibility and sensitivity to context. Improvement in governance practices is possible not only with the help of a liberal paradigm but also with reforms of existing institutions. We also found that informal institutions sometimes are more suitable than formal ones. As Frank Upham[28] has noted, putting all the eggs in the formal basket is often misguided, yet it is the preferred practice in the World Bank and many other donor agencies. The point is that there is no single formula for fair administration of justice.

## Notes

1. The earliest Anglo-Saxon legal compilation was the Laws of Ethelbert, ruler of Kent, who had married a Christian and had himself been converted to Christianity by one the Pope's own emissaries, Augustine. See Harold J. Berman, *Law and Revolution: The Formation of the Western Legal Tradition* (Cambridge, MA: Harvard University Press, 1983), p. 54.

2. For more detail, see Max Rheinstein (ed.), *Max Weber on Law in Economy and Society* (Cambridge MA: Harvard University Press, 1966).

3. Berman, *Law and Revolution*, pp. 54ff.

4. Lon L. Fuller, *The Morality of Law*, 2nd ed (New Haven, CT: Yale University Press, 1964), p. 106.

5. See: Julio Faundez, (ed.), *Good Government and the Rule of Law* (London: Macmillan, 1997), p. 1

6. David M. Trubek and Marc Galanter, "Scholars in Self-Estrangement: Some Reflections on the Crisis in Law and Development Studies in the United States," *Wisconsin Law Review* (1974): 1062.

7. Thomas Carothers, "The Rule of Law Revival," *Foreign Affairs* 77, no. 2 (1998): 95.

8. J. Rawls, *A Theory of Justice* (Cambridge, MA: Harvard University Press, 1972), p. 235

9. Margaret Janet Radin, "Reconsidering the Rule of Law," *Boston Law Review* 69, no. 4 (July 1989): 787.

10. Amartya Sen, "What Is the Role of Legal And Judicial Reform in the Development Process?" *World Bank Legal Conference*, Washington, DC, June 5, 2000, p. 11

11. D. Narayan, R. Patel, K. Schafft, A. Rademacher, and S. Koch-Schulte, *Voices of the Poor: Can Anyone Hear Us?* (Washington, DC: World Bank, 2000).

12. Quoted in R. Messick, "Judicial Reform and Economic Development: A Survey of the Issues," *The World Bank Research Observer* 14, no. 1 (February 1999): 117–136.

13. World Bank, *World Development Report 2002: Building Institutions for Markets* (Washington, DC: World Bank, 2003).

14. Arne Bigsten et al., "Contract Facilities and Dispute Resolution," *Journal of Development Studies* 36, no. 4 (2000): 1–37.

15. Rafael La Porta, Florencio Lopez-de-Silanes, Andrei Shleifer, and Robert W. Vishny "Legal Determinants of External Finance," *Journal of Finance* 52, no. 3 (1997): 1131–1150.

16. J. Hewko, "Foreign Direct Investment: Does the Rule of Law Matter?" *Rule of Law Series Working Paper* (Washington, DC: Carnegie Endowment for International Peace, 2002).

17. Stephen Golub and Kim McQuay, "Legal Empowerment: Advancing Good Governance and Poverty Reduction," in *Law and Policy Reform at the Asian Development Bank* (Manila: Asian Development Bank, 2001).

18. Michael Anderson, "Getting Rights Right," *id21 Insights,* no. 43 (Falmer, Sussex, UK: Institute of Development Studies, September 2002).

19. Ole Norgaard and Karin Hilmer Pedersen, "Development, Law, and Democracy: Exploring a New Relationship," in G. Hyden and O. Elgstrom, eds., *Development and Democracy: What Have We Learnt and How?* (London: Routledge, 2002), pp. 87–105.

20. Lawrence Solum, "Equity and the Rule of Law," in Ian Shapiro, ed., *The Rule of Law* (New York University Press, 1994), pp. 120–148.

21. Michael S. Moore, "A Natural Law Theory of Interpretation," *Southern California Law Review* 58 (1985): 277–398. Carothers, "The Rule of Law Revival," p. 164.

22. World Bank, *World Development Report 2002*, pp. 118–119.

23. Anderson, "Getting Rights Right."

24. See a well written portrait and biography of Justice Nyalali by Jennifer A. Widner, *Building the Rule of Law* (New York: W.W. Norton, 2001).

25. Our question did not make a distinction between signing and ratifying an international treaty, even less the extent to which legal norms taken from international treaties had been implemented. We recognize, therefore, that *adoption* left our respondents a little confused as to what the question implied. Several respondents, however, made an effort to clarify their rating by commenting on the fact that their government had often signed a treaty but done little to live up to its aspirations.

26. Norgaard and Hilmer Pedersen, "Development, Law, and Democracy."

27. Carothers, "The Rule of Law Revival," p. 104.

28. This point was made by Upham at a roundtable organized by the Carnegie Endowment for International Peace in 2002.

# 9

# Conclusions

The previous chapters lead to important questions that we have saved for this concluding assessment regarding the methods and findings of the World Governance Survey. Given the limited number of countries and data, we are cautious in drawing far-reaching and overly specific conclusions. As indicated from the beginning, the purpose has been to test the extent to which governance can be meaningfully measured in ways that add to other governance surveys and studies of democratization. First we discuss lessons learned.

Second we consider what our study says about governance and its relation to democracy and studies of democratization. We began this project without defining what the relation is; we preferred to inductively find out. It is time to clarify how governance and democracy relate.

The third issue we address is more practical: whether we can meaningfully identify the weak spots in the governance realm. As we suggested in previous chapters, some arenas score lower than others. What does that tell us? And what are the implications? Even within each arena there are differences, and scores on some indicators are lower, some higher. We would like to discuss the extent to which there are patterns of special interest for future research and identify issues that may become concerns for consultants and practitioners in the field of governance.

Throughout this study we asked ourselves a question: What is the relationship between the different arenas? We have treated them equally in weight assigned to the indicators, but judging from our results, is it possible to say that some arenas are more crucial for improving governance than others? More specifically, we consider whether any arenas serve as a driving force. These questions have a bearing on research hypotheses for future studies, as well as on how to plan practical ways to improve governance.

We conclude by returning to the beginning. Chapter 1 started with an overview of how governance fits into the international development debate.

It is appropriate that we discuss what this study tells us about the relationship between governance and development. That discussion gives us an opportunity to stage a concluding review of the implications for future research and practice in the governance field.

## Making Sense of Governance

Our study has shown that a focus on governance yields insights that are interesting to scholars and practitioners alike. Design issues are of critical importance. We like to discuss the most important ones here.

We began with the ambition of doing a worldwide study—hence the title of the project. We soon realized that this ambition must remain a long-term goal. We had to settle for a much smaller number of countries—twenty-two in which the survey was initially conducted. We confined ourselves to developing regions, although one industrialized country—a member of the OECD—was included: South Korea. One of the shortcomings we acknowledge is that the sample is small and that countries were not chosen on a scientific basis. We selected countries more pragmatically, responding to opportunities such as funding interest within the United Nations Development Programme, one of the two principal supporters, and the availability of interested academic collaborators. This flaw is not lethal; it is obvious that in any second phase of study the countries could be chosen on more scientific grounds.

Although we did not haggle much over the political-process framework we adopted (we did have long discussions about how much it was system as opposed to process that we wanted to study), the choice of indicators proved time-consuming. In retrospect, we believe that our choice of five general indicators is still correct. It yields interesting information, but we conclude that the choice of indicators and how they relate to the six principles could have been more systematic. There wasn't always the best fit that we had sought. The test of our instrument has suggested that this is a problem that can be fixed. We provide our own revised version of the instrument to indicate what we have concluded. It contains six indicators per arena, an expansion from thirty to thirty-six. All indicators are more consistently accommodated within the six-principle framework. The revised framework is shown in Table 9.1.

Even this version is not cast in stone; based on our research it is a more effective means of making sense of governance and obtaining measures that relate to real-world issues.

As for the choice of respondents, we decided to seek the well-informed who had an understanding of governance issues at the national and international levels. We wish to emphasize that this is not a public opinion survey;

**Table 9.1 Revised Governance Framework with Six Indicators per Arena**

| Principle/ Arena | Participation | Fairness | Decency | Accountability | Transparency | Efficiency |
|---|---|---|---|---|---|---|
| Civil society | Freedom of association | Society free from discrimination | Freedom of expression | Respect for governing rules | Freedom of the media | Input in policymaking |
| Political society | Legislature representative of society | Policy reflective of public preferences | Peaceful competition for political power | Legislators accountable to public | Transparency of political parties | Legislative function affecting policy |
| Government | Intragovernmental consultation | Adequate standard of living for citizens | Personal security of citizens | Security forces subordinated to civilian government | Government provides accurate information | Best use of available resources |
| Bureaucracy | Higher civil servants part of policymaking | Equal access to public services | Civil servants respectful toward citizens | Civil servants accountable for their actions | Clear decisionmaking process | Merit-based system for recruitment |
| Economic society | Consultation with the private sector | Regulations equally applied to all firms | Government respects property rights | Regulating private sector in the public interest | Transparency in formulating economic policy | Obtaining licenses free from corruption |
| Judiciary | Nonformal processes of conflict resolution | Equal access to justice for all citizens | International human rights incorporated in national legal practice | Judicial officers held accountable | Clarity in administering justice | Efficiency of the judicial system |

such an instrument is neither necessary nor justified in order to obtain governance measures. We are not asking for individual preferences but informed opinions about complex issues. That is why we placed a premium on obtaining not only a rating on each indicator but also qualitative information to complement the numerical score. In any future study along these lines, the importance of such complementarity in the data must be stressed.

Another issue we faced was how respondents were selected in each country. We left this to our country coordinators to decide. We should have given more definite instructions, because we found in the end that we did not always get the balance needed among those associated with the state versus other spheres of society. Thus no less than six countries had to be thrown out for inadequacy of numbers of respondents or selection bias in the samples. We believe that even in countries where sampling is difficult because of lack of civil administration data, sampling lists for choosing members of each category of well-informed persons can be made up, however elementary such an exercise would be. Together with a larger number of respondents for each country, the database for studying governance in the future can be strengthened and the analysis made more extensive.

Studying governance can be done in ways that are methodologically feasible and interesting. The basis for reaching stronger substantive conclusions can be improved, but this first step is an encouraging start. It is in that perspective that we discuss the more important and interesting conclusions to draw about the usefulness of applying a governance perspective to the study of development.

## Governance, Democracy, and Development

This study is inductively designed but deductively driven. Given that this is a first attempt to use governance for analytical purposes rather than as a heuristic device for programming specific governance interventions, there is inevitably an exploratory component. Yet it has an underlying theoretical base in a political-process approach. We consistently treated governance as applicable to a political process with inputs and outputs. Our findings relate to the nature of this process, the assumption being that the extent to which rules-in-use are perceived as legitimate matters in two ways: as determinant of *policymaking* and *regime stability*.

Our study tried to strike a balance between theory and practice. We realize that governance is a practical political activity. It is voluntarist in the sense that it involves human choices. In assessing what choices were made and how, we relied on a set of general principles rather than a particular model of democracy or governance. We as much as possible avoided an explicitly normative model in favor of a more empirical—and realistic—

approach to governance. Compared to most other efforts measuring governance we avoided being prescriptive or interventionist in the sense of claiming that one particular rule fits all countries. This doesn't mean that we lost all sense of what is good governance. We provided a set of principles that the vast majority of human beings can agree upon regardless of cultural and national origins. To be sure, political actors end up prioritizing some more than others at particular times. How well they reconcile the possible tensions and conflicts between these principles is reflected in the perceived quality of governance.

Such principles provided the opportunity to apply our survey cross-nationally while acknowledging the importance of national context. The various acts of governance are evaluated not so much in comparison to actors and actions in other countries but in relation to the country's own past. For instance, in our sample Indonesia and Peru recorded significant improvement in governance between 1995 and 2000 because regime changes responded to concerns that citizens had expressed about violation of certain key rules by their governments. Similarly, as discussed in Chapter 2, the Philippines suffered a significant decline in governance quality because of the corrupt nature of the Estrada administration in the late 1990s. These and other cases raise the issue of the relationship among governance, democracy, and development.

Governance and democracy do not measure the same thing. We have maintained throughout that governance measures a broader set of phenomena than democracy does. *Governance* refers to the creation and maintenance of a system of rules that govern the public arena and thus regulate how state, civil society, and market-based actors relate to and interact with each other. In this respect, our measure of governance is thicker and broader than what is typically assessed in studies of democratization, where a minimalist definition of the concept of democracy is preferred. We believe that the relationship between politics and development is better served by this conceptualization; as this study demonstrates, development is not necessarily most effectively achieved by imitating a liberal democratic model.

We can draw interrelated conclusions that are relevant to this point. The first is that rules-in-use vary from country to country as well as from time to time. These rules are historically embedded and are not easily changed. This so-called path dependency observation means that respondents assess rules in terms of not only regime quality but also regime stability. People learn to live with rules even if the rules are not optimal from the individual or group point of view. The second conclusion is that by asking respondents about changes over time we capture another important aspect that is typically overlooked in other indices: the notion that the state of governance changes in response to specific events. The legitimacy of specific rules changes up and down over time, creating opportunities and constraints for political actors. In this respect, the study of governance provides insights into what the opportunities and limitations are for consolidating democracy.

These points are important for understanding the differences that exist between our governance scores, on the one hand, and the Freedom House Index, one of the most frequently used measures of democracy, on the other. The comparison is contained in Table 9.2 below. The left column shows the governance score for the country included in our study with the highest listed at the top of the table, the lowest at the bottom of it. The right column indicates the country's designation in terms of democraticness— *free, partly free,* or *not free.*

As expected, there is variation between the two indices.[1] Not all high-scoring governance countries are also the most democratic, although the latter tend to congregate at the top of our table. Argentina and the Philippines, both of which are among the more democratic in our sample, do not fare particularly well in governance terms. In Argentina, it may be primarily because the rules affecting certain arenas are perceived as being contrary to prevailing principles about transparency and fairness. In the Philippines, the reason seems to be first of all a lack of respect for existing rules.

So what can we say about the relationship between governance, democracy, and development, drawing on the findings of this study? There is an overlap, but we argue that governance is a prerequisite for democracy and development. The empirical research that we have done shows that

**Table 9.2  Comparison of WGS Country Scores with Freedom House Designations, 2000**

| Country | WGS Score | FHI Country Designation |
|---------|-----------|-------------------------|
| Thailand | 100 | Free |
| Chile | 99 | Free |
| India | 98 | Free |
| Jordan | 97.5 | Partly free |
| Tanzania | 91 | Partly free |
| Mongolia | 86 | Partly free |
| Argentina | 83 | Free |
| Bulgaria | 83 | Free |
| China | 82 | Not free |
| Peru | 82 | Partly free |
| Indonesia | 80 | Partly free |
| Kyrgyzstan | 75 | Not free |
| Philippines | 75 | Free |
| Russia | 73 | Partly free |
| Pakistan | 65 | Not free |
| Togo | 62.5 | Partly free |

development stagnation and obstacles to democratization stem from a failure to undertake the necessary steps for establishing a system of rules that legitimate political choices and political behavior. In short, the elements of good governance provide opportunities for democratization and development in a more sustainable fashion. In this respect, getting politics right means a set of normative and institutional changes that transcend the liberal democratic model. It also asks for more than the neoclassical economic model of development typically is concerned about. These conclusions are important for researchers and practitioners alike. They indicate that rules-in-use are inevitably embedded in specific temporal and sociocultural contexts that we cannot ignore if our ambition is to study how state-society relations affect democracy and development. They also tell us that there is more than one path to democracy. Societies tend to prioritize different rules at different times, hence the variation that we find between governance and democracy scores. In this study, China, Jordan, and Thailand are examples of countries where development has been driven by an emphasis on rules that are not identical to those associated with liberal democracy. The Thai case suggests that once the emphasis is laid on rules that promote development there is a tendency for this to gradually spread to the whole spectrum of governance rules. It is for this reason that we are ready to conclude that good governance—in the long run—lays the foundation for a liberal form of democracy.

## The Weak Governance Spots

Because we take a holistic approach to governance—examining each arena/dimension of the political process—we also have a better view of the relative strength and weakness of the various parts. It is inevitable that some parts function better than others, that rules are easier to sustain in some arenas than others. The reverse is also true. If rules that build on any one of the key governance principles we have identified are violated or ignored, the costs and consequences are likely to be higher in some arenas than in others.

The most dramatic events between 1995 and 2000 that happened in countries included in our study were the military coup in Pakistan that brought President Musharaf to power, President Suharto's forced resignation in Indonesia, the degradation of the Estrada administration in the Philippines, and the rapidly growing opposition to the arbitrary and corrupt nature of President Fujimori's government in Peru. These events make a significant dent in the ratings by respondents in these countries, but in no instance did the political regime collapse completely. To be sure, there was street violence in several places, but nowhere did a real transformation of politics take place. This suggests two things. One is that regimes are more durable than is often assumed. Another is that some spots within the regime are weaker than others. These issues we explore here.

We begin by examining the six arenas to see if some can be declared more vulnerable than others. If we go by the average scores per arena, they come out as indicated in Table 9.3.

Even if there has been improvement in each arena from 1995 to 2000, it is clear that the six arenas fall into two distinct categories. *Civil society*, *government*, and *economic society* have scores considerably above the other three. *Political society*, *bureaucracy*, and *judiciary* stand out as the more problematic governance arenas. What does this tell us?

Rules are more politically visible in some arenas than others; a violation in one place doesn't necessarily have the same consequences in another. Based on our study, we conclude—and present as a hypothesis for further research—that the political costs of ignoring and violating rules are higher in arenas where adherence to formal rules is especially important for assessing governance. Our research has confirmed over and over the major governance problem is that formal rules are replaced by informal practices that undermine the credibility of those rules. For instance, elections are not held in a free and fair manner; government officials are not hired or promoted based on merit criteria; judicial officers, including judges, are not immune to bribery; and so on. In all these cases, there is a violation of multiple principles of governance, notably fairness, transparency, and accountability. Softness in adherence to the rules that govern public institutions such as elections, civil service, and judiciary thus tends to have a more dramatic effect on the overall governance assessment than other indicators less directly dependent on the extent to which specific rules are followed.

The other three arenas—civil society, government, and economic society—are all dependent on flexibility and the freedom granted to individuals. Members of voluntary associations want—and need—freedom of assembly; cabinet ministers want flexibility to negotiate and make policy of their choice; and people in business like less rather than more regulation.

**Table 9.3    Summed Up Score Per Governance Arena, 1995 and 2000**

| Governance Arena | 1995 | 2000 |
|---|---|---|
| Civil society | 233 | 242 |
| Political society | 200 | 209 |
| Government | 226 | 231 |
| Bureaucracy | 205.5 | 214 |
| Economic society | 220 | 233.5 |
| Judiciary | 197 | 214 |

As we shall see below, there may be threshold rules that apply also to these arenas, but by and large an assessment of governance is less dependent on strict rule adherence. This does not mean that chaos and anarchy can be allowed in these arenas, but as long as they function reasonably well—and help produce results—the ratings here are not going to be adversely affected in the same way as in the other three arenas.

What we have are two distinct governance challenges. One deals with rule adherence, the other with rule design. Both are important and need to be evaluated in any study of governance. In an era of liberalization and democratization, the issue of design—or redesign—may not be as acute as the issue of adherence, although the case of China, Pakistan, and Togo indicate that the former remains high on the governance agenda in some countries. The principal challenge is the institutionalization of rules (i.e., getting actors to take them seriously and not ignore or violate them). The weak numbers in the governance equation are most immediately related to this set of issues.

This leads us to ask whether some indicators in each arena are conditional for satisfactory and good performance. In other words, is there a threshold that countries must pass in order to make further progress in the governance realm? We believe that there is. Each arena has at least one indicator on which others are in part contingent. Drawing on our findings, we propose that several indicators are foundational for each governance arena (see Table 9.4).

These key indicators fall largely under the rubric of rule of law, confirming that it is critical to good governance. But governance is more than mere adherence to specific rules. The question thus arises whether in any future study of governance, indicators should be weighted differently or, even more radically, should only foundational indicators be included.

Apart from the added technical difficulty of assessing indicators weighted differently, there is the question whether on substantive grounds it is justified. We believe that because each arena contains a range of other governance challenges, it would be wrong to focus on these key indicators

**Table 9.4  Foundational Indicators for Each Governance Arena**

| Arena | Indicator |
| --- | --- |
| Civil society | Freedom of expression; freedom of assembly |
| Political society | Free and fair elections |
| Government | Civil-military relations |
| Bureaucracy | Meritocracy |
| Economic society | Absence of corruption |
| Judiciary | Impartial judgment |

alone, even if using varying weights. Civil society rules have a significant impact on how individual citizens are socialized into politics and how citizens relate to political society. The way the latter is constituted has a bearing on elections as well as the operations of party systems and legislatures. A government must be assessed in terms of how well rules help it achieve security and welfare for citizens. A bureaucracy must be assessed in terms of how well it delivers and how accessible it is to members of the public. Economic society relies on many other rules (e.g., those pertaining to property and consultation). The judiciary faces other challenges than just fair judgment, such as access to justice and the existence of alternative mechanisms for conflict resolution. In short, we are convinced that a broader set of variables is needed to provide a balanced assessment of each arena.

Governance skills in each arena rely on more than the ability to handle a small number of key issues. Once they are taken care of, the real challenges lie elsewhere. That is why there is a need for a broader range of variables. We agree with Sylvia Chan, who writes with reference to liberal democracy that "because theories have generally assumed a unitary product, 'liberal democracy,' they have not theorized adequately about how the processes involved in institutionalizing the 'liberal' part may react with that of the 'democratic' part, and how these in turn are related to other important issues for these countries, for example, economic development."[2] There is more tension between different aspects of democracy than theories focusing on democratization imply, and there is more to the relationship between governance and development than what is captured by these theories alone.

## Is There a Driving Force?

Does our analysis of governance provide us with a set of policy recommendations about what should be done to improve governance practices? More specifically, is there one arena, or a set of indicators, that may be identified as having the ability to influence others? This is of special interest to those who fund governance or work practically with governance issues.

Before we try to answer these questions, it is important to remember that governance is a voluntarist activity. It reflects choices that actors make in the governance realm. How they make decisions depends on circumstances, some economic and cultural, others political. We do not imply that countries are captives of their historical past to such an extent that they cannot change, but we do reject the notion that they are clean slates. For instance, bilateral agencies in the international development community operate on the assumption that what is acceptable to their respective domestic political constituency should also be the prescriptive devices implemented in the field. The result is that many developing countries are recipients of advice on how to improve governance that has little to do with their political realities but is still being peddled because it is part of donor priorities and their wish to demonstrate success.

There are many problems with this approach. It is ethnocentric. It also ignores local preferences and possibilities. And it is not easily sustainable. There is no doubt that a more fine-tuned and responsive approach to the task of improving governance is needed. The first step is to improve the analysis that goes into policymaking on these issues.

Some countries recorded substantial improvements or declines due to single events that affected the governance climate. The change of government in Indonesia in the late 1990s is one such example. The serious deterioration of government performance during the same period in Peru and the Philippines are other cases in point. These and similar examples show the importance of disjunctures that create the conditions for change in rules. They are what students of social movements refer to as shifts in the political opportunity structure.[3] Such shifts apply also more broadly to governance as public opinion changes and thus create possibilities for new governance initiatives.

Some scholars see this as a honeymoon, based on the assumption that political actors who have just come to power enjoy a grace period during the first few months in office. Some discuss this thesis with reference to middle-income countries in Asia and Latin America that were undergoing economic reform in the 1990s.[4] The point is that during the honeymoon period interests associated with the old regime are discredited and disorganized, providing an opportunity for reform that would not otherwise arise.[5] In the longer run the opportunity structure closes, as reformers must appeal to a broader spectrum of potential beneficiaries. Mette Kjaer has convincingly applied this thesis to her study of civil-service reform in Uganda and Tanzania in the 1990s, showing that a new broom (i.e., a new political leader) can make a difference—but only for a while.[6]

Structural conditions that typically shape what action may be considered are not frozen. They are malleable and sometimes change so dramatically that they leave new opportunities for action. Regimes can be changed with greater ease in such circumstances because governance measures enjoy a higher degree of legitimacy. Being able to seize such opportunities to introduce reforms that discredit previous rules is what typically helps enhance the quality of governance.

Donors and practitioners in the governance field are aware of this issue, but they do not always take the trouble to analyze the situation carefully enough to maximize its use. Instead they may rush into action supporting any actor that steps forward. Although this study confirms that opportunity structure is an important variable, we believe that with our holistic approach to governance we offer a more balanced, more clearheaded assessment of the opportunities and constraints in the governance realm as a whole. This way we acknowledge the importance of honeymoon mandates without falling victim to exaggerated optimism.

This leaves us with the question whether, in situations where radically different opportunities do not exist, there is a set of variables that constitutes the driving force behind efforts to improve governance. Our study suggests some issues of interest and relevance to practitioners. The first is that interest in governance is very much influenced by the way that the international community defines approaches to development. We suggested in Chapter 1 that governance has become a development concern because there is a belief that development is sustainable only if owned by local stakeholders, hence the recipe for a participatory approach to development. We also argued that those funding development embrace the notion that getting politics right is a prerequisite for development, hence the interest in good governance as a recipe for reform of macro structures.

Amartya Sen[7] has contributed to this new thinking with his idea of *development as freedom*. Studies of poverty carried out suggest that issues such as personal security, access to justice, and freedom to speak out—all significant governance concerns—are viewed by the poor as being as important as material well-being.[8] The Gallup Millennium Survey, which we cited in Chapter 1, confirmed that human rights are an important concern to ordinary people in developing and developed countries.[9] In short, there is a growing tendency to assume that promoting governance is not merely a means of accelerating development; it is actually the same as fostering development.

With this kind of thinking still prevailing in the international development community, more attention has recently been paid to nongovernmental rather than governmental institutions. Voluntary associations and private enterprises are treated as the most opportune targets for support by various development agencies. Providing incentives for private and voluntary organizations as well as helping them build capacity have become core components of donor policy. With so much both intellectual and material weight being placed on supporting nongovernmental actors, there is reason to assume that such organizations provide a relevant entry point for thinking about improvement in the governance realm. To be sure, many organizations are still weak, and many lack real roots in society. In the business sector, small and medium-sized businesses are often at a disadvantage in competition, as we saw in Chapter 7.

The most serious shortcoming of the civil society arena, however, is the almost complete absence of strong social movements. Civil society scores high because it enjoys freedom of expression and assembly, but, as we saw in Chapter 3, it does not have much policy influence. It doesn't connect to political society. The result is that its overall impact on the political process is small. The international development community cannot be the catalyst of social movements, but to the extent that it is interested in strengthening civil society actors, it should not hesitate to help boost their influence, even if that is controversial.

If civil society is the springboard for improving governance, the real challenges lie in other arenas, notably political society, bureaucracy, and the judiciary. The task here is institutionalization of norms that enhance the credibility of actors in those arenas. Most if not all countries already have legal provisions that prescribe (e.g., free and fair elections, merit for hiring in the civil service, and absolute integrity of judges and court officials). The problem is that while such norms exist on paper, officers do not always follow them in practice. We have shown that in all these arenas this is a major shortcoming. There is still far too much personal discretion in public office. Officeholders have yet to internalize the norms and principles that are enacted.

This is a different problem of institutionalization than the one that Samuel Huntington identified in his seminal work on the challenges of creating political order.[10] The issue in 1968 was that modernization and development rapidly raised popular expectations of what governments should be able to do for citizens. Huntington's thesis was that regimes would crumble because institutions are unable to cope with these demands. The challenge today may still be associated with inflated popular expectations, but not about government as distributor of benefits and resources; rather it is the extent to which it has integrity. The issue is not so much one of political economy—who gets what, when, how—as it is one of governance—what rules matter when and how.

A good number of international organizations recognize the significance of this challenge. For instance, Transparency International, headquartered in Berlin, works on issues related to transparency and accountability in government and in private corporations. It publishes the annual *Index of Perceptions of Corruption*. Since 2001, it has also published an anuual global corruption report in order to highlight issues of concern to the organization as well as substantive findings in different countries around the world.[11] The United Nations Development Programme and many bilateral donor agencies also work on issues of institutionalization.

Drawing on our own study, we believe that this thrust is appropriate. Institutionalization of norms that are compatible with credible conduct in public office is necessary for improving governance and regime stability. For instance, an increasingly cynical citizenry may rise against a government or withdraw from political involvement, allowing misconduct to perpetuate, possibly leading to a military takeover. Institutionalization of civic public norms that make sense in local contexts is part of bringing state and society into more productive exchanges and relationships; that is a more congenial atmosphere for national development.

At the same time, we have reservations about the way this objective is pursued by international organizations. The most important is that it is driven from the outside. These organizations have their own program mandates, some tantamount to a mission. Iraq after the fall of Saddam Hussein is the best example. Although such enthusiasm for the cause may sometimes produce results, it also tends to be antagonistic. For instance, an international consultant or adviser can come across as too abrasive or arrogant. Much of the work backfires or fizzles out once the consultant leaves. The more technical approach that others prefer also has problems. It assumes that governance can be improved by professionally conducted capacity-building workshops or similar mechanisms. Although we have no doubt that individuals participating learn a lot, applying new insights usually proves difficult, if not impossible, because the real-world context is very different from the learning environment. We came across several references to the problems of implementing governance reforms that were initiated with the help of outside agencies.

Another problem with the approach of many agencies is how they collect data. Organizations that cater to the business community tend to rely almost exclusively on subjective perceptions or panels of outside experts. There is little or no effort to incorporate the views of local actors from the country being assessed. We consider this to be a serious shortcoming, especially since assessments by outsiders are being used to rate and rank countries for quality of governance. The consumers of these assessments rarely understand the skewed nature of the data. This bias in reporting encouraged us to carry out the World Governance Survey using a cross section of well-informed persons from each country. We feel increasingly confident in this approach now that we have seen the results of the first phase.

So is there a force driving efforts to improve governance? In an international climate in which participation and ownership of development activities are still considered primary objectives, *civil society* comes closest. But the study has demonstrated that civil society's potential is far from fully tapped. Any push by civil society actors, however, would amount to little without a more effective institutionalization of norms associated with conduct in public office. Political society, bureaucracy, and judiciary are the keys; economic society is also important, as market-based actors interact with government officials and other representatives of the state. Government, in terms of its overall responsibility for national development, is dependent on the governance quality in the other arenas. It obviously has the potential to influence, but our study suggests that even so its influence is limited.

## Implications for Future
## Governance Research and Practice

In terms of future research, we see the benefit of focusing on governance, as broadly defined in this study, as a way to generate new hypotheses that address issues that tend to be ignored by those who focus primarily on democratic transition and consolidation. The lines between authoritarianism and democracy have become blurred, and it is not clear that we are really capturing the interesting and important things in these countries if we are too preoccupied with fitting them into an increasing number of diminished subtypes of democracy. Assessing quality of governance would allow for a new cut and provide a baseline from a set of indicators less directly tied to a particular model like liberal democracy. In this study we made a threefold distinction between high-, medium-, and low-scoring countries. We also used a delineation among these three categories that allowed us to get roughly the same number in each group. In any future study along the same lines it would be preferable to use a more general scale of differentiation. For instance, using the thirty indicators with a 5-point scale, we would recommend the division as illustrated in Table 9.5.

This scale would have reclassified many of the countries included in this study, but we are ready to recommend a scale along these lines to provide a basis for future comparisons of a larger sample of countries, including possibly those that are already supposed to be well-governed.

One of the few things that students of comparative politics tend to agree upon is that democratic (but not necessarily democratizing) countries do not fight each other.[12] There is much less agreement about the extent to which democracy also promotes development. A major reason is that both concepts are broad and include many dimensions. Depending on which combination of dimensions is used, the answer tends to vary. For instance,

**Table 9.5  Proposed Scale for Identifying Quality of Governance**

| Level of Governance Quality | Points on a Scale of 150 |
| --- | --- |
| Very high | 121–150 |
| High | 101–120 |
| Medium | 86–100 |
| Low | 66–85 |
| Very low | 30–65 |

*Note:* We have deliberately made the top and bottom categories wider because there is a tendency in each assessment of this kind to avoid the very highest and lowest scores unless something quite outstanding motivates it.

researchers continue to argue whether it is the level of economic development, the pace of economic growth, or the direction of economic performance that correlates most strongly with democracy. Similarly, there is lack
of consensus on the issue whether the causal link runs from development to
democracy, or vice versa.

Our study confirms the conclusion reached by others that the quality of
political regime is not related to levels of economic growth.[13] As the figures in Table 9.6 show, average GDP growth for 1999-2001 is not necessarily highest among the countries that score high on governance in our survey. Similarly, the low-scoring countries in our study do not all have lower
levels of economic growth.

We need to exercise caution in assuming that the causal connection
between governance and development is unilinear in that direction. We are
so inclined partly because of the methodological limitations of our own
study, partly because our study highlighted the extent to which governance
is contextually determined. The differences in scores among the sixteen
WGS countries are better explained by factors that are specific to each
rather than by objective indicators such as growth in GDP, quality of
human development, or level of economic growth.[14] We disagree, therefore, that regime does not matter in explaining growth and development.

**Table 9.6  WGS Governance Scores and Various Development Indicators**

| Country | WGS Score | GDP per capita, 2000 (PPP U.S.$) | HDI, 2000[a] | Average GDP Growth, 1999-2001[b] |
|---|---|---|---|---|
| Thailand | 100 | 6,402 | 0.762 | 3.71 |
| Chile | 99 | 9,417 | 0.831 | 2.38 |
| India | 98 | 2,358 | 0.577 | 5.17 |
| Jordan | 97.5 | 3,966 | 0.717 | 3.77 |
| Tanzania | 91 | 523 | 0.440 | 4.40 |
| Mongolia | 86 | 1,783 | 0.655 | 1.91 |
| Bulgaria | 83 | 5,710 | 0.779 | 4.23 |
| Argentina | 83 | 12,377 | 0.844 | -2.54 |
| China | 82 | 3,976 | 0.726 | 7.43 |
| Peru | 82 | 4,799 | 0.747 | 1.43 |
| Indonesia | 80 | 3,043 | 0.684 | 3.00 |
| Philippines | 75 | 3,971 | 0.754 | 3.60 |
| Kyrgyzstan | 75 | 2,711 | 0.712 | 4.80 |
| Russia | 73 | 8,377 | 0.781 | 6.47 |
| Pakistan | 65 | 1,928 | 0.499 | 3.83 |
| Togo | 62.5 | 1,442 | 0.493 | 1.06 |

*Sources:* a. Human Development Index issued by the United Nations Development
Programme.
   b. Calculated from data provided by the annual World Development Reports issued by the
World Bank.

We believe that it does—but it depends on how the concept is disaggregated. Our use of regime in the context of governance suggests its potential usefulness.

Although we applaud the development of better governance indicators at the World Bank,[15] margins of error are still considerable in the aggregate data set used. That research confirms how data based on subjective perceptions are more relevant and at least as reliable as objective sources. Yet that approach to data collection and analysis is not the only one. As Daniel Kaufmann himself expressed in May 2003: "No one has [a] monopoly on data in this business."

Our study has drawn on two sources of data: survey ratings and personal comments provided by the respondents, as well as insightful commentary and analysis by the country coordinators. Thus our study draws on quantitative and qualitative sources of data, richer than the cross-sectional studies by the econometricians in the World Bank. Behind each score we have an interesting story line. We realize that there is much more that could have been said in the seven data chapters, but even with the limits we were forced to accept, we consider the WGS to be an important complement to the aggregate dataset produced by the World Bank.

This does not mean that what we have achieved thus far is good enough. We would like to extend our survey in a second phase to a larger number of countries, including countries belonging to the Organization for Economic Cooperation and Development. Our study has shown that good governance is not the privilege of the rich. It occurs in poorer countries. We are interested in comparing ratings from industrial societies to those in the developing world. Our assumption is that in a subjective-perceptions index like we have developed, there is room for interesting surprises. With an increased number of respondents per country, it would be possible to take the analysis of how governance relates to democracy and development a step farther.

We also believe in the value of specific case studies to highlight peculiarities in the aggregate data. There is no single path to democracy; it is important to acknowledge the contextual factors that determine each path. The example of the Asian financial crisis in 1997-1998 is a case in point, as is the economic crisis in Argentina in 2001. Poor implementation of the right policy is not an adequate explanation. Missing is a reference to the value of indigenous institutions and their own dynamics. We share the perspective of a group of Asian governance researchers who point to the value of seeing improved governance not merely as a result of adopting practices from the outside but as the product of strengthening already existing institutions.[16]

Although progress continues to be made in terms of quality of data on governance issues, the research community still has some way to go. Even with further improved data, it is necessary to be cautious in interpreting the relationship between governance and development. Good governance is a prerequisite for progress toward democracy and a sustainable form of development. Even so, we are unable to confirm to the interested policy-maker how exactly this relationship works in the context of specific development policy issues. More research in the future would help throw additional light.

The World Bank is issuing a warning in revealing the decline, not improvement, in governance.[17] This suggests that the very fundament on which democracy and development are being pursued is actually weakening, not growing stronger, as one would have expected given the amount of attention and resources devoted to governance. Future research, with the help of primary data, might probe how far this decline is on a global or regional scale and the associated factors.

## Summary

Having discussed the implications of this study, it may be helpful to reiterate the primary points that we make in this study.

The first is that *the concept of governance is meaningful for comparative studies of politics*. It can be operationalized in ways that make it a useful complement to existing concepts used in empirical assessment of political change. Furthermore, empirical work has taught us lessons that allow us to improve on how to use it in the future. In short, it has stood the test of feasibility.

The second is that *governance provides a broader and more diversified approach to the study of regime issues than the more narrow focus on democracy does*. It offers the opportunity to incorporate into the analysis of political change a larger set of variables that matter for a country's ability to develop, whether this is measured in political, social, or economic terms. By focusing on how state/society/market relations at large are constituted and managed, a governance approach provides data that are crucial for understanding the prospects both for democracy and development.

The third is that *by disaggregating the political process into six arenas and specifying an identical number of indicators for each arena, we have been able to highlight both strengths and weaknesses in existing regimes around the world*. We have also shown that a composite set of indicators from the six arenas suggests that good governance is not necessarily confined to countries with a liberal democratic regime. Good governance comes in different packages, and each has its own implications for the prospects for democracy and development.

The fourth is that *some arenas are perceived as weaker than others*.

Those where the question of adherence to rules is especially critical, like political society, bureaucracy, and judiciary, tend to be the most vulnerable. Others are given higher scores, at least in part because the assessment of rule adherence there tends to be more pragmatic. We conclude that *civil society appears to be the potential engine for improvement in governance*, but it requires that rules in political society, bureaucracy, and judiciary are also clear and taken seriously by concerned actors.

The fifth is that *studies of governance can be carried out effectively without relying on expensive public opinion polls*. We have shown that a cross section of well-informed persons drawn from different walks of life and sectors of society provides a solid base of information for understanding governance issues at the country level. How these respondents are selected matters, and improvement in sampling respondents should be an important aspect of any future governance research.

## Notes

1. One reason for this variation is methodological. Freedom House uses panels of outside experts who are being asked to rate countries according to the 7-point scale because they are knowledgeable about particular countries yet have no stake in scoring them in particular ways. The assumption is that this way, Freedom House can arrive at objective scores. The WGS index is the product of ratings provided by local respondents. The latter have a stake in the country's governance, but not all of them want to inflate the score. Others want to deflate it. Our respondents live with the quality of governance on a day-to-day basis; they do represent different walks of life and positions in society. For example, government officials and parliamentarians often have a higher appreciation of how the country is governed than well-informed persons in other elite categories. This way, we are able to arrive at an average score that represents both critics and supporters of the governance status quo.

2. Sylvia Chan, *Liberalism, Democracy, and Development* (Cambridge, UK: Cambridge University Press, 2002), p. 58.

3. See, e.g., Sidney Tarrow, *Power in Movement* (New York: Cambridge University Press, 1998), pp. 18–20.

4. Stephan Haggard and Robert R. Kaufman, *The Political Economy of Democratic Transitions* (Princeton, NJ: Princeton University Press, 1995).

5. Joan M. Nelson, *Intricate Links: Democratization and Market Reforms in Latin America and Eastern Europe* (New Brunswick: Transaction Publishers, 1994).

6. Mette Kjaer, *The Politics of Civil Service Reform: A Comparative Analysis of Uganda and Tanzania in the 1990s* (Aarhus, Denmark: Politica, 2002).

7. Amartya Sen, *Development as Freedom* (New York: Anchor Books, 1999).

8. See, e.g., D. Narayan, R. Patel, K. Schafft, A. Rademacher, and S. Koch-Schulte, *Voices of the Poor: Can Anyone Hear Us?* (Washington, DC: World Bank, 2000).

9. R. Sprogard and M. James, "Governance and Democracy: The People's View. A Global Opinion Poll," presented at the United Nations University's Millennium Conference, Tokyo, January 19–21, 2000.

10. Samuel P. Huntington, *Political Order in Changing Society* (New Haven, CT: Yale University Press, 1968).

11. The second such report was published in 2003; Transparency International, *Global Corruption Report 2003* (with special focus on access to information) (London: Profile Books, 2003).

12. Even on this issue, however, there is no absolute agreement. See, e.g., Errol Henderson, *Democracy and War: The End of an Illusion?* (Boulder, CO: Lynne Rienner Publishers, 2002).

13. Adam Przeworski and Fernando Limongi, "Political Regimes and Economic Growth," *Journal of Economic Perspectives* 7, no. 3 (1993): 51–69.

14. Acknowledging the limitations of our data, we did perform simple correlations, followed by bivariate and multivariate regressions, using the WGS score as the dependent variable. The results of our correlations and regressions were insignificant.

15. See, e.g., D. Kaufmann, A. Kraay, and P. Zoido-Lobaton, "Governance Matters," *Research Policy Working Paper No. 2196* (Washington, DC: World Bank, 1999); D. Kaufmann, A. Kraay, and P. Zoido-Lobaton, "Governance Matters II: Updated Indicators for 2000/01," *World Bank Policy Research Working Paper No. 2772* (Washington, DC: World Bank, 2002); and Daniel Kaufmann, Aart Kraay, and Massimo Mastruzzi, "Governance Matters III: Governance Indicators for 1996–2002," *Research Policy Working Paper* (Washington, DC: World Bank, May 2003).

16. Yasutami Shimomura (ed.), *The Role of Governance in Asia* (Singapore: Institute of Southeast Asian Studies Press, 2003)

17. Daniel Kaufmann, Aart Kraay, and Massimo Mostruzzi, "Governance Matters III: Governance Indicators for 1996–2002," *Research Policy Working Paper* (Washington, D.C.: World Bank (May 2003).

# Appendix 1:
# Data Collection and Analysis

## Data Collection Strategies

With our goal to collect systematic data on a comprehensive range of governance issues, we had several options. We considered using an international panel of experts or well-informed persons. This would have allowed us to generate data for cross-country comparisons, but it would have been a replication of what others, like the Freedom House, are already doing. We also wanted to avoid the major shortcomings with such panels, namely, their relative superficiality stemming from the coverage of a large number of countries within a limited time frame. We wanted to do something that others have not yet done: collect the opinions of people resident in the countries under consideration while at the same time come up with data for comparative purposes.

We also considered the possibility of conducting a public opinion survey. We rejected this approach, because pretesting had suggested that it was difficult to obtain meaningful and reliable responses from members of the public at large, many of whom lacked the kind of informative perspective that is necessary for participating in the World Governance Survey (WGS). We also realized that public opinion polls would be expensive and that in many countries we would run into problems of sampling.

We had plans to conduct focus-group discussions in three countries as a way of learning what type of data such an approach would generate. Unfortunately, in the end we have a very limited experience to draw from since data were submitted only from two countries—the Philippines and Barbados.[1] Nevertheless, a few things came out clearly, especially from the Philippine study. In terms of strengths, the approach can generate information about the background conditions that determine certain ratings. One obtains a much better sense of the independent variables that determine governance ratings. We used these insights to revise the WGS index, which we will apply in fifty countries in 2005. A second advantage: because a focus group is highly participatory, it has the potential of generating solutions to the problems identified by the group members. The focus group approach also has certain disadvantages that cannot be ignored. It is demanding and requires skilled coordinators. We are not sure that it would be possible to find such coordinators in many countries. Second, since the approach catalyzes collective integrated thinking, it makes individual ratings insignificant. Another drawback is that accuracy suffers, as some individuals may not feel comfortable to speak up in public. A third point is that although it generates more location-specific data, the focus-group approach yields less systematic results. For instance, in the Philippines study, there were marked differences between groups depending on social background and geographic location (e.g., Luzon versus Mindanao). Although we do not reject the idea that the focus-group approach may constitute a complementary approach to data collection, we decided on balance that it would not serve our purposes well. It simply would have left us with more questions than answers when it comes to assessing the data. Our assessment in this regard reflects the consensus view of most researchers (i.e., that focus groups are best used to identify issues and develop surveys rather than as the only source of data).

In the end, we opted for a survey aimed at interviewing a cross-section of well-informed persons (WIPs) in each country. These were individuals who are experienced in and informed about the governance realm. The premise of our approach was that they would be able to provide the most knowledgeable ratings about governance as well as qualitative comments to back up their assessments.

## Implementation of the Survey

The survey was conducted in late 2000 and early 2001 in twenty-two countries that can be described as developing or transitional societies.[2] A country coordinator was identified to implement the survey in each country. These coordinators were in some cases heads of local research and policy institutes working on governance and/or development issues, in others senior researchers located at local universities. The latter were mostly political scientists or economists. The country coordinators were paid U.S.$2,000–3,000 to deliver a minimum of thirty-five completed questionnaires and to prepare a report.[3]

The survey instrument was administered in eight different languages. Translation was done either at United Nations University headquarters or by the country coordinators themselves. Various modes were used to collect the data: face-to-face interviews, faxes, and e-mails. The first option was the most common, but in some countries the others were also used. Country coordinator reports indicate that the response rate was significantly influenced by which method was used.

Our instructions to the country coordinators emphasized that they should select respondents from a cross section of persons representing different perspectives on governance. They should be at least thirty-five years of age and should have significant experience in public life. More specifically, we asked them for a rough balance between the following stakeholder groups:

- High-ranking civil servants
- Long-standing parliamentarians
- Businesspersons
- Senior judges and lawyers
- Respected academics, consultants, or policy advisers
- Heads or senior officials in local NGOs
- Editors or senior reporters in the media
- Any other relevant category

It turned out that it was easier to find such a balance among the cross section of WIPs in some countries than in others. Below is the breakdown of the respondents by country. Clearly, some of our country coordinators had an easier time than others. The countries are presented in the high, medium, and low governance groups that we use in the analysis. As the tables below show (Tables A1, A2, and A3), only a few country coordinators were able to meet our request of interviewing religious leaders. This lack of balance in some of our samples may have contributed to somewhat inflated or deflated assessments of governance at the overall and arena levels. A detailed comparison of the state and nonstate respondents is presented later in this appendix.

Country coordinators had a variety of experiences with response rates. In our survey, the response rates varied from more than 70 percent (China, Jordan, Kyrgyzstan, Samoa, Thailand, and Togo) to a low of 31 percent (Chile). We should also note that some country coordinators were more persistent than others, which was reflected in the final response rates. The average response rate was 57 percent. The details on each country are contained in Table A4.

Because of the unevenness of the data, we were in the end unable to use all of what we collected. We had to remove six poor data quality countries—Barbados, South Korea, Nepal, Nigeria, Papua New Guinea, and Samoa. Four reasons were used to make this decision. The first was that completed questionnaires contained too many missing values. The second was a skewed distribution of stakeholder groups. For example, some coun-

*Appendix I*

**Table A1   Distribution of WGS Stakeholder Groups in the High Governance Countries**

| Stakeholder Group | Thailand | Chile | India | Jordan | Tanzania | Mongolia |
|---|---|---|---|---|---|---|
| Government | 5 | 2 | 5 | 6 | 5 | 5 |
| Business | 5 | 4 | 4 | 6 | 2 | 4 |
| Nongovernmental organizations | 5 | 5 | 2 | 4 | 7 | 9 |
| Parliament | 5 | 3 | 3 | 4 | 2 | 5 |
| Legal | 4 | 3 | 3 | 6 | 2 | 1 |
| International organizations | 4 | 1 | 1 | 0 | 0 | 2 |
| Civil servants | 4 | 1 | 6 | 0 | 1 | 4 |
| Academic | 4 | 4 | 7 | 5 | 5 | 4 |
| Religious | 0 | 2 | 0 | 0 | 0 | 0 |
| Media | 0 | 0 | 3 | 5 | 7 | 0 |
| Others | 5 | 5 | 2 | 4 | 2 | 5 |
| Total | 41 | 30 | 36 | 40 | 33 | 39 |

**Table A2   Distribution of WGS Stakeholder Groups in the Medium Governance Countries**

| Stakeholder Group | Bulgaria | Argentina | Peru | China | Indonesia |
|---|---|---|---|---|---|
| Government | 6 | 4 | 2 | 8 | 5 |
| Business | 7 | 3 | 7 | 0 | 5 |
| Nongovernmental organizations | 4 | 5 | 4 | 1 | 3 |
| Parliament | 7 | 5 | 3 | 0 | 4 |
| Legal | 5 | 7 | 5 | 3 | 3 |
| International organizations | 0 | 0 | 0 | 12 | 2 |
| Civil servants | 0 | 1 | 2 | 4 | 2 |
| Academic | 6 | 4 | 6 | 0 | 5 |
| Religious | 0 | 0 | 1 | 0 | 1 |
| Media | 6 | 6 | 5 | 0 | 2 |
| Others | 0 | 0 | 2 | 5 | 3 |
| Total | 41 | 35 | 37 | 33 | 35 |

tries had too many missing groups, while others lacked an acceptable balance between respondents from state and society. Finally, in some countries such as Barbados, the sample size was just too small. If any of these criteria were not met, a country was removed from the sample. This left us with sixteen countries of sufficiently high data quality to be included here. The response rate for fourteen of the sixteen countries where we currently have response rate information was 57 percent.

**Table A3  Distribution of WGS Stakeholder Groups in the Low Governance Countries**

| Stakeholder Group | Philippines | Russia[a] | Kyrgyzstan | Pakistan | Togo |
|---|---|---|---|---|---|
| Government | 3 | NA | 7 | 4 | 4 |
| Business | 0 | NA | 7 | 5 | 5 |
| Nongovernmental organizations | 8 | NA | 3 | 4 | 5 |
| Parliament | 6 | NA | 3 | 3 | 5 |
| Legal | 2 | NA | 3 | 4 | 5 |
| International organizations | 0 | NA | 3 | 0 | 5 |
| Civil servants | 1 | NA | 7 | 3 | 5 |
| Academic | 8 | NA | 3 | 5 | 5 |
| Religious | 1 | NA | 0 | 0 | 0 |
| Media | 2 | NA | 0 | 1 | 0 |
| Other | 4 | NA | 3 | 4 | 3 |
| Total | 35 | 38 | 39 | 33 | 42 |

Note: a. Stakeholder group information was not available for Russia.

**Table A4  Response Rates and Language Used for the WGS**

| Country/Region | Language | Sample Released | Completed (sample size) | Response Rate |
|---|---|---|---|---|
| Africa | | | | |
| Togo | French | 54 | 42 | 0.78 |
| Tanzania | English | 55 | 33 | 0.60 |
| Nigeria | English | 60 | 38 | 0.63 |
| Asia | | | | |
| China | Chinese | 45 | 37 | 0.82 |
| India | English | 90 | 38 | 0.42 |
| Indonesia | English | 55 | 35 | 0.64 |
| Mongolia | Mongolian | NA | 41 | |
| Nepal | English | 72 | 37 | 0.51 |
| Pakistan | English | 110 | 37 | 0.34 |
| Philippines | English | 70 | 35 | 0.50 |
| Papua New Guinea | English | NA | 37 | |
| Samoa | English | 50 | 37 | 0.74 |
| Thailand | Thai | 50 | 42 | 0.84 |
| Eastern Europe | | | | |
| Bulgaria | Bulgarian | 106 | 42 | 0.40 |
| Russia | Russian | NA | 39 | |
| Kyrgyzstan | Russian | 48 | 40 | 0.83 |
| Middle East | | | | |
| Jordan | Arabic | 55 | 40 | 0.73 |
| Latin America | | | | |
| Argentina | Spanish | 106 | 38 | 0.36 |
| Chile | Spanish | 113 | 35 | 0.31 |
| Barbados | English | 46 | 23 | 0.48 |
| Peru | Spanish | 80 | 37 | 0.46 |
| OECD countries | | | | |
| South Korea | Korean | 60 | 41 | 0.68 |

## Overall WGS and Arena Indices

The WGS questionnaire is composed of thirty indicators. The items are equally divided into six sections covering the six governance arenas introduced in Chapter 1. Each arena has five questions. Respondents were asked to rate various issues concerning governance using the same 5-point response scale: as very high, high, moderate, low, or very low. The WGS index ranges from a low of 30 points to a high or maximum of 150. The six governance arena indices were created by adding the scores of the five items in each arena. These arena indices range from a low of 5 points to a high of 25. Table A5 presents the median, mean, standard deviation, and sample size for the World Governance Survey (WGS2000), the views of our respondents five years earlier, as well as the scores for each arena.

### Reliability

Reliability is a fundamental issue in all research and is especially important in psychological measurement.[4] Scale, or index, reliability is the proportion of variance attributable to the true score of the latent variable, which in this case is governance. Reliability and statistical power are interrelated: as reliability increases, so does the statistical power of the scale. Reliability is inversely related to errors of measurement: the larger the error, the worse the reliability.[5] One way to increase reliability is to increase the number of scale items. In other words, scales with more items are likely to generate

**Table A5**  Medians, Means, and Standard Deviations for WGS 2000 and WGS 1995 and the Six Governance Arenas

| Description | Median | Mean | Standard Deviation | Sample Size |
| --- | --- | --- | --- | --- |
| WGS, 1995 | 81 | 80.17 | 17.03 | 587 |
| WGS, 2000 | 85 | 84.26 | 18.93 | 587 |
| Civil society, 1995 | 15 | 14.49 | 3.13 | 587 |
| Civil society, 2000 | 15 | 15.18 | 3.49 | 587 |
| Political society, 1995 | 13 | 12.51 | 3.69 | 587 |
| Political society, 2000 | 13 | 13.22 | 4.19 | 587 |
| Government, 1995 | 14 | 14.14 | 4.06 | 587 |
| Government, 2000 | 15 | 14.57 | 4.27 | 587 |
| Bureaucracy, 1995 | 13 | 12.93 | 3.57 | 587 |
| Bureaucracy, 2000 | 13 | 13.22 | 3.84 | 587 |
| Economic society, 1995 | 14 | 13.63 | 3.33 | 587 |
| Economic society, 2000 | 15 | 14.55 | 3.44 | 587 |
| Judiciary, 1995 | 12 | 12.49 | 3.67 | 587 |
| Judiciary, 2000 | 13 | 13.52 | 3.83 | 587 |

greater internal consistency. The most common statistical approach to measure reliability is Cronbach's Alpha.[6] Internal consistency is attained when the items, designed to measure the same construct, interrelate with one another.[7] Generally, the more items in a scale or subscale, the higher the Alpha and thus the higher the reliability.

Although the WGS index is not a true attitudinal scale, it does seek to measure a single construct: governance. The WGS index consists of twenty-eight positively and two negatively worded items. The number of questions in the questionnaire is reasonable, with only a couple of respondents complaining that it was too long. The two negatively worded items (Question 3 and Question 23), after reversing the values, were found to be negatively correlated with every other item in the WGS. This may suggest that respondents engaged in what is referred to as satisficing[8] or some other problem.

*Satisficing* occurs when a respondent does not pay close attention to survey questions and takes cognitive shortcuts. Because the first negatively worded item appears in the third question, it is doubtful that satisficing occurred regularly. Sometimes, respondents will answer in the same way to multiple items, or, in some cases, to the entire survey. An examination of the individual responses from each country uncovered only a couple of cases where a respondent entered the same value for every question in the survey. Although there is usually some satisficing in all surveys, there is no indication that the WGS survey had an excessive amount. After a careful systematic analysis of these two items we believe some respondents misinterpreted them, but the evidence does not suggest that all respondents misinterpreted these two negatively worded items.

Another explanation could be the subject matter of these two items. Question 3 concerns discrimination in politics, which is something almost all countries in the world have to one degree or another. Question 23 addresses corruption, which is another issue that few countries totally escape, especially transitional states such as the countries in our sample. In the end, we decided to leave them in our study and include them in all calculations, rather than second-guess our respondents.

The results presented in Table A6 suggest that the WGS index in 1995 and 2000 exhibit very high levels of reliability. Both in 2000 and in 1995

**Table A6   Cronbach's Alpha Reliability Scores for WGS 2000 and WGS 1995**

| WGS Indices | Cronbach's Alpha | Cronbach's Alpha Without q3 and q23 |
|---|---|---|
| WGS 1995 | .93 | .93 |
| WGS 2000 | .93 | .94 |

Cronbach's Alpha score is a very high .93, a perfect score being 1.00. The WGS Alpha scores are well above the threshold of .70, suggested by James Nunally as satisfactory. Alpha scores of .60 and above are commonly used and reported in major academic journals.[9] Removing items Question 3 and Question 23 raised the score only slightly. In Table A6, the Alpha scores for the WGS and the six arenas are displayed for 1995 and 2000. We also present the Alphas with Questions 3 and 23 removed, which were negatively correlated with the other WGS items.

## Validity

A scale or index is valid if it measures what it was designed to measure. Validation usually involves testing a hypothesis about the scale or index. The test that best fits the WGS is the *known groups* validity test. In the case of the WGS we might hypothesize that countries that are considered to have high levels of governance will score higher on the WGS than countries considered to have lower levels. Similarly, the same may be true of different groups of respondents. We have carried out two tests to determine the validity of the WGS. The first is a comparison between our data and that aggregated and presented by the World Bank Institute. The other is between state and nonstate categories of respondents.

## Comparison with World Bank Data

A team led by Daniel Kaufmann at the World Bank Institute has constructed an overall governance measure using numerous indicators collected from fourteen different sources.[10] The World Bank combines these indicators into six different dimensions of governance, namely, voice and accountability, political stability/lack of violence, government effectiveness, regulatory framework, corruption, and rule of law. There is a relatively large overlap with the type of issues that the WGS focuses on.

However, as pointed out in Chapter 1, the World Bank's definitions and indicators are different from those used in the WGS. So to better compare the WGS with the World Bank dimension ratings we looked at the indicators used by the Bank in creating its ratings and created corresponding WGS indicators by including the questions that were the most similar. The construction of these indices is presented below:

- For the voice and accountability dimension we selected the following WGS items to include in the WGS voice and accountability indicator: 1, 2, 3, 4, 6, 7, 8, and 10.

- In the case of political stability/lack of violence we used items 11, 14, and 15.
- For government effectiveness we included items 12, 17, 18, 19, and 20 from the WGS.
- In the regulatory framework dimension we had only item (22) that matched up well with the Bank's indicators.
- For corruption we used items 21 and 23 from the WGS.
- Finally, for the rule of law dimension we used WGS items 5, 21, 26, 27, 28, and 30.

The results are presented in Table A7 and are generally reassuring. The correlations between the various World Bank dimensions and corresponding WGS indices are in the moderate to strong range, except for regulatory framework, where there was only a single item to match up. The results of the correlation test on the 2000 WGS scores and the World Bank's Governance index was .77 with Indonesia and the Philippines included in the analysis, .81 with them removed. We believe in the Philippines the WGS scores reflect a downturn in perceptions of governance caused by the Estrada regime's well-publicized problems. In Indonesia, the higher WGS scores are the result of the end of the Suharto regime.

### State Versus Nonstate Respondents

The results presented in Table A8 suggest that state WIPs (those in government, the parliament, and civil service) rate governance significantly higher than other nonstate WIP groups (the eight remaining stakeholder groups).

**Table A7  World Bank Dimension Scores and Corresponding WGS Measures, 2000**

| Comparing the WGS 2000 with World Bank Indicators 2000 | |
|---|---|
| Indicators | Pearson Correlation Coefficient |
| WB and WGS voice and accountability | .77 |
| WB and WGS political stability | .53 |
| WB and WGS government effectiveness | .59 |
| WB and WGS regulatory framework | .43[a] |
| WB and WGS rule of law | .84 |
| WB and WGS corruption | .61 |
| Overall WB and WGS governance | .77 |

*Note:* a. Significant only at the .09 level.

We expected that WIPs directly connected to the state would likely have higher perceptions of governance.

One can speculate that the state WIPs may suffer from self-evaluation bias. Another way to view these results is that nonstate WIPs are usually more critical of the state of governance. This is an area that provides basis for interesting and insightful analysis of perceptions of governance among different groups of WIPs. The results presented in Table A8 give us confidence that the WGS passes the known groups validity test.

We would like to point out that our research relies and reports on the median values, which reduces the effect of outliers. Unfortunately, this puts us in a difficult situation when we try to use most common statistical tests, such as the Ttest used in Table A8 that compares means. At the aggregate level the differences between the median and the mean statistics are small (usually between 1 to 2 points as shown in Tables A8 and A9). However, when examining specific stakeholder groups and the arenas, especially at the country level, the differences between the median and the mean scores are much greater. Because of these larger differences, no tests of difference were performed at the arena level or country level. However, the median scores for the overall WGS and for each arena, by country, are presented for state and nonstate WIPs in Tables A9, A10, and A11.

**Table A8    Median and Mean Values for WGS 2000 for All Stakeholder Groups**

| Stakeholder Category | WGS 2000 Median | WGS 2000 Mean | Sample Size |
|---|---|---|---|
| Government (state) | 95.0 | 94.0 | 71 |
| Parliament (state) | 90.0 | 91.0 | 58 |
| Civil service (state) | 88.0 | 88.9 | 41 |
| Academics | 85.0 | 82.3 | 71 |
| International organizations | 84.5 | 79.7 | 30 |
| Legal profession | 82.5 | 83.8 | 56 |
| Nongovernmental organizations | 81.0 | 79.7 | 69 |
| Business | 80.0 | 81.0 | 64 |
| Religious | 79.0 | 82.4 | 5 |
| Media | 80.0 | 81.1 | 37 |
| Other (unidentified) | 80.0 | 80.6 | 86 |

**Table A9    Test Results of State and Nonstate WIP Scores, WGS 2000**

| Stakeholder Type | WGS 2000 Median | WGS 2000 Mean |
|---|---|---|
| State | 91 | 91.6[a] |
| Nonstate | 82 | 81.7[a] |

*Note:* a. Significant at the .001 level.

**Table A10  Comparison of State and Nonstate WIPs for High Governance Countries**

| Country | WIP Status | WGS | Civil | Political | Government | Bureaucracy | Economic | Judicial |
|---|---|---|---|---|---|---|---|---|
| Thailand | State | 99.25 | 119 | 16 | 18 | 16 | 16.5 | 16.5 |
| Thailand | Nonstate | 103 | 119 | 16 | 15 | 16 | 16 | 17 |
| Chile | State | 102.5 | 118.5 | 15 | 18.5 | 16 | 19.5 | 15 |
| Chile | Nonstate | 98 | 118 | 16 | 17.5 | 15 | 19 | 15 |
| India | State | 110 | 119 | 18 | 20 | 19.5 | 18 | 16.5 |
| India | Nonstate | 92 | 116 | 15 | 15 | 16 | 16 | 16.5 |
| Jordan | State | 99 | 115.5 | 12.5 | 19 | 16 | 18 | 18 |
| Jordan | Nonstate | 97 | 116 | 14 | 18 | 14.5 | 18.5 | 17 |
| Tanzania | State | 117 | 117.5 | 20.5 | 22.25 | 20.5 | 19 | 20 |
| Tanzania | Nonstate | 85 | 114 | 13 | 16 | 15 | 15 | 13 |
| Mongolia | State | 88.5 | 116 | 16.5 | 16 | 14.5 | 15 | 13 |
| Mongolia | Nonstate | 86 | 115 | 14 | 14 | 14 | 14 | 14 |

**Table A11  Comparison of State and Nonstate WIPs for Medium Governance Countries**

| Country | WIP Status | WGS | Civil | Political | Government | Bureaucracy | Economic | Judicial |
|---|---|---|---|---|---|---|---|---|
| Bulgaria | State | 95 | 16 | 17 | 16 | 14 | 15 | 14 |
| Bulgaria | Nonstate | 80.5 | 14 | 12 | 13.5 | 13 | 15 | 12.5 |
| Argentina | State | 89.5 | 15 | 16.75 | 17 | 12.5 | 14.5 | 12.5 |
| Argentina | Nonstate | 82 | 16 | 12 | 15 | 11 | 13 | 13 |
| Peru | State | 83 | 16 | 15 | 15 | 12 | 14 | 13 |
| Peru | Nonstate | 81 | 15 | 13.5 | 14 | 13.5 | 14 | 12 |
| China | State | 85 | 14 | 12.5 | 16 | 13 | 14 | 12 |
| China | Nonstate | 79 | 13 | 13 | 13 | 12 | 14 | 14 |
| Indonesia | State | 81 | 18 | 17 | 13 | 11 | 13 | 13 |
| Indonesia | Nonstate | 80 | 17 | 14 | 12 | 11 | 12.5 | 12 |

**Table A12  Comparison of State and Nonstate WIPs for Low Governance Countries**

| Country | WIP Status | WGS | Civil | Political | Government | Bureaucracy | Economic | Judicial |
|---|---|---|---|---|---|---|---|---|
| Philippines | State | 80 | 15 | 14 | 13.5 | 14 | 13.5 | 12 |
| Philippines | Nonstate | 73 | 16 | 12 | 10 | 10 | 13 | 13 |
| Russia | NA | 73 | 15 | 12 | 14 | 13 | 12 | 11.5 |
| Kyrgyzstan | State | 86 | 17 | 13 | 16 | 13 | 14 | 13 |
| Kyrgyzstan | Nonstate | 66 | 13 | 11 | 12 | 9.5 | 14 | 10.5 |
| Pakistan | State | 81.75 | 12.5 | 10 | 13.5 | 15.5 | 15.5 | 12 |
| Pakistan | Nonstate | 60.5 | 10 | 7 | 8 | 13 | 13 | 10 |
| Togo | State | 90.5 | 16 | 13.5 | 14.25 | 15 | 16.5 | 16 |
| Togo | Nonstate | 56.5 | 11 | 6 | 8 | 9 | 11.5 | 10 |

## Conclusion

The main conclusion we draw is that our approach to collecting governance data at the national level works. The WGS is also novel for comparative work, in that it draws assessments from a cross section of local experts within each of the survey countries, rather than from outside experts or secondary data. With the help of the respondents' ratings, their qualitative comments, and the country coordinators' reports, our approach generates both quantitative and very rich qualitative data. It is clear that local respondents are particularly well-suited to evaluate the nature of governance in their counties and assess the significance of changes over time. It is also important to add here that out of the 929 persons interviewed in the twenty-two countries originally included, only one actually questioned the framework or method that we used. The vast majority not only supported the idea of making a governance assessment but also commented on the value of its comprehensive nature. The country coordinators also mentioned to us that asking people about governance issues was politically feasible in those countries we had chosen. We realize that there are places where such interviews would be impossible, but we are encouraged by the fact that we could conduct this type of survey in countries such as China, Jordan, and Pakistan. We believe the experience of the project indicates the ability to generate valid and valuable data that for the first time includes the voices of local respondents—despite the contested nature of the governance concept and the considerable methodological problems in collecting data on this set of issues.

## Notes

1. For a comparison of ratings between the focus groups approach and WIP approach in the Philippines, please refer to Appendix 5 in Monica Blagescu, Julius Court, Goran Hyden, Kenneth Mease, and Keiko Suzuki, "Assessing and Analyzing Governance: Lessons from the World Governance Survey Pilot Phase," *United Nations University Governance Project Working Paper No. 2* (Tokyo: United Nations University Press, August 2001).

2. Those countries were (in alphabetical order): Argentina, Barbados, Bulgaria, Chile, China, India, Indonesia, Jordan, Kyrgyzstan, Mongolia, Nepal, Nigeria, Pakistan, Papua New Guinea, Peru, Philippines, Russia, Samoa, South Korea, Tanzania, Thailand, and Togo.

3. In addition, they were required to transcribe the open-ended comments and enter the results of the completed surveys into an Excel® spreadsheet.

4. Robert DeVellis, *Scale Development: Theory and Applications* (Newbury Park, CA: Sage Publications, 1991).

5. Paul Spector, *Summated Rating Scale Construction: An Introduction* (Newbury Park, CA: Sage Publications, 1992).

6. Andrew Comrey, "Factor-Analytic Methods of Scale Development in Personality and Clinical Psychology," *Journal of Consulting and Clinical Psychology* 56, no. 5 (1988): 754–761.

7. George Bohrnstedt, "A Quick Method of Determining the Reliability and Validity of Multiple-Item Scales," *American Sociological Review* 34, no. 4 (1969): 542–548; also Spector, *Summated Rating Scale Construction*.

8. Jon Krosnick, "Satisficing in Surveys: Initial Evidence," in M. T. Braverman and J. K. Slater, eds., *New Directions in Evaluations* (San Francisco: Jossey-Bass, 1996), pp. 29–44.

9. James C. Nunally, *Psychometric Theory* (New York: McGraw Hill, 1978).

10 D. Kaufmann, A. Kraay, and P. Zoido-Lobaton, "Governance Matters," *Research Policy Working Paper No. 2196* (Washington, DC: World Bank, 1999); D. Kaufmann, A. Kraay, and P. Zoido-Lobaton, "Aggregating Governance Indicators," *Policy Research Working Paper No. 2195* (Washington, DC: World Bank, 1999); also D. Kaufmann, A. Kraay, and P. Zoido-Lobaton, "Governance Matters II: Updated Indicators for 2000/01," *World Bank Policy Research Working Paper No. 2772* (Washington, DC: World Bank, 2002). It should be emphasized here that Kaufmann's team continues to expand their database. At the time this volume is being published, their governance research indicators project encompasses twenty-five different sources constructed by eighteen different organizations.

# Appendix 2:
# World Governance Survey

## Governance Perceptions Questionnaire

This survey is the pilot phase of a project to get systematic information on governance for countries around the world. This pilot survey is being conducted in over 20 countries by the United Nations University (UNU) and local partner institutions around the world. The ultimate goal is to better understand what aspects of governance matter most and to provide informed policy advice in this area.

In order that we can make effective comparisons over time and across countries, the survey instrument is a pre-coded, multiple-choice questionnaire. It is important to answer all the questions. Your answers should reflect your experience and perceptions of governance for your country.

We are well aware that these standard questions cannot capture the full complexity of governance issues. Therefore, in addition to indicating which standard answer comes closest to describing your case, please provide additional comments to better explain the situation in your country. Also please add comments if there have been important changes in governance contexts over the last five years, noting the date and nature of these changes. We will take these comments into account when we analyse the findings.

The questionnaire should be filled in by an expert who has extensive experience and can answer questions on the main dimensions of governance in the respective country for the past 5 years. Such an expert should be able to fill in the questionnaire in a maximum of 1 hour. Please contact the country coordinator if you would like further clarification on the aims of the project or regarding specific questions.

Note: The information obtained will
be treated with the strictest confidence.

Coordinator's Name: _____    Country: _____
Name of Expert: _____
Position of Expert:

| | | | | | | | |
|---|---|---|---|---|---|---|---|
| Government | ❑ | Parliament | ❑ | Civil Service | ❑ | Religious | ❑ |
| Business | ❑ | Legal | ❑ | Academia | ❑ | Other | ❑ |
| NGO | ❑ | International Org. | ❑ | Media | ❑ | | |

Experience with governance
issues: _____
_____
_____

Please send me a copy of the country findings. (Provide address below)
_____
_____

Please return all documents to:
Governance Survey—United Nations University
5-53-70 Jingumae, Shibuya-ku, Tokyo, T 150-8925 JAPAN
Tel: 81 3 3499 2811; Fax: 81 3 3499 2810; Email: court@hq.unu.edu

PART I: PARTICIPATION IN THE POLITICAL PROCESS

**1. To what extent do citizens have the freedom of expression?**

*This indicator tries to capture the formal and informal rules that affect people's
opportunities to seek, receive and impart information. This indicator would also
cover how well the media or other formal or informal channels reflect the views of
others than those in power or dominant groups.*

| | 5 years ago | Now |
|---|---|---|
| (5) very high | ❑ | ❑ |
| (4) high | ❑ | ❑ |
| (3) moderate | ❑ | ❑ |
| (2) low | ❑ | ❑ |
| (1) very low | ❑ | ❑ |

Comments: _____
_____

**2. To what degree do citizens have the freedom of peaceful assembly and associ-
ation?**

*This indicator tries to capture the degree of restrictions to people's opportunities to
participate peacefully in the public realm—to join associations or to gather in public. It also includes the right that no one is compelled to belong to an association.*

|  | **5 years ago** | **Now** |
|---|---|---|
| (5) very high | ❏ | ❏ |
| (4) high | ❏ | ❏ |
| (3) moderate | ❏ | ❏ |
| (2) low | ❏ | ❏ |
| (1) very low | ❏ | ❏ |

Comments: _____

---

**3. To what extent is there discrimination in politics?**

*As a governance issue, the level of discrimination is an important indicator of the potential for different groups to enter the political process. Here we refer to distinction according to race, color, sex, language, religion, political or other opinion, national or social origin, property, birth or other status.*

|  | **5 years ago** | **Now** |
|---|---|---|
| (5) very high | ❏ | ❏ |
| (4) high | ❏ | ❏ |
| (3) moderate | ❏ | ❏ |
| (2) low | ❏ | ❏ |
| (1) very low | ❏ | ❏ |

Comments: _____

---

**4. To what extent do governments facilitate public discussion on major shifts in policy?**

*For governments to formulate effective policies there will need to be mechanisms for consultation with different groups in society. Mechanisms to promote participation include consultations with citizens groups, public forums or referendums, for example.*

|  | **5 years ago** | **Now** |
|---|---|---|
| (5) very high | ❏ | ❏ |
| (4) high | ❏ | ❏ |
| (3) moderate | ❏ | ❏ |
| (2) low | ❏ | ❏ |
| (1) very low | ❏ | ❏ |

Comments: _____

---

**5. To what extent do citizens respect the system of rule-making?**

*The support (or lack of it) that citizens provide for the public realm is an important governance issue. Indicators of responsibilities to society would include issues such as payment of taxes, turning out to vote and not committing crime, for example.*

|                | 5 years ago | Now |
|----------------|:-----------:|:---:|
| (5) very high  | ❑ | ❑ |
| (4) high       | ❑ | ❑ |
| (3) moderate   | ❑ | ❑ |
| (2) low        | ❑ | ❑ |
| (1) very low   | ❑ | ❑ |

Comments: _____

---

**We would appreciate any further comments on the issues affecting participation in the political process. What are some priorities for reform in your country? What important issues does the questionnaire not cover?**

_____
_____
_____
_____
_____
_____
_____
_____

PART II: INTEREST AGGREGATION IN THE POLITICAL PROCESS

**6. To what extent is the legislature representative of society?**

*This would cover, for example, the degree to which the legislature contains women or minority groups.*

|                | 5 years ago | Now |
|----------------|:-----------:|:---:|
| (5) very high  | ❑ | ❑ |
| (4) high       | ❑ | ❑ |
| (3) moderate   | ❑ | ❑ |
| (2) low        | ❑ | ❑ |
| (1) very low   | ❑ | ❑ |

Comments: _____

**7. To what degree is there real competition for political power?**

*Competition is often between political parties. But it need not only be the case. For example, there are examples where there is only one party but the level of competition is high within that party. Competition is essentially non-existent in a dictatorship.*

|                | 5 years ago | Now |
|----------------|:-----------:|:---:|
| (5) very high  | ❑ | ❑ |
| (4) high       | ❑ | ❑ |

| | | |
|---|---|---|
| (3) moderate | ❏ | ❏ |
| (2) low | ❏ | ❏ |
| (1) very low | ❏ | ❏ |

Comments: _____

---

## 8. To what extent does the policymaking process fairly reflect public preferences?

*Ideally, interest aggregation implies being able to fairly accommodate competing preferences into public policy. The contrasting situation would be if the views of certain groups were excluded or if policy was primarily formulated in the interests of dominant groups.*

| | 5 years ago | Now |
|---|---|---|
| (5) very high | ❏ | ❏ |
| (4) high | ❏ | ❏ |
| (3) moderate | ❏ | ❏ |
| (2) low | ❏ | ❏ |
| (1) very low | ❏ | ❏ |

Comments: _____

---

## 9. To what extent does the legislative function affect policy content?

*On one hand, the legislature may play a decisive role in shaping policy. In contrast, it might only play a rubber-stamping function.*

| | 5 years ago | Now |
|---|---|---|
| (5) very high | ❏ | ❏ |
| (4) high | ❏ | ❏ |
| (3) moderate | ❏ | ❏ |
| (2) low | ❏ | ❏ |
| (1) very low | ❏ | ❏ |

Comments: _____

---

## 10. To what extent are legislators accountable to the public?

*For many countries, this will refer to the effectiveness of the electoral system. But there could be other ways that legislators might be accountable to the public.*

| | 5 years ago | Now |
|---|---|---|
| (5) very high | ❏ | ❏ |
| (4) high | ❏ | ❏ |
| (3) moderate | ❏ | ❏ |
| (2) low | ❏ | ❏ |
| (1) very low | ❏ | ❏ |

Comments: _____

_____

**We would appreciate any further comments on the issues affecting interest aggregation in the political process. What are some priorities for reform in your country? What important issues does the questionnaire not cover?**

_____

_____

_____

_____

_____

_____

_____


PART III: GOVERNMENT STEWARDSHIP


**11. To what extent is the government committed to ensuring the personal security of citizens?**

*There is a wide range of threats to personal security that governments can influence. These include fear of torture, arbitrary detention, crime, ethnic conflict and domestic violence, for example.*

|                  | **5 years ago** | **Now** |
|------------------|-----------------|---------|
| (5) very high    | ❑               | ❑       |
| (4) high         | ❑               | ❑       |
| (3) moderate     | ❑               | ❑       |
| (2) low          | ❑               | ❑       |
| (1) very low     | ❑               | ❑       |

Comments: _____

_____


**12. To what extent is the government committed to ensuring an adequate standard of living for citizens?**

*Equally important is the issue of how government promotes basic economic and social development. This includes issues such as the right to work and the right to social security, for example.*

|                  | **5 years ago** | **Now** |
|------------------|-----------------|---------|
| (5) very high    | ❑               | ❑       |
| (4) high         | ❑               | ❑       |
| (3) moderate     | ❑               | ❑       |
| (2) low          | ❑               | ❑       |
| (1) very low     | ❑               | ❑       |

Comments: _____

_____

**13. To what extent are leaders encouraged to make tough decisions that are in the national interest?**

*Long-term reforms may be necessary for a country but may have drawbacks in the short term. In contrast, short-term populist measures may be harmful in the long run.*

|  | **5 years ago** | **Now** |
|---|---|---|
| (5) very high | ❑ | ❑ |
| (4) high | ❑ | ❑ |
| (3) moderate | ❑ | ❑ |
| (2) low | ❑ | ❑ |
| (1) very low | ❑ | ❑ |

Comments: _____

_____

**14. To what extent does the military accept its subordination to a civilian government?**

*On one hand, the military may play a professional role without engaging in politics. At the other extreme, the military might be entrenched in power. Or the military may exercise influence by infiltrating the political realm in other ways.*

|  | **5 years ago** | **Now** |
|---|---|---|
| (5) very high | ❑ | ❑ |
| (4) high | ❑ | ❑ |
| (3) moderate | ❑ | ❑ |
| (2) low | ❑ | ❑ |
| (1) very low | ❑ | ❑ |

Comments: _____

_____

**15. To what extent is the government committed to peaceful resolution of internal conflicts?**

*An emphasis on peaceful resolution of conflicts within countries is important for personal security as well as for national stability and economic development. Alternatively, governments may incite or use conflict for reasons that are harmful to the security and life of individual citizens.*

|  | 5 years ago | Now |
|---|---|---|
| (5) very high | ❑ | ❑ |
| (4) high | ❑ | ❑ |
| (3) moderate | ❑ | ❑ |
| (2) low | ❑ | ❑ |
| (1) very low | ❑ | ❑ |

Comments: _____

_____

**We would appreciate any further comments on the issues affecting overall stewardship of the governance realm. What are some priorities for reform in your country? What important issues does the questionnaire not cover?**

_____
_____
_____
_____
_____
_____
_____
_____

PART IV: POLICY IMPLEMENTATION, ESPECIALLY THE BUREAUCRACY

### 16. To what extent are higher civil servants part of the policymaking process?

*The extent to which power is given to specialized agencies to formulate policy indicates a strong role for bureaucrats. The existence of deep layers of political appointments in the bureaucracy would indicate a lesser role.*

|  | 5 years ago | Now |
|---|:---:|:---:|
| (5) very high | ❑ | ❑ |
| (4) high | ❑ | ❑ |
| (3) moderate | ❑ | ❑ |
| (2) low | ❑ | ❑ |
| (1) very low | ❑ | ❑ |

Comments: _____

_____

### 17. To what extent is there a merit-based system for recruitment into the civil service?

*The degree of merit in the rules guiding recruitment has long been regarded as a key issue for successful policy implementation, regulation and provision of services. This could include a specific exam, the need to have objective entry requirements or an independent body on public service employment.*

|  | 5 years ago | Now |
|---|:---:|:---:|
| (5) very high | ❑ | ❑ |
| (4) high | ❑ | ❑ |
| (3) moderate | ❑ | ❑ |
| (2) low | ❑ | ❑ |
| (1) very low | ❑ | ❑ |

Comments: _____

_____

## 18. To what extent are civil servants accountable for their actions?

*The degree of accountability of civil servants—for corruption or other forms of misuse of public office—is an important indicator of governance. Audits, ombudsman institutions, public censure or courts, if effective, are mechanisms of how civil service accountability can be exercised.*

| | 5 years ago | Now |
|---|---|---|
| (5) very high | ❑ | ❑ |
| (4) high | ❑ | ❑ |
| (3) moderate | ❑ | ❑ |
| (2) low | ❑ | ❑ |
| (1) very low | ❑ | ❑ |

Comments: _____

_____

## 19. To what extent are there clear decisionmaking processes in the civil service?

*Clear rules could reduce or eliminate the risk of misuse of public office whereas unclear rules could encourage it. The rules could be in the form of a code of conduct, informal systems or the presence of laws that make official documents open to the public.*

| | 5 years ago | Now |
|---|---|---|
| (5) very high | ❑ | ❑ |
| (4) high | ❑ | ❑ |
| (3) moderate | ❑ | ❑ |
| (2) low | ❑ | ❑ |
| (1) very low | ❑ | ❑ |

Comments: _____

_____

## 20. To what extent is there equal access to public services?

*The state may make extra effort to ensure equal access to public services in remote areas or marginalized groups. In contrast, certain groups or regions may not have any access to services.*

| | 5 years ago | Now |
|---|---|---|
| (5) very high | ❑ | ❑ |
| (4) high | ❑ | ❑ |
| (3) moderate | ❑ | ❑ |
| (2) low | ❑ | ❑ |
| (1) very low | ❑ | ❑ |

Comments: _____

_____

**We would appreciate any further comments on the issues affecting policy imple-
mentation, particularly the bureaucracy. What are some priorities for reform in
your country? What important issues does the questionnaire not cover?**

_____
_____
_____
_____
_____
_____
_____
_____

PART V: RELATIONSHIP BETWEEN THE STATE AND THE MARKET

**21. To what extent do persons in public office promote respect for property
rights?**

*Those in positions of public authority have a vital role in ensuring that property
rights, whether private, common or public, are respected. This would include not
directly appropriating property and by providing protection from crime or other
threats to property.*

|                  | 5 years ago | Now |
|------------------|-------------|-----|
| (5) very high    | ❏           | ❏   |
| (4) high         | ❏           | ❏   |
| (3) moderate     | ❏           | ❏   |
| (2) low          | ❏           | ❏   |
| (1) very low     | ❏           | ❏   |

Comments: _____

_____

**22. To what extent are economic regulations applied equally to firms in the
economy?**

*Applying and enforcing regulations equally is important for the business climate.
The other extreme is where regulations are applied in an ad hoc manner or where
special treatment is given to cronies of those in power.*

|                  | 5 years ago | Now |
|------------------|-------------|-----|
| (5) very high    | ❏           | ❏   |
| (4) high         | ❏           | ❏   |
| (3) moderate     | ❏           | ❏   |
| (2) low          | ❏           | ❏   |
| (1) very low     | ❏           | ❏   |

Comments: _____

---

**23. To what extent is obtaining a business license associated with corrupt transactions?**

*The issue here is whether a business license can be obtained in a straightforward and transparent manner or does it involve a number of other transactions that go contrary to the stated rules and regulations.*

|                  | 5 years ago | Now |
|------------------|:-----------:|:---:|
| (5) very high    | ❑           | ❑   |
| (4) high         | ❑           | ❑   |
| (3) moderate     | ❑           | ❑   |
| (2) low          | ❑           | ❑   |
| (1) very low     | ❑           | ❑   |

Comments: _____

---

**24. To what extent is there consultation on policy between public and private sector actors?**

*Issues relevant here include, among others, the existence and nature of consultation committees and whether firms or business associations are systematically consulted about potential changes in economic policy.*

|                  | 5 years ago | Now |
|------------------|:-----------:|:---:|
| (5) very high    | ❑           | ❑   |
| (4) high         | ❑           | ❑   |
| (3) moderate     | ❑           | ❑   |
| (2) low          | ❑           | ❑   |
| (1) very low     | ❑           | ❑   |

Comments: _____

---

**25. To what extent does the government take the new rules of global trade, finance and technology flows into account when formulating policy?**

*International economic interactions (trade, finance and technology flows) have become an increasingly significant factor in national development. The challenge is how to manage these processes so as to enhance the benefits and reduce the negative effects upon people.*

|                  | 5 years ago | Now |
|------------------|:-----------:|:---:|
| (5) very high    | ❑           | ❑   |
| (4) high         | ❑           | ❑   |
| (3) moderate     | ❑           | ❑   |
| (2) low          | ❑           | ❑   |
| (1) very low     | ❑           | ❑   |

Comments: _____

_____

**We would appreciate any further comments on the issues affecting the relationship between the state and the market. What are some priorities for reform in your country? What important issues does the questionnaire not cover?**

_____
_____
_____
_____
_____
_____
_____
_____

PART VI: DISPUTE RESOLUTION, PARTICULARLY THE JUDICIARY

**26. To what extent is there equal access to justice for citizens?**

*Legal aid and other services may make the judicial arena a more even playing field for all citizens. In contrast, citizens may be prevented from going to court for security, financial or other reasons.*

|  | 5 years ago | Now |
|---|---|---|
| (5) very high | ❏ | ❏ |
| (4) high | ❏ | ❏ |
| (3) moderate | ❏ | ❏ |
| (2) low | ❏ | ❏ |
| (1) very low | ❏ | ❏ |

Comments: _____

_____

**27. To what extent are there clear decisionmaking processes in the judicial system?**

*If procedures are clear and are systematically followed, it is likely to make the role that the judiciary plays more respected. Decisionmaking includes not just what happens in the courtroom but all other aspects associated with a legal case, including for example the way evidence is collected.*

|  | 5 years ago | Now |
|---|---|---|
| (5) very high | ❏ | ❏ |
| (4) high | ❏ | ❏ |
| (3) moderate | ❏ | ❏ |
| (2) low | ❏ | ❏ |
| (1) very low | ❏ | ❏ |

Comments: _____

---

## 28. To what extent are judicial officials accountable for their actions?

*Decisions may not be made in an objective manner, due to reasons of political interference or corruption for example. Mechanisms such as appeal, judicial review and special inquiries, if effective, are examples of how legal service accountability can be exercised.*

|                   | 5 years ago | Now |
|-------------------|:-----------:|:---:|
| (5) very high     | ❏           | ❏   |
| (4) high          | ❏           | ❏   |
| (3) moderate      | ❏           | ❏   |
| (2) low           | ❏           | ❏   |
| (1) very low      | ❏           | ❏   |

Comments: _____

---

## 29. To what extent are international legal norms in the human rights field being incorporated into the national rights regime?

*Partly at stake here is whether governments sign and ratify international human rights conventions. More important, however, is the degree to which the legal profession incorporates the agreed international norms into the national legal system.*

|                   | 5 years ago | Now |
|-------------------|:-----------:|:---:|
| (5) very high     | ❏           | ❏   |
| (4) high          | ❏           | ❏   |
| (3) moderate      | ❏           | ❏   |
| (2) low           | ❏           | ❏   |
| (1) very low      | ❏           | ❏   |

Comments: _____

---

## 30. To what extent are non-judicial processes in place for fair resolution of conflicts?

*Conflicts arise at different levels and societies develop varied institutional arrangements to cater for these eventualities. The extent and importance of such arrangements, through NGOs or community groups for example, is an important governance concern.*

|                   | 5 years ago | Now |
|-------------------|:-----------:|:---:|
| (5) very high     | ❏           | ❏   |
| (4) high          | ❏           | ❏   |
| (3) moderate      | ❏           | ❏   |
| (2) low           | ❏           | ❏   |
| (1) very low      | ❏           | ❏   |

Comments: _____

_____

**We would appreciate any further comments on the issues affecting dispute resolution, especially the judiciary. What are some priorities for reform in your country? What important issues does the questionnaire not cover?**

_____

_____

_____

_____

_____

_____

_____

OTHER GENERAL COMMENTS

**Thank you very much for sharing your expertise. We would appreciate any thoughts you might like to add on the issue of governance in your country. We would also appreciate any suggestions for how to make the questionnaire clearer and more useful.**

_____

_____

_____

_____

_____

_____

_____

_____

_____

_____

_____

_____

_____

_____

_____

_____

_____

_____

_____

_____

_____

# References

Ackerman, Rose. 1999. *Corruption and Government: Causes, Consequences, and Reform.* New York: Cambridge University Press.

Almond, Gabriel A. and Sidney Verba. 1963. *Civic Culture.* Princeton, NJ: Princeton University Press.

Anderson, Michael. 2002. "Getting Rights Right." *id21 Insights*, no. 43 (September). Falmer, Sussex, UK: Institute of Development Studies.

An-Naim, Abdullahi A., and Francis Deng (eds.). 1990. *Human Rights in Africa: Cross-Cultural Perspectives.* Washington, DC: Brookings Institution.

Anonymous. 2003. "All The Spine of a Jellyfish." *The Economist* 366, no. 8308 (January 25–31).

Arat, Zehra. 1991. *Democracy and Human Rights in Developing Countries.* Boulder, CO: Lynne Rienner Publishers.

Arrow, Kenneth J. 1963. *Social Choice and Individual Values.* New York: John Wiley.

Barkan, Joel D. 1995. "Elections in Agrarian Societies." *Journal of Democracy* 6: 106–116.

———. 2000. "Protracted Transitions Among Africa's New Democracies." *Democratization* 7, no. 3: 227–243.

Bauer, Joanne R., and D. A. Bell (eds.). 1999. *The East Asian Challenge for Human Rights.* Cambridge, UK: Cambridge University Press

Beetham, David. 1999. *Democracy and Human Rights.* Cambridge, UK: Polity.

Berman, Harold J. 1983. *Law and Revolution: The Formation of the Western Legal Tradition.* Cambridge, MA: Harvard University Press.

Bigsten, Arne, et al. 2000. "Contract Facilities and Dispute Resolution." *Journal of Development Studies* 36, no. 4: 1–37.

Blagescu, Monica, Julius Court, Goran Hyden, Kenneth Mease, and Keiko Suzuki 2001. "Assessing and Analyzing Governance: Lessons from the World Governance Survey Pilot Phase." *United Nations University Governance Project Working Paper No 2.* Tokyo: United Nations University (August).

Blau, Peter 1963. *The Dynamics of Bureaucracy: A Study of Interpersonal Relations in Two Government Agencies.* Chicago: University of Chicago Press.

———. 1964. *Exchange and Power in Social Life.* London: John Wiley.

Blunt, Peter. 1983. *Organization Theory and Behaviour: An African Perspective.* London: Longman.

Bohrnstedt, George. 1969. "A Quick Method of Determining the Reliability and

Validity of Multiple-Item Scales." *American Sociological Review* 34, no. 4: 542–548.

Caiden, Gerald. 1991. *Administrative Reform Comes of Age.* Berlin and New York: Walter de Gruyter.

Campos, N., and Jeffrey Nugent. 1999. "Development Performance and the Institutions of Governance: Evidence from East Asia and Latin America." *World Development* 27, no. 3: 439–452.

Carothers, Thomas 1998. "The Rule of Law Revival." *Foreign Affairs* 77, no. 2: 92–104.

Chan, Sylvia. 2002. *Liberalism, Democracy, and Development.* Cambridge, UK: Cambridge University Press.

Chong, Alberto, and C. Calderon. 2000. "Causality and Feedback Between Institutional Measures and Economic Growth." *Economics and Politics* 12, no. 1: 69–81.

Chua, Amy. 2003. *World on Fire.* New York: Doubleday.

Civicus. 1994. *Citizens Strengthening Global Civil Society.* Washington, DC: Civicus—World Alliance for Citizen Participation.

Coase, Ronald. 1992. "The Institutional Structure of Production." *American Economic Review* 28, no. 4: 713–720.

Cohen, Ronald, Goran Hyden, and Winston Nagan (eds.). 1993. *Human Rights and Governance in Africa.* Gainesville: University Press of Florida.

Coleman, Jules L., and John Ferejohn. 1998. "Democracy and Social Choice." *Ethics* 97: 6–25.

Collier, David, and Steven Levitsky. 1997. "Democracy with 'Adjectives': Conceptual Innovation in Comparative Research." *World Politics* 49, no. 3 (April): 430–451.

Comrey, Andrew. 1988. "Factor-Analytic Methods of Scale Development in Personality and Clinical Psychology." *Journal of Consulting and Clinical Psychology* 56, no. 5: 754–761.

Coppedge, Michael. 1994. *Strong Parties and Lame Ducks: Presidential Partyarchy and Factionalism in Venezuela.* Stanford, CA: Stanford University Press.

Court, Julius, Petra Kristen, and Beatrice Weder. 1999. "Bureaucratic Structure and Performance: New Evidence from Africa." *United Nations University Working Paper.* Tokyo: United Nations University Press.

Crozier, Michel. 1964. *The Bureaucratic Phenomenon.* Chicago: University of Chicago Press.

Dahl, Robert. 1971. *Polyarchy.* New Haven, CT, and London: Yale University Press.

Daubon, Ramon E., and Herman H. Sanders. 2002. "Operationalizing Social Capital: A Strategy to Enhance Communities" "Capacity for Concert." *International Studies Perspectives,* no. 3: 176–191.

De Alessi, L. 1980. "The Economics of Property Rights: A Review of the Evidence." *Research in Law and Economics* 2: 1–47.

Demsetz, Harold 1967. "Toward a Theory of Property Rights." *American Economic Review* 57: 347–359.

De Soto, Herman. 2002. *The Mystery of Capital: Why Capitalism Triumphs in the West and Fails Everywhere Else.* New York: Random House.

DeVellis, Robert. 1991. *Scale Development: Theory and Applications.* Newbury Park, CA: Sage Publications.

Diamond, Larry. 1999. *Developing Democracy: Towards Consolidation.* Baltimore: Johns Hopkins University Press.

DiPalma, Guiseppe. 1991. *To Craft Democracies: An Essay on Democratic Transitions.* Berkeley: University of California Press.

Dryzek, John. 1990. *Discursive Democracy.* Cambridge, UK: Cambridge University Press.

———. 1996. *Democracy in Capitalist Times: Ideals, Limits, and Struggles.* Oxford, UK: Oxford University Press.

———. 1996. "Political Inclusion and the Dynamics of Democratization." *American Political Science Review* 90, no. 1 :478–487.

Dunn, John. 1985. *Rethinking Modern Political Theory.* Cambridge, UK: Cambridge University Press.

Duverger, Maurice. 1954. *Political Parties: Their Organization and Activity in the Modern State.* New York: Wiley.

Ekeh, Peter. 1975. "Colonialism and the Two Publics: A Theoretical Statement." *Comparative Studies in Society and History* 17, no. 1: 91–117.

Elklit, Jorgen, and Palle Svensson. 1997. "What Makes Elections Free and Fair?" *Journal of Democracy* 8: 32–46.

Elster, Jon. 1998. *Deliberative Democracy.* Cambridge, UK: Cambridge University Press.

Evans, Peter. 1995. *Embedded Autonomy: States and Industrial Transformation.* Princeton, NJ: Princeton University Press.

Evans, Peter, and James E. Rauch. 1999. "Bureaucracy and Growth: A Cross-National Analysis of the Effects of 'Weberian' State Structures on Economic Growth." *American Sociological Review* 64, no. 5 (October): 748–765.

———. 2000. "Bureaucratic Structure and Bureaucratic Performance in Less Developed Countries." *Journal of Public Economics* 75 (January): 49–71.

Faundez, Julio (ed.). 1997. *Good Government and the Rule of Law.* London: Macmillan.

Freedom House. 2001. *Freedom in the World, 2000–2001.* Washington, DC: Freedom House.

Fukuyama, Francis F. 1995. *Trust: The Social Virtues and the Creation of Prosperity.* New York: Free Press.

Fuller, Lon L. 1964. *The Morality of Law,* 2nd ed. New Haven, CT: Yale University Press.

Garreton, Manuel Antonio. 1994. "Human Rights in the Processes of Democratization." *Journal of Latin American Studies* 26: 221–234.

Gellner, Ernest. 1994. *Conditions of Freedom: Civil Society and Its Rivals.* London: Penguin.

Gluckman, Max 1965. *Politics, Law, and Ritual in Tribal Society.* Oxford, UK: Blackwell.

Goldsmith, Adam 1999. "Africa's Overgrown State Reconsidered: Bureaucracy and Economic Growth." *World Politics* 51 (July): 520–546.

Golub, Stephen, and Karl McQuay. 2001. "Legal Empowerment: Advancing Good Governance and Poverty Reduction." *Law and Policy Reform at the Asian Development Bank.* Manila: Asian Development Bank (September).

Gurr, Ted. 1970. *Why Men Rebel.* Princeton, NJ: Princeton University Press.

Haggard, Stephan, and Robert R. Kaufman. 1995. *The Political Economy of Democratic Transitions.* Princeton, NJ: Princeton University Press.

Harbeson, John, Daniel Rothchild, and Naomi Chazan (eds.). 1994. *Civil Society and the State in Africa.* Boulder, CO: Lynne Rienner Publishers.

Hatcher, Larry, and Eric Stephanski. 1994. "A Step by Step Approach to Using the

SAS System for Univariate and Multivariate Statistics." Cry, NC: SAS Institute.

Henderson, Errol. 2002. *Democracy and War: The End of an Illusion?* Boulder, CO: Lynne Rienner Publishers.

Hewitt de Alcantara, Cynthia. 1998. "Uses and Abuses of the Concept of Governance." *International Social Science Journal* 50, no. 1: 105–113.

Hewko, John 2002. "Foreign Direct Investment: Does the Rule of Law Matter?" *Rule of Law Series Working Paper*. Washington, DC: Carnegie Endowment for Peace.

Hobsbawm, Eric J. 1975. "Revolution." Paper presented at the Fourteenth International Congress of Historical Sciences, San Francisco (August).

Holsti, Kalevi J. 1992. "Governance without Government: Polyarchy in 19th Century European International Politics." In James N. Rosenau and Ernst-Otto Cziempel, eds., *Governance Without Government: Order and Change in World Politics*. Cambridge, UK: Cambridge University Press.

Howell, Jude. 1993. *China Opens Its Doors: The Politics of Economic Transition*. Boulder, CO: Lynne Rienner Publishers.

Huntington, Samuel P. 1968. *Political Order in Changing Societies*. New Haven, CT: Yale University Press.

———. 1991. *The Third Wave: Democratization at the End of the 20th Century*. Norman: University of Oklahoma Press.

Hyden, Goran. 1980. *Beyond Ujamaa in Tanzania: Underdevelopment and an Uncaptured Peasantry*. Berkeley: University of California Press; and London: Heinemann Educational Books.

———. 1983. *No Shortcuts to Progress: African Development Management in Perspective*. Berkeley: University of California Press; and London: Heinemann Educational Books.

———. 1992. "The Study of Governance." In Goran Hyden and Michael Bratton, eds., *Governance and Politics in Africa*. Boulder, CO: Lynne Rienner Publishers.

Hyden, Goran, and Ole Elgstrom (eds.). 2002. *Development and Democracy: What Have We Learnt and How?* London and New York: Routledge.

Hyden, Goran, Dele Olowu, and Hastings W. O. Okoth Ogendo (eds.). 2000. *African Perspectives on Governance*. Trenton, NJ: Africa World.

Inglehart, Ronald. 1977. *Silent Revolution*. Princeton, NJ: Princeton University Press.

International Institute for Democracy and Electoral Assistance. 1997. *The International IDEA Handbook of Electoral System Design*. Stockholm: International IDEA.

International Monetary Fund. 1997. *Good Governance: The IMF's Role*. Washington, DC: International Monetary Fund.

Jackson, Robert H., and Carl G. Rosberg. 1982. *Personal Rule in Black Africa*. Berkeley: University of California Press.

Jain, R. B. (ed.). 1989. *Bureaucratic Elites in the Third World*. New Delhi: Gritanjali Publishing House.

Johnson J. J. (ed.). 1962. *The Role of the Military in Underdeveloped Countries*. Princeton, NJ: Princeton University Press.

Joseph, Richard. 1987. *Prebendalism and Democracy in Nigeria*. New York: Cambridge University Press.

Kaufmann, Daniel. 2003. "Rethinking Governance: Empirical Lessons Challenge Orthodoxy." *Policy Research Working Paper*. Washington, DC: World Bank (March).

Kaufmann, Daniel, and Aart Kraay. 2003. "Governance and Growth: Causality Which Way?" *Policy Research Working Paper*. Washington, DC: World Bank (February).

Kaufmann, Daniel, Aart Kraay, and Massimo Mastruzzi. 2003. "Governance Matters III: Governance Indicators for 1996–2002." *Research Policy Working Paper*. Washington, DC: World Bank (May).

Kaufmann, Daniel, Aart Kraay, and Pablo Zoido-Lobaton. 1999. "Aggregating Governance Indicators." *Policy Research Working Paper No. 2195*. Washington, DC: World Bank.

———. 1999. "Governance Matters." *Policy Research Working Paper No. 2196*. Washington, DC: World Bank.

———. 2002. "Governance Matters II." *Policy Research Working Paper No. 2772*. Washington, DC: World Bank.

Keane, John. 1988. *Democracy and Civil Society*. London: Verso.

Kitschelt, Herbert, Z. Mansfeldova, R. Markowski, and Gabor Toka. 1999. *Post-Communist Party Systems: Competition, Representation, and Inter-Party Cooperation*. New York: Cambridge University Press.

Kjaer, Mette. 2002. *The Politics of Civil Service Reform: A Comparative Analysis of Uganda and Tanzania in the 1990s*. Aarhus, Denmark: Politica.

Klitgard, Robert. 1988. *Controlling Corruption*. Berkeley: University of California Press.

Knack, Stephen, and O. Keefer. 1995. "Institutions and Economic Performance: Cross-Country Tests Using Alternative Institutional Measures." *Economics and Politics* 7: 207–227.

Kooiman, Jan (ed.). 1993. *Modern Governance: New Government-Society Interactions*. London: Sage Publications.

Kopytoff, Igor. 1987. *The African Frontier*. Bloomington: Indiana University Press.

Korten, David, and R. Klauss (eds.). 1985. *People-Centered Development: Contributions to Theory and Planning Frameworks*. West Hartford, CT: Kumarian.

Krosnick, Jon. 1996. "Satisficing in Surveys: Initial Evidence." In M. T. Braverman and J. K. Slater, eds., *New Directions in Evaluations*. San Francsico: Jossey-Bass.

Kuznets, Simon. 1955. "Economic Growth and Income Inequality." *American Economic Review* 45, no. 1 (March): 17–26.

Laakso, Marrku, and Rein Taagepera. 1979. "'Effective' Number of Political Parties: A Measure with Application to Western Europe." *Comparative Political Studies* 12, no. 1 (April): 3–27.

Laothamata, Anek. 1992. *Business Association and the New Political Economy of Thailand: From Bureaucratic Polity to Liberal Corporatism*. Boulder, CO: Westview.

La Porta, Rafael, F. Lopez-de-Silanes, A. Shleifer, and R. W. Vishny. 1997. "Legal Determinants of External Finance." *Journal of Finance* 52, no. 3: 1131–1150.

———. 1999. "The Quality of Government." *NBER Working Paper Series No. 6727*. Cambridge, MA: National Bureau of Economic Research.

Lemarchand, Rene. 1972. "Political Clientelism and Ethnicity in Tropical Africa: Competing Solidarities in Nation-Building." *American Political Science Review* 66, no. 1: 68–90.

Levy, Margaret. 1988. *Of Rule and Revenue*. Berkeley: University of California Press.

Leys, Colin T. 1975. *Underdevelopment in Kenya*. London: Heinemann Educational Books; and Berkeley: University of California Press.

Lijphart, Arend. 1977. *Democracy in Plural Societies: A Comparative Exploration*. New Haven, CT: Yale University Press.

Linz, Juan, and Albert Stepan. 1978. *The Breakdown of Democratic Regimes*. Baltimore: Johns Hopkins University Press.

———. 1996. *Problems of Democratic Transition and Consolidation: Southern Europe, South America, and Post-Communist Europe*. Baltimore: Johns Hopkins University Press.

Lipset, Seymour Martin. 1959. "Some Social Requisites of Democracy." *American Political Science Review* 53, no. 1: 69–105.

Lipsky, Michael. 1980. *Street-Level Bureaucracy: Dilemmas of the Individual in Public Services*. New York: Russell Sage Foundation.

Locke, John. 1946. *The Second Treatise of Civil Government*. Oxford, UK: Blackwell.

———. 1960. *Two Treatises of Government*. Cambridge, UK: Cambridge University Press.

Lynn, Laurence E. Jr., Carolyn Heinrich, and C. J. Hill. 1999. "The Empirical Study of Governance: Theories, Models, Methods." Presented at the Workshop for the Empirical Study of Governance. Tucson: University of Arizona.

Mainwaring, Scott. 1993. "Presidentialism, Multipartyism, and Democracy: The Difficult Combination." *Comparative Political Studies* 26, no. 2: 198–225.

Mainwaring, Scott, Guillermo O'Donnell, and J. Samuel Valenzuela. 1992. *Issues in Democratic Consolidation: The New South American Democracies in Comparative Perspective*. South Bend, IN: University of Notre Dame Press.

Mainwaring, Scott, and Timothy R. Scully (eds.). 1995. *Building Democratic Institutions: Party Systems in Latin America*. Stanford, CA: Stanford University Press.

Mamdani, Mahmood. 1996. *Citizen and Subject: Contemporary Africa and the Legacy of Late Colonialism*. Princeton, NJ: Princeton University Press.

March, James G., and Johan P. Olsen. 1998. *Democratic Governance*. New York: Free Press.

Marsh, Ian. 1999. "Economic Governance and Economic Performance." In Ian Marsh, Jean Blondel, and Takashi Inoguchi, eds., *Democracy, Governance, and Economic Performance: East and Southeast Asia*. Tokyo: United Nations University Press.

Mauro, Paolo. 1995. "Corruption and Growth." *Quarterly Journal of Economics*, no. 110: 681–712.

Meier, Marshall, et al. 1985. *Limits to Bureaucratic Growth*. Berlin and New York: Walter de Gruyter.

Messick, Richard 1999. "Judicial Reform and Economic Development: A Survey of the Issues." *The World Bank Research Observer* 145, no. 1 (February): 117–136.

Migdal, Joel. 1988. *Weak States and Strong Societies*. Princeton, NJ: Princeton University Press.

Montesquieu, Charles de. 1970 (1748). *Spirit of the Laws*. New York: Free Press.

Moore, Barrington, Jr. 1966. *The Social Origins of Dictatorship and Democracy*. Boston: Beacon.

———. 1978. *The Social Bases of Obedience and Revolt*. White Plains, NY: M. E. Sharpe.

Moore, Michael S. 1985. "A Natural Law Theory of Interpretation." *Southern California Law Review* 58: 277–398.

Moore, Mick. 1995. "Democracy and Development in Cross-National Perspective." *Democratization* 2, no. 2: 1–19.

———. 1997. "Death Without Taxes: Democracy, State Capacity, and Aid Dependence in the Fourth World." In Gordon White and Mark Robinson, eds., *Towards a Democratic Developmental State*. Oxford, UK: Oxford University Press.

Munck, Gerardo L. 2001. "The Regime Question: Theory Building in Democracy Studies." *World Politics* 54, no. 1 (October): 119–144.

Myrdal, Gunnar. 1968. *Asian Drama: An Inquiry into the Poverty of Nations*. New York: Pantheon.

Narayan, Deepa, R. Patel, K. Schafft, A. Rademacher, and S. Koch-Schulte. 2000. *Voices of the Poor: Can Anyone Hear Us?* Washington, DC: World Bank.

Nelson, Joan M. 1994. *Intricate Links: Market Reform and Democratization in Latin America and Eastern Europe*. New Brunswick, NJ: Transaction Publishers.

Nino, Carlos S. 1996. *The Constitution of Deliberative Democracy*. New Haven, CT: Yale University Press.

Norgaard, Ole, and Karin H. Pedersen. 2002. "Development, Law, and Democracy: Exploring a New Relationship." In Goran Hyden and Ole Elgstrom, eds., *Development and Democracy: What Have We Learnt and How?* London: Routledge.

North, Douglass. 1990. *Institutions, Institutional Change, and Economic Performance*. Cambridge, UK: Cambridge University Press.

Nunally, James C. 1978. *Psychometric Theory*. New York: McGraw Hill.

O'Donnell, Guillermo. 1994. "Delegative Democracy." *Journal of Democracy* 5, no. 1 (January): 55–70.

O'Donnell, Guillermo, and Philippe C. Schmitter. 1986. *Transitions from Authoritarian Rule: Some Tentative Conclusions*, vol. 4. Baltimore: Johns Hopkins University Press.

O'Donnell, Guillermo, Philippe C. Schmitter, and Laurence Whitehead (eds.). 1986. *Transitions from Authoritarian Rule*, 4 vols. Baltimore: Johns Hopkins University Press.

Offe, Claus. 1997. "Micro-Aspects of Democratic Theory: What Makes for Deliberative Competence of Citizens?" In Axel Hadenius, ed., *Democracy's Victory and Crisis*. Cambridge, UK: Cambridge University Press.

Okimoto, Daniel. 1989. *Between MITI and the Market*. Stanford, CA: Stanford University Press.

Olson, Mancur. 1965. *The Logic of Collective Action*. Cambridge, MA: Harvard University Press.

Ostrom, Elinor. 1990. *Governing the Commons: The Evolution of Institutions for Collective Action*. New York: Cambridge University Press.

Pierre, Jon, and Guy Peters. 2000. *Governance, Politics, and the State*. London: Macmillan.

Przeworski, Adam. 1991. *Democracy and the Market*. New York: Cambridge University Press.

Przeworski, Adam, Michael Alvarez, José Antonio Cheibub, and Fernando Limongi. 1996. "What Makes Democracies Endure?" *Journal of Democracy* 7, no. 1: 39–55.

Przeworski Adam, and Fernando Limongi 1993. "Political Regimes and Economic Growth." *Journal of Economic Perspectives* 7, no. 3: 51–69.

Putnam, Robert. 1993. *Making Democracy Work: Civic Traditions in Modern Italy*. Princeton, NJ: Princeton University Press.

———. 2001. *Bowling Alone: The Decline of Social Capital in America*. New York: W. W. Norton.

Radin, Margaret J. 1989. "Reconsidering the Rule of Law." *Boston Law Review* 69, no. 4 (July): 123–145.

Rapley, John. 1996. *Understanding Development: Theory and Practice in the Third World*. Boulder, CO: Lynne Rienner Publishers.

Rawls, John. 1972. *A Theory of Justice*. Cambridge, MA: Harvard University Press.

Redfern, Paul, and Meghnad Desai. 1997. *Global Governance: Ethics and Economics of the World Order*. New York: Pinter.

Reynolds, Arnold. 1995. "The Case for Proportionality." *Journal of Democracy* 6: 117–124

Reynolds, Arnold, and Timothy Sisk (eds.). 1997. *Elections and Conflict Resolution in Africa*. Washington, DC: United States Institute of Peace Press.

Rheinstein, Max (ed.). 1966. *Max Weber on Law in Economy and Society*. Cambridge, MA: Harvard University Press.

Rhodes, R. A. W. 1997. *Understanding Governance: Policy Networks, Governance, and Accountability*. Buckingham, UK: Open University Press.

Rose, Richard. 1994. "Postcommunism and the Problems of Trust." *Journal of Democracy* 5, no. 3 (July): 18–30.

Rosenau, James N., and Ernst-Otto Cziempel (eds.). 1992. *Governance Without Government: Order and Change in World Politics*. Cambridge, UK: Cambridge University Press.

Rueschemeyer, Dietrich, Evelyn Huber Stephens, and John D. Stephens. 1992. *Capitalist Development and Democracy*. Cambridge, UK: Cambridge University Press.

Saich, Tony. 2001. *Governance and Politics of China*. London: Palgrave.

Sartori, Giovanni. 1968. "Political Development and Political Engineering." In John D. Montgomery and Albert O. Hirschman, eds., *Public Policy*. Cambridge, UK: Cambridge University Press.

Schaffer, Bernard. 1969. "The Deadlock in Development Administration." In Colin T. Leys, ed., *Political Change in Developing Countries*. London: Cambridge University Press.

Schumacher, F. E. 1973. *Small Is Beautiful*. New York: Harper & Row.

Scott, James C. 1985. *Weapons of the Weak*. New Haven, CT: Yale University Press.

———. 1999. *Seeing Like a State*. New Haven, CT: Yale University Press.

Sen, Amartya. 1999. *Development as Freedom*. New York: Anchor Books.

———. 2000. "What Is the Role of Legal and Judicial Reform in the Development Process?" Paper presented at the World Bank Legal Conference, Washington, DC (June 5).

Shugart, Matthew, and J. M. Carey. 1992. *Presidents and Assemblies: Constitutional Design and Electoral Dynamics*. Cambridge, UK: Cambridge University Press.

Skocpol, Theda. 1979. *States and Revolutions: A Comparative Analysis of France, Russia and China*. Cambridge, UK: Cambridge University Press.

Spector, Paul. 1992. *Summated Rating Scale Construction: An Introduction*. Newbury Park, CA: Sage Publications.

Sprogard, René, and Meril James. 2000. "Governance and Democracy: The People's View—A Global Opinion Poll." Presented at United Nations University Millennium Conference, Tokyo (January 19–21).

Starr, Paul. 1989. "The Meaning of Privatization." In Sheila B. Kamerman and Alfred J. Kahn, eds., *Privatization and the Welfare State*. Princeton, NJ: Princeton University Press.

Stepan, Alfred, and Cynthia Skach. 1993. "Constitutional Frameworks and Democratic Consolidation: Parliamentarism Versus Presidentialism." *World Politics* 46, no. 1: 1–22.

Stiglitz, Joseph E. 1985. "Information and Economic Analysis: A Perspective." *The Economic Journal* 95 (supplement, conference papers): 21–41.

Tarrow, Sidney. 1998. *Power in Movement*. New York: Cambridge University Press.

Tilly, Charles. 1975. *The Formation of National States in Western Europe*. Princeton, NJ: Princeton University Press.

———. 1990. *Coercion, Capital, and European States, AD 990–1992*. Oxford, UK: Blackwell.

Transparency International. 2003. *Global Corruption Report 2003*. London: Profile Books.

Trubek, David M., and Marc Galanter 1974. "Scholars in Self-Estrangement: Some Reflections on the Crisis in Law and Development Studies in the United States." *Wisconsin Law Review*, no. 4: 1062–1102.

United Nations Development Programme. 1997. *Reconceptualizing Governance*. New York: UNDP.

———. 2000. *Human Development Report*. New York: Oxford University Press.

Van Rijckeghem, Caroline, and Beatrice Weder. 1997. "Corruption and the Rate of Temptation: Do Low Wages in the Civil Service Cause Corruption?" *IMF Working Paper No. 97/73*. Washington, DC: International Monetary Fund.

Weber, Max. 1947. *The Theory of Social and Economic Organizations*. Trans. Talcott Parsons. New York: Free Press.

Weiss, Linda. 1998. *The Myth of the Powerless State: Governing the Economy in a Global Era*. Cambridge, UK: Polity; and Ithaca, NY: Cornell University Press.

Widner, Jennifer A. 2001. *Building the Rule of Law*. New York: W.W. Norton.

Williamson, Oliver. 1995. "The Institutions of Governance of Economic Development and Reform." In *Proceedings of the World Bank Annual Conference on Development Economics 1994*. Washington, DC: World Bank.

World Bank. 1981. *Accelerated Development in Sub-Saharan Africa*. Washington, DC: World Bank.

———. 1992. *Governance and Development*. Washington, DC: World Bank.

———. 1993. *The East Asian Miracle: Economic Growth and Public Policy*. New York: Oxford University Press.

———. 1997. *World Development Report 1997: The State in a Changing World*. New York: Oxford University Press.

———. 2002. *World Development Report 2002: Building Institutions for Markets*. New York: Oxford University Press 2002.

Young, Crawford. 1982. *Ideology and Development in Africa*. New Haven, CT: Yale University Press.

Zakaria, Fareed. 1997. "The Rise of Illiberal Democracy." *Foreign Affairs* 76 (November–December): 22–43.

Zolberg, Aristide. 1969. *One-Party Government in the Ivory Coast*. Princeton, NJ: Princeton University Press.

# Index

Abdullah II (king of Jordan), 37, 114
Accountability, 25, 63, 64; in civil service, 134–135; civil society and, 64*tab*, 66, 67, 68; of elected officials, 83, 93–94; in electoral systems, 80; of legislatures, 83; in political society, 80, 93–94; rules for, 125
Afghanistan, 42
Africa, 1; bureaucracy in, 52; civil service in, 124, 125; democratization in, 89; development in, 8; economic society changes over time in, 154; electoral systems in, 80; independence in, 8; lack of technical capacity for development in, 9; legal systems in, 170; military in, 105, 115; modernization in, 8; neopatrimonialism in, 80; party systems in, 79; slave trade in, 60; structural adjustment programs in, 9; weakness of bureaucracy in, 121
Amin, Idi, 116
Anderson, Michael, 168
Arat, Zehra, 61
Argentina, 1; access to justice in, 177; accountability in, 127; accountability of elected officials in, 85; application of economic regulations in, 156; bureaucracy in, 46*tab*, 127, 128*tab;* bureaucratic changes over time, 130*tab;* civilian control in, 40, 41, 115; civil service recruitment in, 133; civil society changes over time in, 68*tab;* civil society in, 46*tab*,

64*tab*, 66; civil society influence on policy in, 66; conflict resolution in, 116; corruption in, 40, 42, 52, 152, 156, 157; decisionmaking processes in civil service in, 135; democracy in, 36, 66; economic crisis in, 40, 41, 72, 115–116, 128; economic society changes over time in, 153*tab*, 154; economic society in, 42, 46*tab*, 52, 144, 151*tab*, 152; elections in, 90–91; electoral mechanisms in, 40; governance changes over time, 44, 46*tab*, 109*tab;* governance scores, 38, 38*fig*, 40, 192*tab*, 202*tab;* government adjustment to globalization, 159; government in, 46*tab*, 107*tab;* government/private sector consultation in, 157; incorporation of international legal norms in, 181; judicial changes over time in, 176*tab*, 177; judiciary in, 46*tab*, 53, 173*tab*, 174–175; lack of transparency in, 127; *listas sabanas* in, 90–91; military in, 40, 41, 115; national interest in, 108, 113; personal security in, 111; policymaking in, 72; political society changes over time in, 87*tab;* political society in, 46*tab*, 50, 84*tab;* public preferences in policies in, 90–91; public sector reform in, 128; representativeness of legislature in, 85; respect for property rights in, 154; transition in, 38; trust in elected officials in, 93

247

cial, 143; free, 143; functioning, 146; information about, 146; invisible hand of, 146; liberalization, 143; participation in, 167; reduction of state role in, 121; reform, 38; relations with state, 4, 21–22, 36, 39
Marshall Plan, 7, 8
Marx, Karl, 59, 100, 101
Marxism, 102
Media: watchdog role of, 93
Military: in Argentina, 40, 41, 115; in Brazil, 115; in Chile, 36, 40, 41, 115; coups, 105; effectiveness in implementation of policy, 105; human rights and, 115; in Indonesia, 51, 105, 115; in Nigeria, 115; in Pakistan, 42, 50, 68, 86, 89, 107, 115, 193; in Peru, 40; in Philippines, 43, 105; political stability and, 105; politicization of, 105; professionalism in, 115; readiness to accept civilian control, 107; relations with civil authority, 104–105; in South Korea, 105; state relations with, 20; in Taiwan, 105; in Thailand, 36, 105; in Togo, 107
Millenium Development, 29*n8*
Mkapa, Benjamin, 114, 129
Modernization, 8; commitment to, 114
Mongolia, 1; access to justice in, 178; accountability of elected officials in, 83; bureaucracy in, 46*tab*, 127, 128*tab;* bureaucratic changes over time, 130*tab;* central planning in, 37; civil society changes over time in, 68*tab;* civil society in, 46*tab*, 64*tab*, 66; communist regime in, 37; corruption in, 156; decisionmaking in judicial system in, 178; democratization in, 37; economic society changes over time in, 153, 153*tab;* economic society in, 42, 46*tab*, 150, 151*tab*, 152; elections in, 90–91; governance changes over time in, 44, 46*tab*, 109*tab;* governance scores, 34, 34*fig*, 35, 35*fig*, 37, 192*tab*, 202*tab;* government adjustment to globalization, 159; government in, 46*tab*, 107*tab;* influence of legislature in, 85, 92; judicial changes over time in, 176, 176*tab;* judiciary in,

46*tab*, 173*tab;* market economy in, 37; new constitution, 37; nongovernmental organizations in, 65; personal security in, 111; political society changes over time in, 87*tab;* political society in, 46*tab*, 84*tab;* public preferences in policies in, 90–91; reform process in, 37; relations with China, 37; representation for women, 88; social homogeneity in, 66; social welfare in, 113; transparency in, 127
Montesinos, Valdimiro, 40, 110, 176
Montesquieu, Charles de, 22, 100
Moore, Barrington, 102
Musharaf, Pervez, 86, 193
Myrdal, Gunnar, 49

Neoliberalism, 112
Neopatrimonialism, 80, 90
Nepotism, 127
New Zealand: electoral reform in, 81
Nigeria: civilian control in, 115; military in, 105, 115
Norgaard, Ole, 183
Norms: conflict resolution and, 77; contextual, 4; importance of, 24; universal, 4, 14; for working together, 14
North, Douglass, 21, 143, 144
North Korea: socialist law in, 169

OECD. *See* Organization for Economic Cooperation and Development
Olson, Mancur, 61
Organization for Economic Cooperation and Development (OECD), 123
Organizations: aid, 2; bilateral, 10; creation of, 62; international, 2; political parties as, 88; popular, 67; private sector, 8, 88; state, 121; trade, 69; voluntary, 8
Organizations, nongovernmental, 10, 85, 180, 181

Paine, Thomas, 58, 59
Pakistan, 1; access to justice in, 177; access to public services in, 136, 137; application of economic regulations in, 155; autocratic regime in, 67; bureaucracy in, 46*tab*, 128, 128*tab;* bureaucratic changes over

# About the Book

Although governance has been the focus of a considerable body of literature on democratic transitions and consolidation, data to support the claim that the concept is a useful one has been lacking. Now, however, *Making Sense of Governance* clearly shows the utility of research on governance, presenting empirical evidence from sixteen developing countries.

The authors focus on six arenas: civil, political, and economic society and the executive, bureaucracy, and judiciary. Demonstrating conclusively for the first time that perceptions of governance by local stakeholders are realistic indicators of the nature and quality of a political regime, they also reveal the dynamic nature of governance and to what extent it correlates with socioeconomic variables.

This comprehensive study is based on interviews in Argentina, Bulgaria, Chile, China, India, Indonesia, Jordan, Kyrgyzstan, Mongolia, Pakistan, Peru, Philippines, Russia, Tanzania, Thailand, and Togo.

**Goran Hyden** is Distinguished Professor of Political Science at the University of Florida. His many publications include, most recently, *Development and Democracy: What Have We Learned and How?* and *Media and Democracy in Africa.* He is coeditor (with Michael Bratton) of the seminal *Governance and Politics in Africa.* **Julius Court** is research officer at the Overseas Development Institute, London. He is coauthor of *Governing Globalization: New Roles and Functions for the UN and Bretton Woods Institutions.* **Kenneth Mease** is in the research faculty of the Department of Economics at the University of Florida. He served for two years as senior adviser to the UN University's World Governance Assessment project.